EURIPIDES

HECUBA

EDITED WITH INTRODUCTION,
NOTES AND VOCABULARY
BY MICHAEL TIERNEY
(Late Professor of Greek, University College, Dublin)

PUBLISHED BY BRISTOL CLASSICAL PRESS
GENERAL EDITOR: JOHN H. BETTS

This impression 2004
This edition published in 1979 by
Bristol Classical Press
an imprint of
Gerald Duckworth & Co. Ltd.
90-93 Cowcross Street, London EC1M 6BF
Tel: 020 7490 7300
Fax: 020 7490 0080
inquiries@duckworth-publishers.co.uk
www.ducknet.co.uk

First published by Browne and Nolan 1946
© 1946 by M.Tierney

A catalogue record for this book is available
from the British Library

ISBN 0 906515 17 3

Printed and bound in Great Britain by
Antony Rowe Ltd, Eastbourne

Cover illustration: woman tearing her hair in mourning,
from an Attic red-figure style funeral vase (*loutrophoros*)
by the Kleophrades Painter, ca. 480 BC; Louvre, Paris.
[Drawing by Jean Bees]

CONTENTS

FOREWORD

THIS edition is primarily intended for junior students. For this reason I have used Murray's standard Oxford text, omitting the *apparatus criticus*, and confining textual discussion to such points as affect the sense and are therefore treated in the commentary. Whenever Murray's text has seemed to me unacceptable, I have not hesitated to say so, but I have offered no emendations or alterations of my own. Even beginners may find textual questions to have some interest when it is shown how they are related to the meaning. I have cut down grammatical notes to the minimum, and made the vocabulary as brief as possible, believing that the sooner the student is taught to use a dictionary the better. On the other hand, it may be thought that I have given too frequent quotations of, or references to, parallels from other texts whether in point of idiom or of meaning. My reason is a desire to help in awakening the student's literary interest—which I take to be the chief object of his learning Greek—at as early a stage as possible.

For the commentary I have drawn extensively on Weil's edition in his *Sept Tragédies d'Euripide*, on Méridier's edition in the Budé series (especially his introductory notice) and on the school editions of Hadley (Pitt Press Series) and Jeffery (University Tutorial Series). In compiling the vocabulary, my indebtedness to the school editions of Bond and Walpole (Macmillan) and Upcott (Bell) will be obvious. For the Introduction, a new work, Philip

Whaley Harsh's *Handbook of Classical Drama* (Stanford University Press, California, 1944), came into my hands at exactly the right moment, and I should like to recommend its inclusion in every school library. On the difficult question of the choral metres, which I have tried as far as possible to elucidate, I owe most to Wilamowitz, *Griechische Verskunst*, and Schroeder, *Euripidis Cantica*, but have on occasion departed from both.

To Mr. W. H. Porter of Cork, and Professor T. A. Sinclair of Belfast, who have helped in the work of proof-correction, I return my warmest thanks.

Michael Tierney.

January, 1946.

INTRODUCTION

I—TRAGEDY.

EARLY DEVELOPMENT.—Aristotle tells us that Tragedy sprang from the Dithyramb, an elaborate ritual consisting of a song and dance performed by a Chorus of fifty in honour of the god Dionysus. The subject of the Dithyramb was originally a sacred story concerning the god's wonderful birth or his punishment of those who refused his worship, and the dance which formed part of it was of an imitative character. Early in the sixth century B.C., other stories began to be occasionally used instead of those concerning Dionysus. From about 535, in connection with the Athenian spring festival called the Great Dionysia, the leader of the Chorus became separated from it and took on the function of an actor (Greek ὑποκριτής, "answerer," so called because he answered the song of the Chorus with a speech in recitative style). The first to take this revolutionary step was THESPIS, after whom associations of actors are still called Thespians. The new kind of performance initiated by him was called *Tragedy* (τραγῳδία), a word which means "goat-song," because the Dithyramb from which it took its origin was associated with the sacrifice of a goat, an animal supposed to incarnate the god. The more general word *Drama* means simply "action" and was applied from an early date to the whole combination of sacrifice, song, and imitative dance.

vii

AESCHYLUS.—Real drama in our sense was not possible until a second actor was introduced beside the first, thus permitting the development of *dialogue*. This was the work of AESCHYLUS, who thus became the second founder of Tragedy. Born in 525 B.C., he was active as a dramatist from about 500 till his death in 456. As well as making dialogue the vehicle for dramatic action, he also carried further the tendency to substitute heroic subjects for Dionysiac, thus becoming a pioneer in the development of the *plot*. He is said to have described his tragedies as "slices from the great banquet of Homer." After him, the history of Tragedy is in one aspect that of the victory of plot and dialogue over dance and song, of the actor over the Chorus.

SOPHOCLES.—His great successor, SOPHOCLES (born 495, active from 468 to 406), is credited by Aristotle with the introduction of a third actor and scene-painting. He is also said to have finally fixed the number of the Chorus at fifteen : the Chorus in Tragedy seems to have been always smaller than in the Dithyramb, and was only twelve before Sophocles. In his hands, Tragedy may be said to have reached its classic perfection of form and style. It had become the chief literary expression of the Attic genius, in which the already very rich material of Greek epic and lyric poetry was further enriched, expanded, and used as a medium for the most profound poetic treatment of contemporary problems.

THE THEATRE.—The theatre (θέατρον, "show-place ") in which tragedies were produced at the Great Dionysia was part of the sacred precinct of the god, whose priest had a special front seat at performances. In the fifth century it was a semicircular hollow, south of the Acropolis Hill, its sides and back slopes filled with tiers of wooden seats. In the centre of the hollow was the flat circular dancing-floor (ὀρχήστρα, whence our *orchestra*) round an altar (θυμέλη) of the god. On the far side of the orchestra from the audience was the wooden booth (σκηνή, whence our *scene*), in front of which the actors performed. It now seems certain that there was no stage, only at most some steps leading up from the orchestra to the front of the booth. The Chorus performed its dances round the θυμέλη, the actors moved and spoke before the σκηνή, which served as background and was decorated with appropriate paintings. Elaborate scenery was unknown, and changes of scene were very rare, but certain mechanical devices were in use, and Aeschylus in particular was famous for his partiality to them. An example of such a device was the μηχανή (*machina*, machine), by means of which gods, ghosts, and other preternatural beings were swung or made hover above the σκηνή (cp. l. 32 of this play).

PLAY-PRODUCTION.—Tragedies were produced in competition, and prizes were awarded on the verdict of a committee of ten judges. A poet wishing to compete applied to the Archon Eponymus, who appointed a Choregus (χορηγός), a rich citizen who bore the expense of training and dressing the Chorus. Normally the poet himself taught the Chorus and actors their parts ; hence the verb διδάσκειν is equivalent to the English verb " to produce," in reference to a play. Each poet competed with four plays, three of which were tragedies and the fourth a play called a Satyric Drama, in which a tragic plot was treated in burlesque fashion. The three tragedies were known as a *trilogy*, the group of four plays as a *tetralogy*.

SPECIAL FEATURES.—The differences between ancient and modern Tragedy were very wide indeed. Ancient Tragedy formed part of a religious festival, was played in the open air in daylight, and consisted, for about a third of its length, of a series of elaborate semi-ritual hymns sung by the Chorus to the accompaniment of specially-composed music and a complicated dance. The poet was at once dramatist, composer, choreographer, and producer, and in early times chief actor as well ; the first poet to give up acting in person, we are told, was Sophocles, on account of the weakness of his voice. As there were only three actors, dialogue as well as lyrics had a formal quality. Actors and Chorus alike wore masks, and the former had special high-soled shoes to increase their height. Plots were almost invariably drawn from heroic legend, but it is a mistake to suppose that their outlines were always well known. On the contrary, the poets exercised the greatest freedom of invention, and it was in order to give the audience some idea of the story that devices like the Prologue and the *Deus ex Machina*, so beloved by Euripides, were used. The three great dramatists have never been excelled and rarely equalled for their power of producing suspense, surprise, and excitement in an audience, and they exploited many varied means, both literary and theatrical, for this purpose. Owing to the number of citizens trained every year for the competing Choruses, a high level of technical competence was widely diffused. This gave the whole Attic drama a communal character entirely foreign to our theatre, and kept the standard of criticism very high.

II—EURIPIDES.

LIFE.—The last of the three great tragic poets was born, according to tradition, on the island of Salamis, and on the very day of the great naval victory won there over the Persian fleet (September, 480 B.C.). His father's name was Mnesarchus, his mother's Cleito, and in spite of certain stories deriving from the jibes of comic poets, his family was probably well-to-do. He seems to have come early under the influence of the philosopher Anaxagoras, and among his friends were the latter's disciple, Archelaos, the Sophists Protagoras and Prodicus, and Socrates, who was at least ten years his junior. At any rate, the doctrines of all these men are constantly reflected in his extant work ; and in the Alexandrian *Life* of him by Satyrus, discovered in 1912, we are told that in his play, *The Cretans*, he sketched the whole philosophy of Anaxagoras in three lyric periods. Even in his lifetime he had a reputation for learning, and is one of the earliest Greeks said to have possessed a library. His first trilogy, *Daughters of Pelias* (including the story of Medea), was produced in 455, a year after the death of Aeschylus ; but he won no prize till 442, and was put first only five times in his life. After 408, he retired from Athens to the court of King Archelaos of Macedon, in whose honour he wrote a play, *Archelaos*, now lost. He died at Pella in the summer of 406, having been torn to pieces, according to one legend, by the hunting-dogs of his royal host. After his death, his son produced at Athens his three last plays, *Bacchae*, *Iphigeneia in Aulis*, and the lost *Alcmeon in Corinth*. There is a touching story that on the news of his death the veteran Sophocles appeared in the theatre in mourning, and that the audience wept.

HIS REPUTATION.—Euripides seems to have enjoyed in his lifetime only a limited popularity among his own people. He was particularly obnoxious to conservative Athenians because of his unorthodox views on religion and morality. This is evident from the frequent severe criticisms of his work found in the comedies of Aristophanes (*Acharnians*, *Thesmophoriazusae*, and especially *Frogs*). On the other hand his plays seem to have been well liked by the common people, and outside Athens his fame was very great even in his lifetime. Thus we are told that some of the Athenian prisoners at Syracuse in 413 were saved because they knew his work by heart ; and Milton has familiarised English readers with the story of how

the repeated air
Of sad Electra's poet had the power
To save th' Athenian walls from ruin bare

after Lysander's victory in 404. In the century after his death, the fame of Euripides spread all over Greece. His influence on the New Comedy (late fourth and third centuries) was enormous, and through this and the much later tragedies of Seneca he became one of the chief indirect sources of modern drama. An amusing story from Lucian tells how on one occasion in the time of King Lysimachus (306–281 B.C.) the people of Abdera in Thrace, after an epidemic of some kind of influenza, were seized with a craze for singing and recitation, and went about pale and thin repeating a famous speech of Perseus from his *Andromeda* (now lost) about the power of Love.

His Work.—Our present text of Euripides goes back ultimately to a selection of ten of his plays made for school use in the second century A.D., and to the chance survival of nine others from an edition of his collected works in alphabetical order. This gives us nineteen plays out of a recorded total of ninety-two. One of the nineteen is a Satyric Drama, *The Cyclops*, another, *Rhesus*, seems to have been worked over, perhaps by his son. The ten plays above referred to are : *Hecuba, Orestes, Phoenissae, Hippolytus, Medea, Alcestis, Andromache, Rhesus, Troades, Bacchae.* The nine are : *Helen, Electra, Heracles, Heracleidae, Cyclops, Hiketides (Suppliant Women), Ion, Tauric Iphigeneia, Iphigeneia in Aulis.* We possess also a large number of fragments from plays now lost, but quoted extensively in ancient works ; and in recent times considerable additional fragments have been recovered from papyri, giving us large parts of *Antiope, Hypsipyle,* and two plays called *Melanippe.*

CHRONOLOGY OF PLAYS.—The following is a list of the plays of Euripides of which the dates are recorded :

455 : *Peliades* (trilogy).

438 : *Cretan Women, Alcmeon in Psophis, Telephus, Alcestis.*

431 : *Medea, Philoctetes, Dictys, Theristae.*

428 : *Hippolytus.*

415 : *Alexandros, Palamedes, Troades, Sisyphus.*

412 : *Andromeda, Helen.*

408 : *Orestes.*

406 : *Bacchae, Iphigeneia in Aulis, Alcmeon in Corinth* (all posthumously produced).

It will be noted that we have records of several

Tetralogies and of one complete Trilogy. The list for 415 is especially noteworthy as giving us the only complete Euripidean Tetralogy dealing with a continuous subject of which one play has been preserved. Normally there was no connection between the plots of the plays which made up his Tetralogies. The earliest extant play, *Alcestis*, is not strictly a tragedy, but stands in a class by itself. Though serious in tone, it took the place of a Satyric Drama, and like some of the poet's latest plays (see below) has a happy ending.

Probable dates for other extant plays are: *Heracleidae* : before 427 ; *Andromache* : 426 ; *Hecuba* : before 423 ; *Heracles* : before 422 ; *Suppliant Women* (*Hiketides*) : 421 ; *Ion* : 417 ; *Electra* : 413 ; *Tauric Iphigeneia* : 411–09 ; *Phoenissae* (with *Oinomaos* and *Chrysippus*) : 409. *Hypsipyle* and *Antiope* were probably produced along with *Orestes* in 408. The date of *The Cyclops* is quite uncertain, and *Rhesus* may belong to the fourth century. There are a few other plays, now lost, which we can only date as early (before 420) or late (after 420). Early are probably *Bellerophon, Cresphontes, Cretans, Oineus, Phoinix, Stheneboia, Theseus, Thyestes.* Late are probably *Alope, Antigone, Auge, Ixion, Oedipus.*

DEVELOPMENT.—We are obviously not in a position to form any final judgment on the development of Euripides as a dramatist. The earliest of his extant tragedies, *Medea*, was written when he was nearly fifty, and we know very little of what preceded it. It is, however, both possible and helpful to attempt a general classification of the plays known to us.

1. After *Alcestis* comes a group of great tragedies in which women especially are shown in the grip of some

overmastering passion such as revenge (*Medea*) or love
(Phaedra in *Hippolytus*). Such plays as *The Cretans*
and *Stheneboia*, in which old legendary love-affairs
were presented in this way, with great realism and
a rich display of rhetorical skill, particularly shocked
the poet's conservative critics, who also took exception
to his presentation in *Telephus* of a king disguised in
rags as a beggar.

2. With the beginning of the Peloponnesian War in
432, Euripides seems to have entered on a strongly
patriotic phase. Already in *Medea* we get a splendid
chorus (824, f.) in praise of Athens. The next ten
years saw a series of tragedies, from *Heracleidae* to
The Suppliant Women, in which the glory of Athens
is a leading theme and is accompanied by denunciation of Sparta, as in *Andromache*. To this class
belonged the lost *Aigeus*, *Theseus*, *Erechtheus*, and we
find the same theme prominent in *Heracles* and in
the somewhat later *Ion*. During this phase, too,
Euripides developed greatly his very characteristic
fondness for obscure Attic legends and cults as
subjects for his plays.

3. During the period from the Peace of Nicias to
the Athenian disaster in Sicily (421–413) the poet's
mind seems to have turned against war and even
against patriotism, and he seems definitely to have
abandoned all idea of purpose or meaning in the world.
This extreme pessimism is felt for the first time in
Hecuba, when Talthybius suggests that Chance, not
Zeus, is supreme (see note on 491). In *Heracles* it
runs side by side with the poet's still vigorous
Athenian patriotism : an old tale, little if at all used
for tragic purposes, is altered so as to give it a very
pessimistic turn, and ridicule is thrown on " the

wretched tales of poets " which have so far been the groundwork of Tragedy. The Trilogy containing *The Troades* was perhaps the supreme expression of this pessimism ; in its depiction of the hopeless and meaningless horrors of war it is almost the exact contrary to the earlier patriotic plays. In *Electra* we find another manifestation of the same spirit. Here a famous legend, which had served Aeschylus as material for the noblest spiritual teaching, is presented as a human problem in a cold, rational, " modern " light, and found not noble but horrible.

4. This belief in the sovereign power of Chance is combined with a view which Euripides took over from the Sophists and which we find recurring in all stages of his work : the view that religious practices and the doctrines which justified or explained them were not *natural* but *conventional*. This view was expressed in the famous antithesis between φύσις (nature or growth) and νόμος (law or convention) which we find touched upon in almost every one of his plays (see note, 592-602). Its effect on Euripides was to make him reject, not merely such accidental manifestations of Greek paganism as oracles and blood-sacrifices, but the whole pagan pantheon, and substitute for it a kind of Deist belief in an inscrutable Power, which could as readily be identified with Chance as with anything purposeful or rational. Unfortunately, in thus rejecting a very imperfect religion, Euripides was also rejecting the whole complex of beliefs which made Tragedy possible. Blind Chance, as Aristotle was to perceive, is more suitable to be a comic than a tragic force. The plays of the period from 413 to the death of Euripides are no longer tragedies in the old sense of the word.

though they preserve the tragic form, and though the poet's skill in plot-construction, and his power of devising highly dramatic situations, are almost more brilliant than ever. They are plays of romantic and sensational adventure like *Helen* and *Tauric Iphigeneia*, exciting dramas of intrigue like *Ion* (whose date is perhaps a few years earlier), *Electra*, *Orestes* and *Iphigeneia in Aulis*, or colourful and emotional " cavalcades " like *The Phoenissae*. In almost all, Chance is the driving force of the action, and there is a strong tendency to happy endings and poetic justice. Plots depart more than ever from the old canonical forms (never very fixed, as we have seen), while the Chorus becomes an interesting and beautiful survival, largely external to the action. In the end its songs are altogether irrelevant interludes at certain points, and the plots have become so original that it needs only a short step to abandon the traditional names of the characters. With all this went a continuous advance in realism and refinement of dialogue. These various developments found their natural term in the New Comedy, and Menander is the real successor of Euripides.

III—*HECUBA*.

STRUCTURE.—Like *Heracles*, which may have been a companion piece (see below), *Hecuba* is in structure a " diptych " ; that is to say, it contains two successive themes loosely linked together and given unity by the predominance in both of a single character. The play is sometimes criticised for this looseness of structure, but one of its attractions is the great subtlety and skill with which the defect, if it be a defect, is mitigated.

The two parts are of almost exactly equal length. The drama of Polyxena's fate ends at line 656, with the end of the Second Stasimon, and the remaining 639 lines are devoted to Hecuba's discovery of the fate of Polydorus and her revenge on his murderer. Each part has the chief features of an Aristotelian plot, Recognition, Reversal, Messenger's Narrative, and Dirge. There are, of course, subtle differences : thus in the first part the Dirge is a prolongation of the Parodos and is joined in by Hecuba, Polyxena, and the Chorus, while in the second it is almost a monologue by the odious victim, Polymestor. So too the Narrative in the first part is spoken by the Herald, Talthybius, while in the second Polymestor, isolated and without sympathisers, speaks it himself. Each part also has its own Agon or Debate ; but in the second part this is duplicated. There is a close resemblance between Hecuba's debate with Odysseus in the first part and her debate with Agamemnon in the second, but whereas the earlier one ends in failure for the queen, the later ends in her success. It is followed by her debate with Polymestor, which takes the standard form of a trial-scene.

UNITY OF PLAY.—Unity is ensured principally by the character of Hecuba herself. In this respect the play closely resembles *The Troades*, produced nearly ten years later. There also Hecuba is continuously present, and the separate divisions of the action (in this case three) are united by reference to her. But whereas *The Troades* is a powerful and moving series of vivid *tableaux*, *Hecuba* is a single cumulative process in which every stage leads towards the queen's terrible revenge. Her character thus makes the play an interesting half-way-house between *Medea*, which

is pure revenge-drama, and *The Troades*, which is
a panorama of the fall of Troy.

A second device for mitigating the looseness of the
plot is the Prologue spoken by the ghost of Polydorus.
Usually the speaker of the Euripidean Prologue is
an omniscient god, and its purpose is very often to
set the background for an unfamiliar plot. Polydorus,
by his phantom presence, is here himself the background for the second part of the play ; but his
speech is carefully confined to the chief event of the
first part, the sacrifice of Polyxena. We get from him
no hint of the drastic action his mother will take
on finding his body. The Prologue is followed by
Hecuba's announcement of her double dream, in
which the fates of both her children, and thus the
two parts of the play, are again darkly joined. There
are many other scarcely visible links : thus the body
of Polydorus is found by an old servant sent to fetch
water for Polyxena's burial, and on first seeing it
his mother thinks she still sees Polyxena's corpse. So
too the presence of Agamemnon, all-important in the
second part, is motivated by his desire to speed
Polyxena's burial.

SOURCES OF PLOT.—It is generally agreed that
Euripides took the outline of the plot for the first
part of *Hecuba* from a lost tragedy of Sophocles,
Polyxena. We are in fact told this by the Scholiast
on line 1 : τὰ περὶ Πολυξένην ἔστιν εὑρεῖν παρὰ
Σοφοκλεῖ ἐν Πολυξένῃ. Sophocles in turn had many
predecessors. The story was first told in the Cyclic
epic called *Sack of Ilion*, and figured afterwards in
poems by Stesichorus, Ibycus, and Simonides.[1] In
Sophocles, as well as in his sources, the ghost of

---

[1] Full account in Pearson: *Fragments of Sophocles*, vol. II, 161, f.

Achilles played a very important part, and the scene in which it appeared is highly praised in the treatise *On the Sublime*. Euripides varies the effect by having the story of this famous apparition told by another ghost invented by himself. A slighter addition made by Euripides to his Sophoclean materia. is the willing acceptance of her fate by the heroine,[1] a characteristic which joins her to a long line of Euripidean heroines, from Alcestis down.

If the story of Polyxena's sacrifice owes much to Sophocles, that of Polymestor's crime and Hecuba's revenge is almost entirely original. There is no trace of it in earlier literature, and certain details in later accounts (such as that in *Aeneid* iii, 41, f.), suggest that at most Euripides may have drawn on a local Thracian legend which explained the presence on the Chersonese coast of an oracle of Polydorus and a cairn for Hecuba. We are justified in thinking that the whole of the revenge is an example of the poet's own invention. It abounds in striking devices like the " asides " in the scene with Agamemnon (see note at head of Third Epeisodion, 658–904) and the well-sustained suspense regarding the nature of the punishment of Polymestor.

The location of the play on the Thracian side of the Hellespont is rendered necessary by the use of the ghost of Polydorus for the Prologue ; but it has led Euripides into a slight difficulty regarding the sacrifice of Polyxena. In all earlier versions of the story, the tomb of Achilles, where the sacrifice took place, was on the Asiatic side, close to Troy. We are carefully kept in the dark in the play (narrative of

---

[1] I here follow Méridier's suggestion; see note 2, p. 170, in the introductory *Notice* to his edition of the play.

Talthybius, 518, f.) as to whether or not the whole
Greek host *returned* to the Asiatic side for the
sacrifice. The Scholiast is puzzled by this silence ;
his note on line 521 is a good example of intelligent
ancient criticism : παρῆν μὲν ὄχλος· αἴτημα σκηνικόν.
πῶς γὰρ τοῦ ᾿Αχιλλέως ἐν τῇ Τροίᾳ θανόντος τοὺς
῞Ελληνάς φησι πρὸ τοῦ τύμβου αὐτοῦ θύειν ἐν
Χερρονήσῳ ὄντας ;

DATE.—The date of *Hecuba* is partly fixed by the
parody of line 172 in Aristophanes' *Clouds*, line 1165.
As *The Clouds* was first produced in 423, and as there
is no reason for believing this passage to belong to a
later edition, we thus have that year as a *terminus
ante quem* for *Hecuba*. A rather weaker *terminus
post quem* is afforded by the reference in the First
Stasimon (see note, 455–65) to the Delian festival
revived during the winter of 426-5. It is also possible
that there is in the Second Stasimon (see note, 650)
a reference to the Spartan defeat at Sphacteria in 425.
These indications together point to the spring of 424 as
the most likely date for the first production of *Hecuba*.
It is probable that *Heracles* was produced also in that
year, as suggested by Parmentier in his edition of the
latter play. (*Notice*, p. 16.) If the two belonged to
the same Tetralogy, this would account for some
curious parallels between them. Such are their
" diptych " structure, their references to Chance as
supreme over human affairs, and the fact that the
revived Delian festival, mentioned above, is also
referred to in *Heracles* (line 687).

IV—METRES.

1. IAMBIC TRIMETER.—This is the ordinary metre of dialogue. Aristotle calls it the most conversational of all metres, and says that it took the place of the less refined Trochaic Tetrameter. As its name indicates, it consists of three Iambic *metra* :

$$\overset{\smile}{-}\; {-}\; \smile\; {-}\; \mid\; \overset{\smile}{-}\; {-}\; \smile\; {-}\; \mid\; \overset{\smile}{-}\; {-}\; \smile\; \overset{\smile}{-}\; \mid\; ,$$

but it is commonly scanned as consisting of six *feet*. The first syllable of each metron and the last syllable of the Trimeter may be either short or long (*syllaba anceps*). This is usually expressed by saying that a Spondee (— —) can take the place of an Iambus in the first, third, and fifth foot. A Dactyl (— ⌣ ⌣) may take the place of the Spondee at the beginning of the first and second metron (first and third foot) and an Anapaest (⌣ ⌣ —) at the beginning of the first. With proper names, Anapaests may be used instead of any Iambus except the last. " *Resolution* " (the substitution of three short syllables for an Iambus) was allowed sparingly by Aeschylus, Sophocles and in his early plays by Euripides ; from *Hecuba* on it may occur anywhere except in the third metron (fifth or sixth foot). *Caesura* (division of words within a foot) occurs always in the second metron, in its first or second foot or in both (third or fourth foot of the line). When a line is divided between two speakers (ἀντιλαβή, see 1284, 1285) the break coincides with the Caesura.

If the first syllable of the third metron is long, it must not be followed by a Caesura. This is the rule known as " Porson's Pause " ; it can also be expressed by saying that if a Trimeter ends with a word in the form of a Cretic (— ⌣ —) the syllable preceding that word must be short (the fifth foot must be an Iambus). The only exception allowed is when the word preceding the Cretic is itself a word of one syllable.

2. ANAPAESTIC VERSE.—The Anapaest (⌣ ⌣ —) was regarded as a marching rhythm, and is regularly used for the song sung by the Chorus as it takes its place in the orchestra or goes off at the end. In *Hecuba* the queen enters before the Chorus and both chant in Anapaests ; so does the Chorus as it goes off (59-153, 1293-5). The exchange between Hecuba and Polyxena in the Parodos (154—215) is in a peculiar form of Anapaestic rhythm in which Spondees predominate, thus making it akin to Dochmiac (see below).

Anapaests are scanned like lyric verse, in *cola*, which are normally Dimeters, though Monometers occur frequently. Spondees may take the place of Anapaests all through, and Dactyls in all places except the last. Only the last syllable remains fixed ; it must be always long. This feature gives a sequence of Anapaestic Dimeters the appearance of being continuous, and is called *Synapheia* or " linking." A sequence of Anapaests normally ends in a Dimeter which is a syllable short, or *catalectic*. It thus consists of three Anapaests or their equivalents, followed by a single syllable which may be either short or long (*syllaba anceps*). This catalectic Dimeter is called a Paroemiac, because of its frequent use as a verse-form for proverbs (παροιμίαι), as in οἶνος καὶ παῖδες ἀληθεῖς.

3. DOCHMIAC VERSE.—This derives its name from the Greek word δόχμιος, " aslant," because metricians in trying to analyse it felt that it cut across all their

rules. Its characteristic is its extreme irregularity, which makes it well fitted for the expression of great emotion. Unknown except in Tragedy, it is there the normal metre of the dirge (κομμός, θρῆνος). Its basis is the Dochmiac Metron which may be analysed into a combination of Iambics and Cretics ($\smile$ — — $\smile$ —), or Trochees and Cretics (— $\smile$ — $\smile$ —), but over thirty different forms of this basic metron occur. Like all lyric metres it is usually composed in Dimeters ; what gives it its irregular appearance is the fact that resolution of longs into two shorts and the reverse substitution of a long for two shorts are universally allowed. The Bacchius ($\smile$ — — or — — $\smile$), the Tribrach ($\smile$ $\smile$ $\smile$) and even the Choriamb (— $\smile$ $\smile$ —), frequently occur among Dochmiac metra, which may also consist entirely of short or long syllables. The latter or spondaic form is almost indistinguishable from a variety of the Anapaestic Dimeter, and is to be found in the scene between Hecuba and Polyxena at the end of the Parodos (154–215). This is very effective for the expression of abject grief. Often Dochmiacs occur in scenes of excitement combined with or answered by Iambic Trimeters ; an example is the scene 681–722, which is really a Kommos for Polydorus. The chant of the Chorus, 1024–33, and the wild lament of Polymestor, 1056–1106, are further examples of this rhythm.

4. LYRIC METRES.—The simplest lyric metres were the Iambic and the Trochaic. Of these the latter does not occur in *Hecuba*, the former only in combination with the Aeolic rhythms which are preponderant. As with other metres, the normal Iambic colon was the Dimeter :

$$\stackrel{\smile}{-} - \smile - \mid \stackrel{\smile}{-} - \smile \stackrel{\smile}{-} \mid$$

but Trimeters also occur, always in irregular forms, permitting constant resolution. In Iambic Dimeters, the *Cretic* or *Bacchius* (— ◡ — or ◡ — —) are very frequently found substituted for one metron, as at 629–30, 634.

Aeolic rhythm is based on the Choriamb (— ◡ ◡—), which is usually found associated with four free syllables in the Aeolic or Choriambic Dimeter, as at 469–471, 636, 645, etc. Catalectic forms are frequent, the Choriamb being preceded or followed by two syllables as at 637, 646. Other catalectic forms have special names, such as the *Adonius* (— ◡ ◡ — —), where only one syllable follows the Choriamb, and the *Versus Aristophanicus* (— ◡ ◡ — ◡ — —. *Lydia dic per omnes*) where three syllables, a Bacchius, follow it. Examples are 450, 461.

A favourite variety of the Choriambic Dimeter has the Choriamb in the middle, preceded and followed by two syllables. This is the colon called *Glyconic*, after Glycon, an unknown poet. Examples are 445, 447, 448, 635, 905, 910–12. A catalectic form is called *Pherecratic* after a famous comic poet. Examples are 444, 909. Another form, called *Telesillean* after an Argive poetess, has dropped its first syllable (acephaly). Examples are 451, 466, 467. A still shorter form of this colon has dropped both first and last syllables. It is known as the *Reizianum*, after the German scholar, Reiz, who identified it. In this play it does not occur in isolation, but at 655 is preceded by an Anapaest to make a kind of Trimeter (χέρα δρύπτεταί τε παρειάν. ◡ ◡ — / ◡ — — ◡ ◡ — —).

The Dimeter could also be lengthened by various other means. One such lengthened Dimeter is seen at

631, where a syllable has been added to the end of the Glyconic. This is a well-known colon, called *Hipponacteum* after the satirist Hipponax. At 652 we find two short syllables prefixed to the Versus Aristophanicus, and at 913–14 a Cretic. A similar verse is 951–2, where the Versus Aristophanicus is preceded by a Dactyl. This is best known as the last colon of the Alcaic stanza : *virginibus puerisque canto*. Another well-known colon of this kind is 446, where three syllables ($\smile$ — —) have been added to the end of the Glyconic. This colon was used by Sappho, and is called the Sapphic Hendecasyllabic, but is better known as *Phalaecian*, after a much later poet. It became a favourite Latin metre, and is well known from Catullus and Martial (*cui dono lepidum novum libellum ?*). A form of this with resolution is seen at 453.

In the Third Stasimon, at 931, 941 and 945, occurs sporadically in conjunction with Iambics a colon which was very common in non-dramatic lyric. This is known as *Hemiepes*, and is really the half of the second verse of an elegiac couplet, consisting of two dactyls and a long syllable (— $\smile$ $\smile$ — $\smile$ $\smile$ —). In conjunction with the *Epitrite* (— $\smile$ — —) it was made the basis of Pindar's most frequent colon, the *Dactylo-Epitritic*. Here it occurs also in the Epode of the Second Stasimon, where in combination with an Iambic metron, it makes up the *Iambelegus*, a favourite colon with Horace.

In analysing choral metres, we first rely on the fact that the lyrics are built up in strophic form, strophe and antistrophe corresponding syllable for syllable. This structure was taken over by Tragedy from the great choral lyric of Stesichorus (about 600 B.C.) and his successors, Simonides and Pindar. It is known as the *triadic* structure because of the triad consisting of strophe, antistrophe, and epode. The Epode could be added or omitted at the will of the poet; thus in this play the First Stasimon has no epode, but the second and third have. Within the strophe the poet had complete freedom in the variation of his cola, being controlled only by the musical accompaniment. Except for this freedom, the rhythms were very similar to the more fixed types found in the earlier Alcaic and Sapphic stanzas imitated by Horace, and the same cola were used in choral lyric, but with very much greater variety. The normal cola were Dimeters, but on occasion Trimeters were combined with them. Instead of being composed in fixed and rigid stanzas, cola were built up into *periods* within the strophe. As will be seen from the analysis prefixed to each ode, the periods are very frequently hard for us to recognise.

ΕΚΑΒΗ

ΥΠΟΘΕΣΙΣ ΕΚΑΒΗΣ

Μετὰ τὴν Ἰλίου πολιορκίαν οἱ μὲν Ἕλληνες εἰς τὴν ἀντιπέραν Τρῳάδος Χερρόνησον καθωρμίσθησαν· Ἀχιλλεὺς δὲ νυκτὸς ὁραθεὶς σφάγιον ᾔτει μίαν τῶν θυγατέρων τοῦ Πριάμου. οἱ μὲν οὖν Ἕλληνες τιμῶντες τὸν ἥρωα Πολυξένην ἀποσπάσαντες Ἑκάβης ἐσφαγίασαν· Πολυμήστωρ δὲ ὁ τῶν Θρᾳκῶν βασιλεὺς ἕνα τῶν Πριαμιδῶν Πολύδωρον ἔσφαξεν. εἰλήφει δὲ 5 τοῦτον παρὰ τοῦ Πριάμου ὁ Πολυμήστωρ εἰς παρακαταθήκην μετὰ χρημάτων. ἁλούσης δὲ τῆς πόλεως, κατασχεῖν αὐτοῦ βουλόμενος τὸν πλοῦτον φονεύειν ὥρμησε καὶ φιλίας δυστυχούσης ὠλιγώρησεν. ἐκριφέντος δὲ τοῦ σώματος εἰς τὴν θάλασσαν, κλύδων πρὸς τὰς τῶν αἰχμαλωτίδων σκηνὰς αὐτὸν ἐξέβαλεν, Ἑκάβη δὲ τὸν νεκρὸν θεασαμένη ἐπέγνω· κοινω- 10 σαμένη δὲ τὴν γνώμην Ἀγαμέμνονι, Πολυμήστορα σὺν τοῖς παισὶν αὐτοῦ ὡς ἑαυτὴν μετεπέμψατο, κρύπτουσα τὸ γεγονός, ὡς ἵνα θησαυροὺς ἐν Ἰλίῳ μηνύσῃ αὐτῷ· παραγενομένων δὲ τοὺς μὲν υἱοὺς κατέσφαξεν, αὐτὸν δὲ τῆς ὁράσεως ἐστέρησεν. ἐπὶ δὲ τῶν Ἑλλήνων λέγουσα τὸν κατήγορον ἐνίκησεν· ἐκρίθη γὰρ οὐκ ἄρξαι ὠμότητος, ἀλλ' ἀμύνασθαι τὸν κατάρξαντα. 15

ΤΑ ΤΟΥ ΔΡΑΜΑΤΟΣ ΠΡΟΣΩΠΑ

ΠΟΛΥΔΩΡΟΥ ΕΙΔΩΛΟΝ

ΕΚΑΒΗ

ΧΟΡΟΣ [ΑΙΧΜΑΛΩΤΙΔΩΝ
    ΓΥΝΑΙΚΩΝ]

ΠΟΛΥΞΕΝΗ

ΟΔΥΣΣΕΥΣ

ΤΑΛΘΥΒΙΟΣ

ΘΕΡΑΠΑΙΝΑ

ΑΓΑΜΕΜΝΩΝ

ΠΟΛΥΜΗΣΤΩΡ

ΕΚΑΒΗ

ΠΟΛΥΔΩΡΟΥ ΕΙΔΩΛΟΝ

Ἥκω νεκρῶν κευθμῶνα καὶ σκότου πύλας
λιπών, ἵν' Ἅιδης χωρὶς ᾤκισται θεῶν,
Πολύδωρος, Ἑκάβης παῖς γεγὼς τῆς Κισσέως
Πριάμου τε πατρός, ὅς μ', ἐπεὶ Φρυγῶν πόλιν
κίνδυνος ἔσχε δορὶ πεσεῖν Ἑλληνικῷ,⁣   5
δείσας ὑπεξέπεμψε Τρωικῆς χθονὸς
Πολυμήστορος πρὸς δῶμα Θρηκίου ξένου,
ὃς τήν⟨δ'⟩ ἀρίστην Χερσονησίαν πλάκα
σπείρει, φίλιππον λαὸν εὐθύνων δορί.
πολὺν δὲ σὺν ἐμοὶ χρυσὸν ἐκπέμπει λάθρᾳ⁣   10
πατήρ, ἵν', εἴ ποτ' Ἰλίου τείχη πέσοι,
τοῖς ζῶσιν εἴη παισὶ μὴ σπάνις βίου.
νεώτατος δ' ἦ Πριαμιδῶν, ὃ καί με γῆς
ὑπεξέπεμψεν· οὔτε γὰρ φέρειν ὅπλα
οὔτ' ἔγχος οἷός τ' ἦ νέῳ βραχίονι.⁣   15
ἕως μὲν οὖν γῆς ὄρθ' ἔκειθ' ὁρίσματα
πύργοι τ' ἄθραυστοι Τρωικῆς ἦσαν χθονὸς
Ἕκτωρ τ' ἀδελφὸς οὑμὸς εὐτύχει δορί,
καλῶς παρ' ἀνδρὶ Θρηκὶ πατρῴῳ ξένῳ
τροφαῖσιν ὥς τις πτόρθος ηὐξόμην, τάλας·⁣   20
ἐπεὶ δὲ Τροία θ' Ἕκτορός τ' ἀπόλλυται
ψυχή, πατρῷα θ' ἑστία κατεσκάφη,
αὐτὸς δὲ βωμῷ πρὸς θεοδμήτῳ πίτνει
σφαγεὶς Ἀχιλλέως παιδὸς ἐκ μιαιφόνου,
κτείνει με χρυσοῦ τὸν ταλαίπωρον χάριν⁣   25
ξένος πατρῷος καὶ κτανὼν ἐς οἶδμ' ἁλὸς
μεθῆχ', ἵν' αὐτὸς χρυσὸν ἐν δόμοις ἔχῃ.

3

4 ΕΚΑΒΗ

κεῖμαι δ' ἐπ' ἀκταῖς, ἄλλοτ' ἐν πόντου σάλῳ,
πολλοῖς διαύλοις κυμάτων φορούμενος,
ἄκλαυτος ἄταφος· νῦν δ' ὑπὲρ μητρὸς φίλης   30
Ἑκάβης ἀίσσω, σῶμ' ἐρημώσας ἐμόν,
τριταῖον ἤδη φέγγος αἰωρούμενος,
ὅσονπερ ἐν γῆ τῆδε Χερσονησίᾳ
μήτηρ ἐμὴ δύστηνος ἐκ Τροίας πάρα.
πάντες δ' Ἀχαιοὶ ναῦς ἔχοντες ἥσυχοι   35
θάσσουσ' ἐπ' ἀκταῖς τῆσδε Θρῃκίας χθονός·
ὁ Πηλέως γὰρ παῖς ὑπὲρ τύμβου φανεὶς
κατέσχ' Ἀχιλλεὺς πᾶν στράτευμ' Ἑλληνικόν,
πρὸς οἶκον εὐθύνοντας ἐναλίαν πλάτην·
αἰτεῖ δ' ἀδελφὴν τὴν ἐμὴν Πολυξένην   40
τύμβῳ φίλον πρόσφαγμα καὶ γέρας λαβεῖν.
καὶ τεύξεται τοῦδ', οὐδ' ἀδώρητος φίλων
ἔσται πρὸς ἀνδρῶν· ἡ πεπρωμένη δ' ἄγει
θανεῖν ἀδελφὴν τῷδ' ἐμὴν ἐν ἤματι.
δυοῖν δὲ παίδοιν δύο νεκρὼ κατόψεται   45
μήτηρ, ἐμοῦ τε τῆς τε δυστήνου κόρης.
φανήσομαι γάρ, ὡς τάφου τλήμων τύχω,
δούλης ποδῶν. πάροιθεν ἐν κλυδωνίῳ.
τοὺς γὰρ κάτω σθένοντας ἐξῃτησάμην
τύμβου κυρῆσαι κᾁς χέρας μητρὸς πεσεῖν.   50
τοὐμὸν μὲν οὖν ὅσονπερ ἤθελον τυχεῖν
ἔσται· γεραιᾷ δ' ἐκποδὼν χωρήσομαι
Ἑκάβῃ· περᾷ γὰρ ἥδ' ὑπὸ σκηνῆς πόδα
Ἀγαμέμνονος, φάντασμα δειμαίνουσ' ἐμόν.
φεῦ·
ὦ μῆτερ ἥτις ἐκ τυραννικῶν δόμων   55
δούλειον ἦμαρ εἶδες, ὡς πράσσεις κακῶς
ὅσονπερ εὖ ποτ'· ἀντισηκώσας δέ σε
φθείρει θεῶν τις τῆς πάροιθ' εὐπραξίας.

ΕΚΑΒΗ

ἄγετ', ὦ παῖδες, τὴν γραῦν πρὸ δόμων,
ἄγετ' ὀρθοῦσαι τὴν ὁμόδουλον,   60
Τρῳάδες, ὑμῖν, πρόσθε δ' ἄνασσαν·
λάβετε φέρετε πέμπετ' ἀείρετέ μου
γεραιᾶς χειρὸς προσλαζύμεναι·
κἀγὼ σκολιῷ σκίπωνι χερὸς   65
διερειδομένα σπεύσω βραδύπουν
ἤλυσιν ἄρθρων προτιθεῖσα.
ὦ στεροπὰ Διός, ὦ σκοτία νύξ,
τί ποτ' αἴρομαι ἔννυχος οὕτω
δείμασι, φάσμασιν; ὦ πότνια Χθών,   70
μελανοπτερύγων μῆτερ ὀνείρων,
ἀποπέμπομαι ἔννυχον ὄψιν,
ἣν περὶ παιδὸς ἐμοῦ τοῦ σῳζομένου κατὰ Θρήκην
ἀμφὶ Πολυξείνης τε φίλης θυγατρὸς δι' ὀνείρων   75
[εἶδον γὰρ] φοβερὰν [ὄψιν ἔμαθον] ἐδάην.
ὦ χθόνιοι θεοί, σώσατε παῖδ' ἐμόν,
ὃς μόνος οἴκων ἄγκυρ' ἔτ' ἐμῶν   80
τὴν χιονώδη Θρήκην κατέχει
ξείνου πατρίου φυλακαῖσιν.
ἔσται τι νέον·
ἥξει τι μέλος γοερὸν γοεραῖς.
οὔποτ' ἐμὰ φρὴν ὧδ' ἀλίαστος   85
φρίσσει, ταρβεῖ.
ποῦ ποτε θείαν Ἑλένου ψυχὰν
καὶ Κασάνδραν ἐσίδω, Τρῳάδες,
ὥς μοι κρίνωσιν ὀνείρους;
εἶδον γὰρ βαλιὰν ἔλαφον λύκου αἵμονι χαλᾷ   90
σφαζομέναν, ἀπ' ἐμῶν γονάτων σπασθεῖσαν ἀνοίκτως.
καὶ τόδε δεῖμά μοι· ἦλθ' ὑπὲρ ἄκρας
τύμβου κορυφᾶς
φάντασμ' Ἀχιλέως· ᾔτει δὲ γέρας
τῶν πολυμόχθων τινὰ Τρωιάδων.   95

ἀπ' ἐμᾶς ἀπ' ἐμᾶς οὖν τόδε παιδὸς
πέμψατε, δαίμονες, ἱκετεύω.

ΧΟΡΟΣ

Ἑκάβη, σπουδῇ πρός σ' ἐλιάσθην
τὰς δεσποσύνους σκηνὰς προλιποῦσ',
ἵν' ἐκληρώθην [καὶ προσετάχθην]   100
δούλη, πόλεως ἀπελαυνομένη
τῆς Ἰλιάδος, λόγχης αἰχμῇ
δοριθήρατος πρὸς Ἀχαιῶν,
οὐδὲν παθέων ἀποκουφίζουσ',
ἀλλ' ἀγγελίας βάρος ἀραμένη   105
μέγα σοί τε, γύναι, κῆρυξ ἀχέων.
ἐν γὰρ Ἀχαιῶν πλήρει ξυνόδῳ
λέγεται δόξαι σὴν παῖδ' Ἀχιλεῖ
σφάγιον θέσθαι· τύμβου δ' ἐπιβὰς
οἶσθ' ὅτε χρυσέοις ἐφάνη σὺν ὅπλοις,   110
τὰς ποντοπόρους δ' ἔσχε σχεδίας
λαίφη προτόνοις ἐπερειδομένας
τάδε θωΰσσων·
Ποῖ δή, Δαναοί, τὸν ἐμὸν τύμβον
στέλλεσθ' ἀγέραστον ἀφέντες;   115
πολλῆς δ' ἔριδος συνέπαισε κλύδων,
δόξα δ' ἐχώρει δίχ' ἀν' Ἑλλήνων
στρατὸν αἰχμητήν, τοῖς μὲν διδόναι
τύμβῳ σφάγιον, τοῖς δ' οὐχὶ δοκοῦν.
ἦν δ' ὁ τὸ μὲν σὸν σπεύδων ἀγαθὸν   120
τῆς μαντιπόλου Βάκχης ἀνέχων
λέκτρ' Ἀγαμέμνων·
τὼ Θησείδα δ', ὄζω Ἀθηνῶν,
δισσῶν μύθων ῥήτορες ἦσαν·
γνώμῃ δὲ μιᾷ συνεχωρείτην,   125
τὸν Ἀχίλλειον τύμβον στεφανοῦν
αἵματι χλωρῷ, τὰ δὲ Κασάνδρας

λέκτρ' οὐκ ἐφάτην τῆς Ἀχιλείας
πρόσθεν θήσειν ποτὲ λόγχης.
σπουδαὶ δὲ λόγων κατατεινομένων 130
ἦσαν ἴσαι πως, πρὶν ὁ ποικιλόφρων
κόπις ἡδυλόγος δημοχαριστὴς
Λαερτιάδης πείθει στρατιὰν
μὴ τὸν ἄριστον Δαναῶν πάντων
δούλων σφαγίων εἵνεκ' ἀπωθεῖν, 135
μηδέ τιν' εἰπεῖν παρὰ Φερσεφόνῃ
στάντα φθιμένων
ὡς ἀχάριστοι Δαναοὶ Δαναοῖς
τοῖς οἰχομένοις ὑπὲρ Ἑλλήνων
Τροίας πεδίων ἀπέβησαν. 140
ἥξει δ' Ὀδυσεὺς ὅσον οὐκ ἤδη,
πῶλον ἀφέλξων σῶν ἀπὸ μαστῶν
ἔκ τε γεραιᾶς χερὸς ὁρμήσων.
ἀλλ' ἴθι ναούς, ἴθι πρὸς βωμούς,
ἵζ' Ἀγαμέμνονος ἱκέτις γονάτων, 145
κήρυσσε θεοὺς τούς τ' οὐρανίδας
τούς θ' ὑπὸ γαῖαν.
ἢ γάρ σε λιταὶ διακωλύσουσ'
ὀρφανὸν εἶναι παιδὸς μελέας,
ἢ δεῖ σ' ἐπιδεῖν τύμβου προπετῆ 150
φοινισσομένην αἵματι παρθένον
ἐκ χρυσοφόρου
δειρῆς νασμῷ μελαναυγεῖ.

Εκ. οἲ ἐγὼ μελέα, τί ποτ' ἀπύσω ;   [στρ.
     ποίαν ἀχώ, ποῖον ὀδυρμόν, 155
     δειλαία δειλαίου γήρως,
         δουλείας [τᾶς] οὐ τλατᾶς,
         [τᾶς] οὐ φερτᾶς ; οἴμοι.
     τίς ἀμύνει μοι ; ποία γέννα,
     ποία δὲ πόλις ; φροῦδος πρέσβυς, 160

φροῦδοι παῖδες.
ποίαν ἢ ταύταν ἢ κείναν
στείχω; †ποῖ δ' ἦσω; † ποῦ τις θεῶν
†ἢ δαιμόνων† ἐπαρωγός;
ὦ κάκ' ἐνεγκοῦσαι,   165
Τρῳάδες ὦ κάκ' ἐνεγκοῦσαι
πήματ', ἀπωλέσατ' ὠλέσατ'· οὐκέτι μοι βίος
ἀγαστὸς ἐν φάει.
ὦ τλάμων ἄγησαί μοι πούς,
ἄγησαι τᾷ γηραιᾷ   170
πρὸς τάνδ' αὐλάν· ὦ τέκνον, ὦ παῖ,
δυστανοτάτας [ματέρος]—ἔξελθ' ἔξελθ'
οἴκων—ἄιε ματέρος αὐδάν.
[ὦ τέκνον ὡς εἰδῇς οἵαν οἵαν   175
ἀίω φάμαν περὶ σᾶς ψυχᾶς.]

ΠΟΛΥΞΕΝΗ
                              ἰώ·
          μᾶτερ μᾶτερ τί βοᾷς; τί νέον
          καρύξασ' οἴκων μ' ὥστ' ὄρνιν
              θάμβει τῷδ' ἐξέπταξας;
Εκ.   οἴμοι τέκνον.   180
Πλ.   τί με δυσφημεῖς; φροίμιά μοι κακά.
Εκ.   αἰαῖ σᾶς ψυχᾶς.
Πλ.   ἐξαύδα· μὴ κρύψῃς δαρόν·
          δειμαίνω δειμαίνω, μᾶτερ,
              τί ποτ' ἀναστένεις . . .   ι5
Εκ.   [ὦ] τέκνον τέκνον μελέας ματρὸς . . .
Πλ.   τί ⟨δὲ⟩ τόδ' ἀγγελεῖς;
Εκ.   σφάξαι σ' Ἀργείων κοινὰ
          συντείνει πρὸς τύμβον γνώμα
              Πηλείᾳ γέννᾳ.   190
Πλ.   οἴμοι μᾶτερ, πῶς φθέγγῃ
          ἀμέγαρτα κακῶν; μάνυσόν μοι,
              μάνυσον, μᾶτερ.

Εκ. αὐδῶ, παῖ, δυσφήμους φήμας·
     ἀγγέλλουσ' 'Αργείων δόξαι   195
     ψήφῳ τᾶς σᾶς περί μοι ψυχᾶς.

Πλ. ὦ δεινὰ παθοῦσ', ὦ παντλάμων,   [ἀντ.
     ὦ δυστάνου μᾶτερ βιοτᾶς
     οἵαν οἵαν αὖ σοι λώβαν
         ἐχθίσταν ἀρρήταν τ'   200
             ὦρσέν τις δαίμων ;
     οὐκέτι σοι παῖς ἅδ' οὐκέτι δὴ
     γήρᾳ δειλαίῳ δειλαία
     συνδουλεύσω.
     σκύμνον γάρ μ' ὥστ' οὐριθρέπταν   205
     μόσχον δειλαία δειλαίαν
     . . . . . ἐσόψῃ,
         χειρὸς ἀναρπαστὰν
     σᾶς ἄπο λαιμότομόν τ' 'Αίδᾳ
     γᾶς ὑποπεμπομέναν σκότον, ἔνθα νεκρῶν μέτα
         τάλαινα κείσομαι.   210
     καὶ σοῦ μέν, μᾶτερ, δυστάνου
         κλαίω πανδύρτοις θρήνοις,
     τὸν ἐμὸν δὲ βίον λώβαν λύμαν τ'
     οὐ μετακλαίομαι, ἀλλὰ θανεῖν μοι
     ξυντυχία κρείσσων ἐκύρησεν.   215

Χο. καὶ μὴν 'Οδυσσεὺς ἔρχεται σπουδῇ ποδός,
    'Εκάβη, νέον τι πρὸς σὲ σημανῶν ἔπος.

ΟΔΥΣΣΕΥΣ
     γύναι, δοκῶ μέν σ' εἰδέναι γνώμην στρατοῦ
     ψῆφόν τε τὴν κρανθεῖσαν· ἀλλ' ὅμως φράσω.
     ἔδοξ' 'Αχαιοῖς παῖδα σὴν Πολυξένην   220
     σφάξαι πρὸς ὀρθὸν χῶμ' 'Αχιλλείου τάφου.
     ἡμᾶς δὲ πομποὺς καὶ κομιστῆρας κόρης

τάσσουσιν εἶναι· θύματος δ' ἐπιστάτης
ἱερεύς τ' ἐπέσται τοῦδε παῖς Ἀχιλλέως.
οἶσθ' οὖν ὃ δρᾶσον; μήτ' ἀποσπασθῇς βίᾳ   225
μήτ' ἐς χερῶν ἄμιλλαν ἐξέλθῃς ἐμοί·
γίγνωσκε δ' ἀλκὴν καί παρουσίαν κακῶν
τῶν σῶν. σοφόν τοι κἂν κακοῖς ἃ δεῖ φρονεῖν.
Εκ. αἰαῖ· παρέστηχ', ὡς ἔοικ', ἀγὼν μέγας,
πλήρης στεναγμῶν οὐδὲ δακρύων κενός.   230
κἄγωγ' ἄρ' οὐκ ἔθνησκον οὗ μ' ἐχρῆν θανεῖν,
οὐδ' ὤλεσέν με Ζεύς, τρέφει δ', ὅπως ὁρῶ
κακῶν κάκ' ἄλλα μείζον' ἢ τάλαιν' ἐγώ.
εἰ δ' ἔστι τοῖς δούλοισι τοὺς ἐλευθέρους
μὴ λυπρὰ μηδὲ καρδίας δηκτήρια   235
ἐξιστορῆσαι, σοὶ μὲν εἰρῆσθαι χρεών,
ἡμᾶς δ' ἀκοῦσαι τοὺς ἐρωτῶντας τάδε.
Οδ. ἔξεστ', ἐρώτα· τοῦ χρόνου γὰρ οὐ φθονῶ.
Εκ. οἶσθ' ἡνίκ' ἦλθες Ἰλίου κατάσκοπος,
δυσχλαινίᾳ τ' ἄμορφος, ὀμμάτων τ' ἄπο   240
φόνου σταλαγμοὶ σὴν κατέσταζον γένυν ;
Οδ. οἶδ'· οὐ γὰρ ἄκρας καρδίας ἔψαυσέ μου.
Εκ. ἔγνω δέ σ' Ἑλένη καὶ μόνη κατεῖπ' ἐμοί ;
Οδ. μεμνήμεθ' ἐς κίνδυνον ἐλθόντες μέγαν.
Εκ. ἦψω δὲ γονάτων τῶν ἐμῶν ταπεινὸς ὤν ;   245
Οδ. ὥστ' ἐνθανεῖν γε σοῖς πέπλοισι χεῖρ' ἐμήν.
Εκ. ἔσωσα δῆτά σ' ἐξέπεμψά τε χθονός ;
Οδ. ὥστ' εἰσορᾶν γε φέγγος ἡλίου τόδε.
Εκ. τί δῆτ' ἔλεξας δοῦλος ὢν ἐμὸς τότε ;
Οδ. πολλῶν λόγων εὑρήμαθ', ὥστε μὴ θανεῖν.   250
Εκ. οὔκουν κακύνῃ τοῖσδε τοῖς βουλεύμασιν,
ὃς ἐξ ἐμοῦ μὲν ἔπαθες οἷα φῂς παθεῖν,
δρᾷς δ' οὐδὲν ἡμᾶς εὖ, κακῶς δ' ὅσον δύνῃ ;
ἀχάριστον ὑμῶν σπέρμ', ὅσοι δημηγόρους
ζηλοῦτε τιμάς· μηδὲ γιγνώσκοισθέ μοι,   255
οἳ τοὺς φίλους βλάπτοντες οὐ φροντίζετε,

ἦν τοῖσι πολλοῖς πρὸς χάριν λέγητέ·τι.
ἀτὰρ τί δὴ σόφισμα τοῦθ' ἡγούμενοι
ἐς τήνδε παῖδα ψῆφον ὥρισαν φόνου ;
πότερα τὸ χρῆν σφ' ἐπήγαγ' ἀνθρωποσφαγεῖν   260
πρὸς τύμβον, ἔνθα βουθυτεῖν μᾶλλον πρέπει ;
ἢ τοὺς κτανόντας ἀνταποκτεῖναι θέλων
ἐς τήνδ' Ἀχιλλεὺς ἐνδίκως τείνει φόνον ;
ἀλλ' οὐδὲν αὐτὸν ἥδε γ' εἴργασται κακόν.
Ἑλένην νιν αἰτεῖν χρῆν τάφῳ προσφάγματα·   265
κείνη γὰρ ὤλεσέν νιν ἐς Τροίαν τ' ἄγει.
εἰ δ' αἰχμαλώτων χρή τιν' ἔκκριτον θανεῖν
κάλλει θ' ὑπερφέρουσαν, οὐχ ἡμῶν τόδε·
ἡ Τυνδαρὶς γὰρ εἶδος ἐκπρεπεστάτη,
ἀδικοῦσά θ' ἡμῶν οὐδὲν ἧσσον ηὑρέθη.   270
τῷ μὲν δικαίῳ τόνδ' ἁμιλλῶμαι λόγον·
ἃ δ' ἀντιδοῦναι δεῖ σ' ἀπαιτούσης ἐμοῦ,
ἄκουσον. ἥψω τῆς ἐμῆς, ὡς φής, χερὸς
καὶ τῆσδε γραίας προσπίτνων παρηίδος·
ἀνθάπτομαί σου τῶνδε τῶν αὐτῶν ἐγὼ   275
χάριν τ' ἀπαιτῶ τὴν τόθ' ἱκετεύω τέ σε,
μή μου τὸ τέκνον ἐκ χερῶν ἀποσπάσῃς,
μηδὲ κτάνητε· τῶν τεθνηκότων ἅλις.
ταύτῃ γέγηθα κἀπιλήθομαι κακῶν·
ἥδ' ἀντὶ πολλῶν ἐστί μοι παραψυχή,   280
πόλις, τιθήνη, βάκτρον, ἡγεμὼν ὁδοῦ.
οὐ τοὺς κρατοῦντας χρὴ κρατεῖν ἃ μὴ χρεών,
οὐδ' εὐτυχοῦντας εὖ δοκεῖν πράξειν ἀεί·
κἀγὼ γὰρ ἦ ποτ', ἀλλὰ νῦν οὐκ εἴμ' ἔτι,
τὸν πάντα δ' ὄλβον ἦμαρ ἕν μ' ἀφείλετο.   285
ἀλλ', ὦ φίλον γένειον, αἰδέσθητί με,
οἴκτιρον· ἐλθὼν δ' εἰς Ἀχαιικὸν στρατὸν
παρηγόρησον, ὡς ἀποκτείνειν φθόνος
γυναῖκας, ἃς τὸ πρῶτον οὐκ ἐκτείνατε
βωμῶν ἀποσπάσαντες, ἀλλ' ᾠκτίρατε.   290

νόμος δ' ἐν ὑμῖν τοῖς τ' ἐλευθέροις ἴσος
καὶ τοῖσι δούλοις αἵματος κεῖται πέρι.
τὸ δ' ἀξίωμα, κἂν κακῶς λέγῃ, τὸ σὸν
πείσει· λόγος γὰρ ἔκ τ' ἀδοξούντων ἰὼν
κἀκ τῶν δοκούντων αὐτὸς οὐ ταὐτὸν σθένει. 295
Χο. οὐκ ἔστιν οὕτω στερρὸς ἀνθρώπου φύσις,
ἥτις γόων σῶν καὶ μακρῶν ὀδυρμάτων
κλύουσα θρήνους οὐκ ἂν ἐκβάλοι δάκρυ.
Οδ. Ἑκάβη, διδάσκου μηδὲ τῷ θυμουμένῳ
τὸν εὖ λέγοντα δυσμενῆ ποιοῦ φρενός. 300
ἐγὼ τὸ μὲν σὸν σῶμ' ὑφ' οὗπερ εὐτύχουν
σῴζειν ἕτοιμός εἰμι κοὐκ ἄλλως λέγω·
ἃ δ' εἶπον εἰς ἅπαντας οὐκ ἀρνήσομαι,
Τροίας ἁλούσης ἀνδρὶ τῷ πρώτῳ στρατοῦ
σὴν παῖδα δοῦναι σφάγιον ἐξαιτουμένῳ. 305
ἐν τῷδε γὰρ κάμνουσιν αἱ πολλαὶ πόλεις,
ὅταν τις ἐσθλὸς καὶ πρόθυμος ὢν ἀνὴρ
μηδὲν φέρηται τῶν κακιόνων πλέον.
ἡμῖν δ' Ἀχιλλεὺς ἄξιος τιμῆς, γύναι,
θανὼν ὑπὲρ γῆς Ἑλλάδος κάλλιστ' ἀνήρ. 310
οὔκουν τόδ' αἰσχρόν, εἰ βλέποντι μὲν φίλῳ
χρώμεσθ', ἐπεὶ δ' ὄλωλε, μὴ χρώμεσθ' ἔτι ;
εἶεν· τί δῆτ' ἐρεῖ τις, ἤν τις αὖ φανῇ
στρατοῦ τ' ἄθροισις πολεμίων τ' ἀγωνία ;
πότερα μαχούμεθ' ἢ φιλοψυχήσομεν, 315
τὸν κατθανόνθ' ὁρῶντες οὐ τιμώμενον ;
καὶ μὴν ἔμοιγε ζῶντι μέν, καθ' ἡμέραν
κεἰ σμίκρ' ἔχοιμι, πάντ' ἂν ἀρκούντως ἔχοι·
τύμβον δὲ βουλοίμην ἂν ἀξιούμενον
τὸν ἐμὸν ὁρᾶσθαι· διὰ μακροῦ γὰρ ἡ χάρις. 320
εἰ δ' οἰκτρὰ πάσχειν φής, τάδ' ἀντάκουέ μου·
εἰσὶν παρ' ἡμῖν οὐδὲν ἧσσον ἄθλιαι
γραῖαι γυναῖκες ἠδὲ πρεσβῦται σέθεν,
νύμφαι τ' ἀρίστων νυμφίων τητώμεναι,

ὧν ἥδε κεύθει σώματ' Ἰδαία κόνις.   325
τόλμα τάδ'. ἡμεῖς δ', εἰ κακῶς νομίζομεν
τιμᾶν τὸν ἐσθλόν, ἀμαθίαν ὀφλήσομεν·
οἱ βάρβαροι δὲ μήτε τοὺς φίλους φίλους
ἡγεῖσθε, μήτε τοὺς καλῶς τεθνηκότας
θαυμάζεθ', ὡς ἂν ἡ μὲν Ἑλλὰς εὐτυχῇ,   330
ὑμεῖς δ' ἔχηθ' ὅμοια τοῖς βουλεύμασιν.
Χο. αἰαῖ· τὸ δοῦλον ὡς κακὸν πέφυκ' ἀεὶ
τολμᾷ θ' ἃ μὴ χρή, τῇ βίᾳ νικώμενον.
Εκ. ὦ θύγατερ, οὑμοὶ μὲν λόγοι πρὸς αἰθέρα
φροῦδοι μάτην ῥιφέντες ἀμφὶ σοῦ φόνου·   335
σὺ δ', εἴ τι μείζω δύναμιν ἢ μήτηρ ἔχεις,
σπούδαζε πάσας ὥστ' ἀηδόνος στόμα
φθογγὰς ἱεῖσα, μὴ στερηθῆναι βίου.
πρόσπιπτε δ' οἰκτρῶς τοῦδ' Ὀδυσσέως γόνυ
καὶ πεῖθ'—ἔχεις δὲ πρόφασιν· ἔστι γὰρ τέκνα   340
καὶ τῷδε—τὴν σὴν ὥστ' ἐποικτῖραι τύχην.
Πλ. ὁρῶ σ', Ὀδυσσεῦ, δεξιὰν ὑφ' εἵματος
κρύπτοντα χεῖρα καὶ πρόσωπον ἔμπαλιν
στρέφοντα, μή σου προσθίγω γενειάδος.
θάρσει· πέφευγας τὸν ἐμὸν Ἱκέσιον Δία·   345
ὡς ἕψομαί γε τοῦ τ' ἀναγκαίου χάριν
θανεῖν τε χρήζουσ'· εἰ δὲ μὴ βουλήσομαι,
κακὴ φανοῦμαι καὶ φιλόψυχος γυνή.
τί γάρ με δεῖ ζῆν; ᾗ πατὴρ μὲν ἦν ἄναξ
Φρυγῶν ἁπάντων· τοῦτό μοι πρῶτον βίου·   350
ἔπειτ' ἐθρέφθην ἐλπίδων καλῶν ὕπο
βασιλεῦσι νύμφη, ζῆλον οὐ σμικρὸν γάμων
ἔχουσ', ὅτου δῶμ' ἑστίαν τ' ἀφίξομαι·
δέσποινα δ' ἡ δύστηνος Ἰδαίαισιν ἦ
γυναιξὶ †παρθένοις τ' ἀπόβλεπτος μέτα,†   355
ἴση θεοῖσι πλὴν τὸ κατθανεῖν μόνον·
νῦν δ' εἰμὶ δούλη. πρῶτα μέν με τοὔνομα
θανεῖν ἐρᾶν τίθησιν οὐκ εἰωθὸς ὄν·

ἔπειτ' ἴσως ἂν δεσποτῶν ὠμῶν φρένας
τύχοιμ' ἄν, ὅστις ἀργύρου μ' ὠνήσεται,   360
τὴν Ἑκτορός τε χἀτέρων πολλῶν κάσιν,
προσθεὶς δ' ἀνάγκην σιτοποιὸν ἐν δόμοις,
σαίρειν τε δῶμα κερκίσιν τ' ἐφεστάναι
λυπρὰν ἄγουσαν ἡμέραν μ' ἀναγκάσει·
λέχη δὲ τἀμὰ δοῦλος ὠνητός ποθεν   365
χρανεῖ, τυράννων πρόσθεν ἠξιωμένα.
οὐ δῆτ'· ἀφίημ' ὀμμάτων ἐλευθέρων
φέγγος τόδ', Ἅιδη προστιθεῖσ' ἐμὸν δέμας.
ἄγου μ', Ὀδυσσεῦ, καὶ διέργασαί μ' ἄγων·
οὔτ' ἐλπίδος γὰρ οὔτε του δόξης ὁρῶ   370
θάρσος παρ' ἡμῖν ὥς ποτ' εὖ πρᾶξαί με χρή.
μῆτερ, σὺ δ' ἡμῖν μηδὲν ἐμποδὼν γένῃ,
λέγουσα μηδὲ δρῶσα· συμβούλου δέ μοι
θανεῖν πρὶν αἰσχρῶν μὴ κατ' ἀξίαν τυχεῖν.
ὅστις γὰρ οὐκ εἴωθε γεύεσθαι κακῶν,   375
φέρει μέν, ἀλγεῖ δ' αὐχέν' ἐντιθεὶς ζυγῷ·
θανὼν δ' ἂν εἴη μᾶλλον εὐτυχέστερος
ἢ ζῶν· τὸ γὰρ ζῆν μὴ καλῶς μέγας πόνος.
Χο. δεινὸς χαρακτὴρ κἀπίσημος ἐν βροτοῖς
ἐσθλῶν γενέσθαι, κἀπὶ μεῖζον ἔρχεται   380
τῆς εὐγενείας ὄνομα τοῖσιν ἀξίοις.
Εκ. καλῶς μὲν εἶπας, θύγατερ, ἀλλὰ τῷ καλῷ
λύπη πρόσεστιν. εἰ δὲ δεῖ τῷ Πηλέως
χάριν γενέσθαι παιδὶ καὶ ψόγον φυγεῖν
ὑμᾶς, Ὀδυσσεῦ, τήνδε μὲν μὴ κτείνετε,   385
ἡμᾶς δ' ἄγοντες πρὸς πυρὰν Ἀχιλλέως
κεντεῖτε, μὴ φείδεσθ'· ἐγὼ 'τεκον Πάριν,
ὃς παῖδα Θέτιδος ὤλεσεν τόξοις βαλών.
Οδ. οὐ σ', ὦ γεραιά, κατθανεῖν Ἀχιλλέως
φάντασμ' Ἀχαιούς, ἀλλὰ τήνδ', ᾐτήσατο.   390
Εκ. ὑμεῖς δέ μ' ἀλλὰ θυγατρὶ συμφονεύσατε,
καὶ δὶς τόσον πῶμ' αἵματος γενήσεται

γαία νεκρῷ τε τῷ τάδ' ἐξαιτουμένῳ.
Οδ. ἅλις κόρης σῆς θάνατος, οὐ προσοιστέος
 ἄλλος πρὸς ἄλλῳ· μηδὲ τόνδ' ὠφείλομεν.   395
Εκ. πολλή γ' ἀνάγκη θυγατρὶ συνθανεῖν ἐμέ.
Οδ. πῶς; οὐ γὰρ οἶδα δεσπότας κεκτημένος.
Εκ. ὁποῖα κισσὸς δρυός, ὅπως τῆσδ' ἔξομαι.
Οδ. οὔκ, ἤν γε πείθῃ τοῖσι σοῦ σοφωτέροις.
Εκ. ὡς τῆσδ' ἑκοῦσα παιδὸς οὐ μεθήσομαι.   400
Οδ. ἀλλ' οὐδ' ἐγὼ μὴν τήνδ' ἄπειμ' αὐτοῦ λιπών.
Πλ. μῆτερ, πιθοῦ μοι· καὶ σύ, παῖ Λαερτίου,
 χάλα τοκεῦσιν εἰκότως θυμουμένοις,
 σύ τ', ὦ τάλαινα, τοῖς κρατοῦσι μὴ μάχου.
 βούλῃ πεσεῖν πρὸς οὖδας ἑλκῶσαί τε σὸν   405
 γέροντα χρῶτα πρὸς βίαν ὠθουμένη,
 ἀσχημονῆσαί τ' ἐκ νέου βραχίονος
 σπασθεῖσ', ἃ πείσῃ; μὴ σύ γ'· οὐ γὰρ ἄξιον.
 ἀλλ', ὦ φίλη μοι μῆτερ, ἡδίστην χέρα
 δός καὶ παρειὰν προσβαλεῖν παρηίδι·   410
 ὡς οὔποτ' αὖθις, ἀλλὰ νῦν πανύστατον
 ἀκτῖνα κύκλον θ' ἡλίου προσόψομαι.
 τέλος δέχῃ δὴ τῶν ἐμῶν προσφθεγμάτων.
 ὦ μῆτερ, ὦ τεκοῦσ', ἄπειμι δὴ κάτω,
Εκ. ὦ θύγατερ, ἡμεῖς δ' ἐν φάει δουλεύσομεν.   415
Πλ. ἄνυμφος ἀνυμέναιος ὧν μ' ἐχρῆν τυχεῖν,
Εκ. οἰκτρὰ σύ, τέκνον, ἀθλία δ' ἐγὼ γυνή.
Πλ. ἐκεῖ δ' ἐν Ἅιδου κείσομαι χωρὶς σέθεν.
Εκ. οἴμοι· τί δράσω; ποῖ τελευτήσω βίον;
Πλ. δούλη θανοῦμαι, πατρὸς οὖσ' ἐλευθέρου.   420
Εκ. ἡμεῖς δὲ πεντήκοντά γ' ἄμμοροι τέκνων.
Πλ. τί σοι πρὸς Ἕκτορ' ἢ γέροντ' εἴπω πόσιν;
Εκ. ἄγγελλε πασῶν ἀθλιωτάτην ἐμέ.
Πλ. ὦ στέρνα μαστοί θ', οἵ μ' ἐθρέψαθ' ἡδέως.
Εκ. ὦ τῆς ἀώρου θύγατερ ἀθλίας τύχης.   425
Πλ. χαῖρ', ὦ τεκοῦσα, χαῖρε Κασάνδρα τ' ἐμοί,

Εκ. χαίρουσιν ἄλλοι, μητρὶ δ' οὔκ ἔστιν τόδε.
Πλ. ὅ τ' ἐν φιλίπποις Θρηξὶ Πολύδωρος κάσις.
Εκ. εἰ ζῇ γ'· ἀπιστῶ δ'· ὧδε πάντα δυστυχῶ.
Πλ. ζῇ καὶ θανούσης ὄμμα συγκλήσει τὸ σόν.   430
Εκ. τέθνηκ' ἔγωγε πρὶν θανεῖν κακῶν ὕπο.
Πλ. κόμιζ', 'Οδυσσεῦ, μ' ἀμφιθεὶς κάρα πέπλοις.
      ὡς πρὶν σφαγῆναί γ' ἐκτέτηκα καρδίαν
      θρήνοισι μητρὸς τήνδε τ' ἐκτήκω γόοις.
      ὦ φῶς· προσειπεῖν γὰρ σὸν ὄνομ' ἔξεστί μοι,   435
      μέτεστι δ' οὐδὲν πλὴν ὅσον χρόνον ξίφους
      βαίνω μεταξὺ καὶ πυρᾶς 'Αχιλλέως.
Εκ. οἲ 'γώ, προλείπω· λύεται δέ μου μέλη.
      ὦ θύγατερ, ἅψαι μητρός, ἔκτεινον χέρα,
      δός· μὴ λίπῃς μ' ἄπαιδ'. ἀπωλόμην, φίλαι. . . .   440
      ὡς τὴν Λάκαιναν σύγγονον Διοσκόροιν
      'Ελένην ἴδοιμι· διὰ καλῶν γὰρ ὀμμάτων
      αἴσχιστα Τροίαν εἷλε τὴν εὐδαίμονα.

Χο. —   αὔρα, ποντιὰς αὔρα,   [στρ.
            ἅτε ποντοπόρους κομί-   445
      ζεις θοὰς ἀκάτους ἐπ' οἶδμα λίμνας,
            ποῖ με τὰν μελέαν πορεύ-
            σεις ; τῷ δουλόσυνος πρὸς οἶ-
            κον κτηθεῖσ' ἀφίξομαι ; ἢ
                  Δωρίδος ὅρμον αἴας ;   450
            ἢ Φθιάδος, ἔνθα τὸν
            καλλίστων ὑδάτων πατέρα
      φασὶν 'Απιδανὸν πεδία λιπαίνειν ;

            ἢ νάσων, ἁλιήρει   [ἀντ.
            κώπᾳ πεμπομέναν τάλαι-   456
      ναν, οἰκτρὰν βιοτὰν ἔχουσαν οἴκοις,
            ἔνθα πρωτόγονός τε φοῖ-
            νιξ δάφνα θ' ἱερούς ἀνέ-

σχε πτόρθους Λατοῖ φίλα ὠ-   460
δῖνος ἄγαλμα Δίας;
σὺν Δηλιάσιν τε κού-
ραισιν Ἀρτέμιδος θεᾶς
χρυσέαν ἄμπυκα τόξα τ' εὐλογήσω;   465

ἢ Παλλάδος ἐν πόλει   [στρ.
τὰς καλλιδίφρους Ἀθα-
ναίας ἐν κροκέῳ πέπλῳ
ζεύξομαι ἆρα πώλους ἐν
δαιδαλέαισι ποικίλλουσ'   470
ἀνθοκρόκοισι πήναις, ἢ
Τιτάνων γενεὰν
τὰν Ζεὺς ἀμφιπύρῳ κοιμί-
ζει φλογμῷ Κρονίδας;

ὤ μοι τεκέων ἐμῶν,   [ἀντ.
ὤ μοι πατέρων χθονός θ',   476
ἃ καπνῷ κατερείπεται,
τυφομένα, δορίκτητος
Ἀργείων· ἐγὼ δ' ἐν ξεί-
νᾳ χθονὶ δὴ κέκλημαι δού-   480
λα, λιποῦσ' Ἀσίαν,
Εὐρώπας θεραπνᾶν ἀλλά-
ξασ' Ἀίδα θαλάμους.

ΤΑΛΘΥΒΙΟΣ
ποῦ τὴν ἄνασσαν δή ποτ' οὖσαν Ἰλίου
Ἑκάβην ἂν ἐξεύροιμι, Τρῳάδες κόραι;   485
Χο. αὕτη πέλας σου νῶτ' ἔχουσ' ἐπὶ χθονί,
Ταλθύβιε, κεῖται ξυγκεκλημένη πέπλοις.
Τα. ὦ Ζεῦ, τί λέξω; πότερά σ' ἀνθρώπους ὁρᾶν;
ἢ δόξαν ἄλλως τήνδε κεκτῆσθαι μάτην,
[ψευδῆ, δοκοῦντας δαιμόνων εἶναι γένος]   490

τύχην δὲ πάντα τὰν βροτοῖς ἐπισκοπεῖν ;
οὐχ ἥδ᾽ ἄνασσα τῶν πολυχρύσων Φρυγῶν,
οὐχ ἥδε Πριάμου τοῦ μέγ᾽ ὀλβίου δάμαρ ;
καὶ νῦν πόλις μὲν πᾶσ᾽ ἀνέστηκεν δορί,
αὐτὴ δὲ δούλη γραῦς ἄπαις ἐπὶ χθονὶ   495
κεῖται, κόνει φύρουσα δύστηνον κάρα.
φεῦ φεῦ· γέρων μέν εἰμ᾽, ὅμως δέ μοι θανεῖν
εἴη πρὶν αἰσχρᾷ περιπεσεῖν τύχῃ τινί.
   ἀνίστασ᾽, ὦ δύστηνε, καὶ μετάρσιον
πλευρὰν ἔπαιρε καὶ τὸ πάλλευκον κάρα.   500
Εκ. ἔα· τίς οὗτος σῶμα τοὐμὸν οὐκ ἐᾷ
κεῖσθαι ; τί κινεῖς μ᾽, ὅστις εἶ, λυπουμένην ;
Τα. Ταλθύβιος ἥκω Δαναϊδῶν ὑπηρέτης,
᾽Αγαμέμνονος πέμψαντος, ὦ γύναι, μέτα.
Εκ. ὦ φίλτατ᾽, ἆρα κἄμ᾽ ἐπισφάξαι τάφῳ   505
δοκοῦν ᾽Αχαιοῖς ἦλθες ; ὡς φίλ᾽ ἂν λέγοις.
σπεύδωμεν, ἐγκονῶμεν· ἡγοῦ μοι, γέρον.
Τα. σὴν παῖδα κατθανοῦσαν ὡς θάψῃς, γύναι,
ἥκω μεταστείχων σε· πέμπουσιν δέ με
δισσοί τ᾽ ᾽Ατρεῖδαι καὶ λεὼς ᾽Αχαιικός.   510
Εκ. οἴμοι, τί λέξεις ; οὐκ ἄρ᾽ ὡς θανουμένους
μετῆλθες ἡμᾶς, ἀλλὰ σημανῶν κακά ;
ὄλωλας, ὦ παῖ, μητρὸς ἁρπασθεῖσ᾽ ἄπο·
ἡμεῖς δ᾽ ἄτεκνοι τοὐπὶ σ᾽· ὦ τάλαιν᾽ ἐγώ.
πῶς καί νιν ἐξεπράξατ᾽ ; ἆρ᾽ αἰδούμενοι ;   515
ἢ πρὸς τὸ δεινὸν ἤλθεθ᾽ ὡς ἐχθράν, γέρον,
κτείνοντες ; εἰπέ, καίπερ οὐ λέξων φίλα.
Τα. διπλᾶ με χρῄζεις δάκρυα κερδᾶναι, γύναι,
σῆς παιδὸς οἴκτῳ· νῦν τε γὰρ λέγων κακὰ
τέγξω τόδ᾽ ὄμμα, πρὸς τάφῳ θ᾽ ὅτ᾽ ὤλλυτο.   520
παρῆν μὲν ὄχλος πᾶς ᾽Αχαιικοῦ στρατοῦ
πλήρης πρὸ τύμβου σῆς κόρης ἐπὶ σφαγάς·
λαβὼν δ᾽ ᾽Αχιλλέως παῖς Πολυξένην χερὸς
ἔστησ᾽ ἐπ᾽ ἄκρου χώματος, πέλας δ᾽ ἐγώ·

λεκτοί τ' 'Αχαιῶν ἔκκριτοι νεανίαι,   525
σκίρτημα μόσχου σῆς καθέξοντες χεροῖν,
ἔσποντο.   πλῆρες δ' ἐν χεροῖν λαβὼν δέπας
πάγχρυσον αἴρει χειρὶ παῖς 'Αχιλλέως
χοὰς θανόντι πατρί· σημαίνει δέ μοι
σιγὴν 'Αχαιῶν παντὶ κηρῦξαι στρατῷ.   530
κἀγὼ καταστὰς εἶπον ἐν μέσοις τάδε·
Σιγᾶτ', 'Αχαιοί, σῖγα πᾶς ἔστω λεώς,
σίγα σιώπα· νήνεμον δ' ἔστησ' ὄχλον.
ὁ δ' εἶπεν· 'Ω παῖ Πηλέως, πατὴρ δ' ἐμός,
δέξαι χοάς μοι τάσδε κηλητηρίους,   535
νεκρῶν ἀγωγούς· ἐλθὲ δ', ὡς πίῃς μέλαν
κόρης ἀκραιφνὲς αἷμ', ὅ σοι δωρούμεθα
στρατός τε κἀγώ· πρευμενὴς δ' ἡμῖν γενοῦ
λῦσαί τε πρύμνας καὶ χαλινωτήρια
νεῶν δὸς ἡμῖν † πρευμενοῦς † τ' ἀπ' 'Ιλίου   540
νόστου τυχόντας πάντας ἐς πάτραν μολεῖν.
    τοσαῦτ' ἔλεξε, πᾶς δ' ἐπηύξατο στρατός.
εἶτ' ἀμφίχρυσον φάσγανον κώπης λαβὼν
ἐξεῖλκε κολεοῦ, λογάσι δ' 'Αργείων στρατοῦ
νεανίαις ἔνευσε παρθένον λαβεῖν.   545
ἡ δ', ὡς ἐφράσθη, τόνδ' ἐσήμηνεν λόγον·
'Ω τὴν ἐμὴν πέρσαντες 'Αργεῖοι πόλιν,
ἑκοῦσα θνήσκω· μή τις ἅψηται χροὸς
τοὐμοῦ· παρέξω γὰρ δέρην εὐκαρδίως.
ἐλευθέραν δέ μ', ὡς ἐλευθέρα θάνω,   550
πρὸς θεῶν, μεθέντες κτείνατ'· ἐν νεκροῖσι γὰρ
δούλη κεκλῆσθαι βασιλὶς οὖσ' αἰσχύνομαι.
    λαοὶ δ' ἐπερρόθησαν, 'Αγαμέμνων τ' ἄναξ
εἶπεν μεθεῖναι παρθένον νεανίαις.
[οἱ δ', ὡς τάχιστ' ἤκουσαν ὑστάτην ὄπα,   555
μεθῆκαν, οὗπερ καὶ μέγιστον ἦν κράτος.]
κἀπεὶ τόδ' εἰσήκουσε δεσποτῶν ἔπος,
λαβοῦσα πέπλους ἐξ ἄκρας ἐπωμίδος

ἔρρηξε λαγόνας ἐς μέσας παρ' ὀμφαλόν,
μαστούς τ' ἔδειξε στέρνα θ' ὡς ἀγάλματος 560
κάλλιστα, καὶ καθεῖσα πρὸς γαῖαν γόνυ
ἔλεξε πάντων τλημονέστατον λόγον·
'Ιδού, τόδ', εἰ μὲν στέρνον, ὦ νεανία,
παίειν προθυμῇ, παῖσον, εἰ δ' ὑπ' αὐχένα
χρῄζεις, πάρεστι λαιμὸς εὐτρεπὴς ὅδε. 565
ὃ δ' οὐ θέλων τε καὶ θέλων οἴκτῳ κόρης,
τέμνει σιδήρῳ πνεύματος διαρροάς·
κρουνοὶ δ' ἐχώρουν. ἣ δὲ καὶ θνῄσκουσ' ὅμως
πολλὴν πρόνοιαν εἶχεν εὐσχήμων πεσεῖν,
κρύπτουσ' ἃ κρύπτειν ὄμματ' ἀρσένων χρεών. 570
ἐπεὶ δ' ἀφῆκε πνεῦμα θανασίμῳ σφαγῇ,
οὐδεὶς τὸν αὐτὸν εἶχεν 'Αργείων πόνον·
ἀλλ' οἱ μὲν αὐτῶν τὴν θανοῦσαν ἐκ χερῶν
φύλλοις ἔβαλλον, οἱ δέ πληροῦσιν πυρὰν
κορμοὺς φέροντες πευκίνους, ὁ δ' οὐ φέρων 575
πρὸς τοῦ φέροντος τοιάδ' ἤκουεν κακά·
῾Εστηκας, ὦ κάκιστε, τῇ νεάνιδι
οὐ πέπλον οὐδὲ κόσμον ἐν χεροῖν ἔχων;
οὐκ εἶ τι δώσων τῇ περίσσ' εὐκαρδίῳ
ψυχήν τ' ἀρίστῃ; τοιάδ' ἀμφὶ σῆς λέγων 580
παιδὸς θανούσης, εὐτεκνωτάτην τέ σε
πασῶν γυναικῶν δυστυχεστάτην θ' ὁρῶ.
Χο. δεινόν τι πῆμα Πριαμίδαις ἐπέζεσεν
πόλει τε τῇ μῇ θεῶν ἀνάγκαισιν τόδε.
Εκ. ὦ θύγατερ, οὐκ οἶδ' εἰς ὅ τι βλέψω κακῶν, 585
πολλῶν παρόντων· ἢν γὰρ ἅψωμαί τινος,
τόδ' οὐκ ἐᾷ με, παρακαλεῖ δ' ἐκεῖθεν αὖ
λύπη τις ἄλλη διάδοχος κακῶν κακοῖς
καὶ νῦν τὸ μὲν σὸν ὥστε μὴ στένειν πάθος
οὐκ ἂν δυναίμην ἐξαλείψασθαι φρενός· 590
τὸ δ' αὖ λίαν παρεῖλες ἀγγελθεῖσά μοι
γενναῖος. οὔκουν δεινόν, εἰ γῆ μὲν κακὴ

τυχοῦσα καιροῦ θεόθεν εὖ στάχυν φέρει,
χρηστὴ δ' ἀμαρτοῦσ' ὧν χρεὼν αὐτὴν τυχεῖν
κακὸν δίδωσι καρπόν, ἀνθρώποις δ' ἀεί   595
ὁ μὲν πονηρὸς οὐδὲν ἄλλο πλὴν κακός,
ὁ δ' ἐσθλὸς ἐσθλός, οὐδὲ συμφορᾶς ὕπο
φύσιν διέφθειρ', ἀλλὰ χρηστός ἐστ' ἀεί ;
ἆρ' οἱ τεκόντες διαφέρουσιν ἢ τροφαί ;
ἔχει γε μέντοι καὶ τὸ θρεφθῆναι καλῶς   600
δίδαξιν ἐσθλοῦ· τοῦτο δ' ἤν τις εὖ μάθῃ,
οἶδεν τό γ' αἰσχρόν, κανόνι τοῦ καλοῦ μαθών,
καὶ ταῦτα μὲν δὴ νοῦς ἐτόξευσεν μάτην·
σὺ δ' ἐλθὲ καὶ σήμηνον 'Αργείοις τάδε,
μὴ θιγγάνειν μοι μηδέν', ἀλλ' εἴργειν ὄχλον,   605
τῆς παιδός.   ἔν τοι μυρίῳ στρατεύματι
ἀκόλαστος ὄχλος ναυτική τ' ἀναρχία
κρείσσων πυρός, κακὸς δ' ὁ μή τι δρῶν κακόν.
σὺ δ' αὖ λαβοῦσα τεῦχος, ἀρχαία λάτρι,
βάψασ' ἔνεγκε δεῦρο ποντίας ἁλός,   610
ὡς παῖδα λουτροῖς τοῖς πανυστάτοις ἐμήν,
νύμφην τ' ἄνυμφον παρθένον τ' ἀπάρθενον,
λούσω προθῶμαί θ'—ὡς μὲν ἀξία, πόθεν ;
οὐκ ἂν δυναίμην· ὡς δ' ἔχω—τί γὰρ πάθω ;—
κόσμον τ' ἀγείρασ' αἰχμαλωτίδων πάρα,   615
αἵ μοι πάρεδροι τῶνδ' ἔσω σκηνωμάτων
ναίουσιν, εἴ τις τοὺς νεωστὶ δεσπότας
λαθοῦσ' ἔχει τι κλέμμα τῶν αὐτῆς δόμων.
ὦ σχήματ' οἴκων, ὦ ποτ' εὐτυχεῖς δόμοι,
ὦ πλεῖστ' ἔχων κάλλιστά τ', εὐτεκνώτατε   620
Πρίαμε, γεραιά θ' ἥδ' ἐγὼ μήτηρ τέκνων,
ὡς ἐς τὸ μηδὲν ἥκομεν, φρονήματος
τοῦ πρὶν στερέντες.   εἶτα δῆτ' ὀγκούμεθα,
ὁ μέν τις ἡμῶν πλουσίοις ἐν δώμασιν,
ὁ δ' ἐν πολίταις τίμιος κεκλημένος.   625
τὰ δ' οὐδὲν ἄλλως, φροντίδων βουλεύματα

γλώσσης τε κόμποι. κεῖνος ὀλβιώτατος,
ὅτῳ κατ' ἦμαρ τυγχάνει μηδὲν κακόν.

Χο.   ἐμοὶ χρῆν συμφοράν,   [στρ.
    ἐμοὶ χρῆν πημονὰν γενέσθαι,   630
    Ἰδαίαν ὅτε πρῶτον ὕλαν
    Ἀλέξανδρος εἰλατίναν
    ἐτάμεθ', ἅλιον ἐπ' οἶδμα ναυστολήσων
    Ἑλένας ἐπὶ λέκτρα, τὰν   635
    καλλίσταν ὁ χρυσοφαὴς
    Ἅλιος αὐγάζει.

    πόνοι γὰρ καὶ πόνων   [ἀντ.
    ἀνάγκαι κρείσσονες κυκλοῦνται   640
    κοινὸν δ' ἐξ ἰδίας ἀνοίας
    κακὸν τᾷ Σιμουντίδι γᾷ
    ὀλέθριον ἔμολε συμφορά τ' ἀπ' ἄλλων.
    ἐκρίθη δ' ἔρις, ἃν ἐν Ἴ-
    δᾳ κρίνει τρισσὰς μακάρων   645
    παῖδας ἀνὴρ βούτας,
ἐπὶ δορὶ καὶ φόνῳ καὶ ἐμῶν μελάθρων λώβᾳ· [ἐπῳδ.
στένει δὲ καί τις ἀμφὶ τὸν εὔροον Εὐρώταν   650
Λάκαινα πολυδάκρυτος ἐν δόμοις κόρα,
    πολιάν τ' ἐπὶ κρᾶτα μάτηρ
    τέκνων θανόντων
    † τίθεται χέρα δρύπτεται παρειάν,†   655
    δίαιμον ὄνυχα τιθεμένα σπαραγμοῖς.

ΘΕΡΑΠΑΙΝΑ

    γυναῖκες, Ἑκάβη ποῦ ποθ' ἡ παναθλία,
    ἡ πάντα νικῶσ' ἄνδρα καὶ θῆλυν σποράν
    κακοῖσιν; οὐδεὶς στέφανον ἀνθαιρήσεται.   660
Χο. τί δ', ὦ τάλαινα σῆς κακογλώσσου βοῆς;
    ὡς οὔποθ' εὕδει λυπρά σου κηρύγματα.

Θε. Ἑκάβη φέρω τόδ' ἄλγος· ἐν κακοῖσι δὲ
οὐ ῥᾴδιον βροτοῖσιν εὐφημεῖν στόμα.
Χο. καὶ μὴν περῶσα τυγχάνει δόμων ὕπερ 665
ἥδ', ἐς δὲ καιρὸν σοῖσι φαίνεται λόγοις·
Θε. ὦ παντάλαινα κἄτι μᾶλλον ἢ λέγω,
δέσποιν', ὄλωλας κοὐκέτ' εἶ, βλέπουσα φῶς,
ἄπαις ἄνανδρος ἄπολις ἐξεφθαρμένη.
Εκ. οὐ καινὸν εἶπας, εἰδόσιν δ' ὠνείδισας. 670
ἀτὰρ τί νεκρὸν τόνδε μοι Πολυξένης
ἥκεις κομίζουσ', ἧς ἀπηγγέλθη τάφος
πάντων Ἀχαιῶν διὰ χερὸς σπουδὴν ἔχειν ;
Θε. ἥδ' οὐδὲν οἶδεν, ἀλλά μοι Πολυξένην
θρηνεῖ, νέων δὲ πημάτων οὐχ ἅπτεται. 675
Εκ. οἲ 'γὼ τάλαινα· μῶν τὸ βακχεῖον κάρα
τῆς θεσπιῳδοῦ δεῦρο Κασάνδρας φέρεις ;
Θε. ζῶσαν λέλακας, τὸν θανόντα δ' οὐ στένεις
τόνδ'· ἀλλ' ἄθρησον σῶμα γυμνωθὲν νεκροῦ
εἴ σοι φανεῖται θαῦμα καὶ παρ' ἐλπίδας. 680
Εκ. οἴμοι, βλέπω δὴ παῖδ' ἐμὸν τεθνηκότα,
Πολύδωρον, ὅν μοι Θρῇξ ἔσῳζ' οἴκοις ἀνήρ.
ἀπωλόμην δύστηνος, οὐκέτ' εἰμὶ δή.
ὦ τέκνον τέκνον,
αἰαῖ, κατάρχομαι γόων, 685
βακχεῖον ἐξ ἀλάστορος
ἀρτιμαθῆ νόμον.
Θε. ἔγνως γὰρ ἄτην παιδός, ὦ δύστηνε σύ ;
Εκ. ἄπιστ' ἄπιστα, καινὰ καινὰ δέρκομαι.
ἕτερα δ' ἀφ' ἑτέρων κακὰ κακῶν κυρεῖ· 690
οὐδέ ποτ' ἀστένακτος ἀδάκρυτος ἁ-
μέρα [μ'] ἐπισχήσει.
Χο. δείν', ὦ τάλαινα, δεινὰ πάσχομεν κακά.
Εκ. ὦ τέκνον τέκνον ταλαίνας ματρός,
τίνι μόρῳ θνήσκεις, 695
τίνι πότμῳ κεῖσαι ;
πρὸς τίνος ἀνθρώπων ;

Θε. οὐκ οἶδ'· ἐπ' ἀκταῖς νιν κυρῶ θαλασσίαις . . .
Εκ. ἔκβλητον, ἢ πέσημα φοινίου δορός,
    ἐν ψαμάθῳ λευρᾷ ; 700
Θε. πόντου νιν ἐξήνεγκε πελάγιος κλύδων.
Εκ. ὤμοι, αἰαῖ, ἔμαθον ἔνυπνον ὀμμάτων
    ἐμῶν ὄψιν· οὔ με παρέβα
    φάσμα μελανόπτερον, τὰν ἐσεῖδον ἀμφὶ σέ, 705
    ὦ τέκνον, οὐκέτ' ὄντα Διὸς ἐν φάει.
Χο. τίς γάρ νιν ἔκτειν' ; οἶσθ' ὀνειρόφρων φράσαι ;
Εκ. ἐμὸς ἐμὸς ξένος, Θρήκιος ἱππότας, 710
    ἵν' ὁ γέρων πατὴρ ἔθετό νιν κρύψας.
Χο. οἴμοι, τί λέξεις ; χρυσὸν ὡς ἔχοι κτανών ;
Εκ. ἄρρητ' ἀνωνόμαστα, θαυμάτων πέρα,
    οὐχ ὅσι' οὐδ' ἀνεκτά. ποῦ δίκα ξένων ; 715
    ὦ κατάρατ' ἀνδρῶν, ὡς διεμοιράσω
    χρόα, σιδαρέῳ τεμὼν φασγάνῳ
    μέλεα τοῦδε παιδὸς οὐδ' ᾤκτισας. 720
Χο. ὦ τλῆμον, ὥς σε πολυπονωτάτην βροτῶν
    δαίμων ἔθηκεν ὅστις ἐστί σοι βαρύς.
    ἀλλ' εἰσορῶ γὰρ τοῦδε δεσπότου δέμας
    Ἀγαμέμνονος, τοὐνθένδε σιγῶμεν, φίλαι. 725

ΑΓΑΜΕΜΝΩΝ

    Ἑκάβη, τί μέλλεις παῖδα σὴν κρύπτειν τάφῳ
    ἐλθοῦσ', ἐφ' οἷσπερ Ταλθύβιος ἤγγειλέ μοι
    μὴ 'θιγγάνειν σῆς μηδέν' Ἀργείων κόρης ;
    ἡμεῖς μὲν οὖν εἰῶμεν οὐδ' ἐψαύομεν·
    σὺ δὲ σχολάζεις, ὥστε θαυμάζειν ἐμέ. 730
    ἥκω δ' ἀποστελῶν σε· τἀκεῖθεν γὰρ εὖ
    πεπραγμέν' ἐστίν—εἴ τι τῶνδ' ἐστὶν καλῶς.
    ἔα· τίν' ἄνδρα τόνδ' ἐπὶ σκηναῖς ὁρῶ
    θανόντα Τρώων ; οὐ γὰρ Ἀργεῖον πέπλοι
    δέμας περιπτύσσοντες ἀγγέλλουσί μοι. 735
Εκ. δύστην', ἐμαυτὴν γὰρ λέγω λέγουσα σέ,

Ἑκάβη, τί δράσω; πότερα προσπέσω γόνυ
Ἀγαμέμνονος τοῦδ᾽ ἢ φέρω σιγῇ κακά;
Αγ. τί μοι προσώπῳ νῶτον ἐγκλίνασα σὸν
    δύρῃ, τὸ πραχθὲν δ᾽ οὐ λέγεις ;—τίς ἔσθ᾽ ὅδε ;   740
Εκ. ἀλλ᾽, εἴ με δούλην πολεμίαν θ᾽ ἡγούμενος
    γονάτων ἀπώσαιτ᾽, ἄλγος ἂν προσθείμεθ᾽ ἄν.
Αγ. οὔτοι πέφυκα μάντις, ὥστε μὴ κλύων
    ἐξιστορῆσαι σῶν ὁδὸν βουλευμάτων.
Εκ. ἆρ᾽ ἐκλογίζομαί γε πρὸς τὸ δυσμενὲς   745
    μᾶλλον φρένας τοῦδ᾽, ὄντος οὐχὶ δυσμενοῦς ;
Αγ. εἴ τοί με βούλῃ τῶνδε μηδὲν εἰδέναι,
    ἐς ταὐτὸν ἥκεις· καὶ γὰρ οὐδ᾽ ἐγὼ κλύειν.
Εκ. οὐκ ἂν δυναίμην τοῦδε τιμωρεῖν ἄτερ
    τέκνοισι τοῖς ἐμοῖσι. τί στρέφω τάδε ;   750
    τολμᾶν ἀνάγκη, κἂν τύχω κἂν μὴ τύχω.—
    Ἀγάμεμνον, ἱκετεύω σε τῶνδε γουνάτων
    καὶ σοῦ γενείου δεξιᾶς τ᾽ εὐδαίμονος . . .
Αγ. τί χρῆμα μαστεύουσα ; μῶν ἐλεύθερον
    αἰῶνα θέσθαι ; ῥᾴδιον γάρ ἐστί σοι.   755
Εκ. οὐ δῆτα· τοὺς κακοὺς δὲ τιμωρουμένη
    αἰῶνα τὸν σύμπαντα δουλεύειν θέλω.
Αγ. καὶ δὴ τίν᾽ ἡμᾶς εἰς ἐπάρκεσιν καλεῖς ;
Εκ. οὐδέν τι τούτων ὧν σὺ δοξάζεις, ἄναξ.—
    ὁρᾷς νεκρὸν τόνδ᾽, οὗ καταστάζω δάκρυ ;   760
Αγ. ὁρῶ· τὸ μέντοι μέλλον οὐκ ἔχω μαθεῖν.
Εκ. τοῦτόν ποτ᾽ ἔτεκον κἄφερον ζώνης ὕπο.
Αγ. ἔστιν δὲ τίς σῶν οὗτος, ὦ τλῆμον, τέκνων ;
Εκ. οὐ τῶν θανόντων Πριαμιδῶν ὑπ᾽ Ἰλίῳ.
Αγ. ἦ γάρ τιν᾽ ἄλλον ἔτεκες ἢ κείνους, γύναι ;   765
Εκ. ἀνόνητά γ᾽, ὡς ἔοικε, τόνδ᾽ ὃν εἰσορᾷς.
Αγ. ποῦ δ᾽ ὢν ἐτύγχαν᾽, ἡνίκ᾽ ὤλλυτο πτόλις ;
Εκ. πατήρ νιν ἐξέπεμψεν ὀρρωδῶν θανεῖν.
Αγ. ποῖ τῶν τότ᾽ ὄντων χωρίσας τέκνων μόνον ;
Εκ. ἐς τήνδε χώραν, οὗπερ ηὑρέθη θανών.   770

Αγ. πρὸς ἄνδρ' ὃς ἄρχει τῆσδε Πολυμήστωρ χθονός ;
Εκ. ἐνταῦθ' ἐπέμφθη πικροτάτου χρυσοῦ φύλαξ.
Αγ. θνῄσκει δὲ πρὸς τοῦ καὶ τίνος πότμου τυχών ;
Εκ. τίνος γ' ὑπ' ἄλλου ; Θρῄξ νιν ὤλεσε ξένος.
Αγ. ὦ τλῆμον· ἦ που χρυσὸν ἡράσθη λαβεῖν ;   775
Εκ. τοιαῦτ', ἐπειδὴ συμφορὰν ἔγνω Φρυγῶν.
Αγ. ηὗρες δὲ ποῦ νιν ; ἢ τίς ἤνεγκεν νεκρόν ;
Εκ. ἥδ', ἐντυχοῦσα ποντίας ἀκτῆς ἔπι.
Αγ. τοῦτον ματεύουσ' ἢ πονοῦσ' ἄλλον πόνον ;
Εκ. λούτρ' ᾤχετ' οἴσουσ' ἐξ ἁλὸς Πολυξένῃ.   780
Αγ. κτανών νιν, ὡς ἔοικεν, ἐκβάλλει ξένος.
Εκ. θαλασσόπλαγκτόν γ', ὧδε διατεμὼν χρόα.
Αγ. ὦ σχετλία σὺ τῶν ἀμετρήτων πόνων.
Εκ. ὄλωλα κοὐδὲν λοιπόν, Ἀγάμεμνον, κακῶν.
Αγ. φεῦ φεῦ· τίς οὕτω δυστυχὴς ἔφυ γυνή ;   785
Εκ. οὐκ ἔστιν, εἰ μὴ τὴν Τύχην αὐτὴν λέγοις.
    ἀλλ' ὧνπερ οὕνεκ' ἀμφὶ σὸν πίπτω γόνυ
    ἄκουσον. εἰ μὲν ὅσιά σοι παθεῖν δοκῶ,
    στέργοιμ' ἄν· εἰ δὲ τοὔμπαλιν, σύ μοι γενοῦ
    τιμωρὸς ἀνδρός, ἀνοσιωτάτου ξένου,   790
    ὃς οὔτε τοὺς γῆς νέρθεν οὔτε τοὺς ἄνω
    δείσας δέδρακεν ἔργον ἀνοσιώτατον,
    κοινῆς τραπέζης πολλάκις τυχὼν ἐμοί,
    ξενίας τ' ἀριθμῷ πρῶτ' ἔχων ἐμῶν φίλων,
    τυχὼν δ' ὅσων δεῖ—. καὶ λαβὼν προμηθίαν   795
    ἔκτεινε· τύμβου δ', εἰ κτανεῖν ἐβούλετο,
    οὐκ ἠξίωσεν, ἀλλ' ἀφῆκε πόντιον.
    ἡμεῖς μὲν οὖν δοῦλοί τε κἀσθενεῖς ἴσως·
    ἀλλ' οἱ θεοὶ σθένουσι χὡ κείνων κρατῶν
    Νόμος· νόμῳ γὰρ τοὺς θεοὺς ἡγούμεθα   800
    καὶ ζῶμεν ἄδικα καὶ δίκαι' ὡρισμένοι·
    ὃς ἐς σ' ἀνελθὼν εἰ διαφθαρήσεται,
    καὶ μὴ δίκην δώσουσιν οἵτινες ξένους
    κτείνουσιν ἢ θεῶν ἱερὰ τολμῶσιν φέρειν,

οὐκ ἔστιν οὐδὲν τῶν ἐν ἀνθρώποις ἴσον.　805
ταῦτ᾽ οὖν ἐν αἰσχρῷ θέμενος αἰδέσθητί με·
οἴκτιρον ἡμᾶς, ὡς †γραφεύς† τ᾽ ἀποσταθεὶς
ἰδοῦ με κἀνάθρησον οἷ᾽ ἔχω κακά.
τύραννος ἦ ποτ᾽, ἀλλὰ νῦν δούλη σέθεν,
εὔπαις ποτ᾽ οὖσα, νῦν δὲ γραῦς ἄπαις θ᾽ ἅμα,　810
ἄπολις ἔρημος, ἀθλιωτάτη βροτῶν . . .
　οἴμοι τάλαινα, ποῖ μ᾽ ὑπεξάγεις πόδα ;
ἔοικα πράξειν οὐδέν· ὦ τάλαιν᾽ ἐγώ.
τί δῆτα θνητοὶ τἆλλα μὲν μαθήματα
μοχθοῦμεν ὡς χρὴ πάντα καὶ ματεύομεν,　815
Πειθὼ δὲ τὴν τύραννον ἀνθρώποις μόνην
οὐδέν τι μᾶλλον ἐς τέλος σπουδάζομεν
μισθοὺς διδόντες μανθάνειν, ἵν᾽ ἦν ποτε
πείθειν ἅ τις βούλοιτο τυγχάνειν θ᾽ ἅμα ;
πῶς οὖν ἔτ᾽ ἄν τις ἐλπίσαι πράξειν καλῶς ;　820
οἱ μὲν γὰρ ὄντες παῖδες οὐκέτ᾽ εἰσί μοι,
αὕτη δ᾽ ἐπ᾽ αἰσχροῖς αἰχμάλωτος. οἴχομαι·
καπνὸν δὲ πόλεως τόνδ᾽ ὑπερθρῴσκονθ᾽ ὁρῶ.
　καὶ μήν—ἴσως μὲν τοῦ λόγου κενὸν τόδε,
Κύπριν προβάλλειν· ἀλλ᾽ ὅμως εἰρήσεται·　825
πρὸς σοῖσι πλευροῖς παῖς ἐμὴ κοιμίζεται
ἡ φοιβάς, ἣν καλοῦσι Κασάνδραν Φρύγες.
ποῦ τὰς φίλας δῆτ᾽ εὐφρόνας δείξεις, ἄναξ,
ἢ τῶν ἐν εὐνῇ φιλτάτων ἀσπασμάτων
χάριν τίν᾽ ἕξει παῖς ἐμή, κείνης δ᾽ ἐγώ ;　830
[ἐκ τοῦ σκότου τε τῶν τε νυκτερησίων
φίλτρων μεγίστη γίγνεται βροτοῖς χάρις.]
ἄκουε δή νυν· τὸν θανόντα τόνδ᾽ ὁρᾷς ;
τοῦτον καλῶς δρῶν ὄντα κηδεστὴν σέθεν
δράσεις. ἑνός μοι μῦθος ἐνδεὴς ἔτι.　835
εἴ μοι γένοιτο φθόγγος ἐν βραχίοσι
καὶ χερσὶ καὶ κόμαισι καὶ ποδῶν βάσει
ἢ Δαιδάλου τέχναισιν ἢ θεῶν τινος,

ὡς πάνθ' ὁμαρτῇ σῶν ἔχοιντο· γουνάτων
κλαίοντ', ἐπισκήπτοντα παντοίους λόγους.   840
ὦ δέσποτ', ὦ μέγιστον Ἕλλησιν φάος,
πιθοῦ, παράσχες χεῖρα τῇ πρεσβύτιδι
τιμωρόν, εἰ καὶ μηδέν ἐστιν, ἀλλ' ὅμως.
ἐσθλοῦ γὰρ ἀνδρὸς τῇ δίκῃ θ' ὑπηρετεῖν
καὶ τοὺς κακοὺς δρᾶν πανταχοῦ κακῶς ἀεί.   845
Χο. δεινόν γε, θνητοῖς ὡς ἅπαντα συμπίτνει,
καὶ τὰς ἀνάγκας οἱ νόμοι διώρισαν,
φίλους τιθέντες τούς γε πολεμιωτάτους
ἐχθρούς τε τοὺς πρὶν εὐμενεῖς ποιούμενοι.
Αγ. ἐγὼ σὲ καὶ σὸν παῖδα καὶ τύχας σέθεν,   850
Ἑκάβη, δι' οἴκτου χεῖρά θ' ἱκεσίαν ἔχω,
καὶ βούλομαι θεῶν θ' οὕνεκ' ἀνόσιον ξένον
καὶ τοῦ δικαίου τήνδε σοι δοῦναι δίκην,
εἴ πως φανείη γ' ὥστε σοί τ' ἔχειν καλῶς,
στρατῷ τε μὴ δόξαιμι Κασάνδρας χάριν   855
Θρῄκης ἄνακτι τόνδε βουλεῦσαι φόνον.
ἔστιν γὰρ ᾗ ταραγμὸς ἐμπέπτωκέ μοι·
—Τὸν ἄνδρα τοῦτον φίλιον ἡγεῖται στρατός,
τὸν κατθανόντα δ' ἐχθρόν· εἰ δὲ σοὶ φίλος
ὅδ' ἐστί, χωρὶς τοῦτο κοὺ κοινὸν στρατῷ.—   860
πρὸς ταῦτα φρόντιζ'· ὡς θέλοντα μέν μ' ἔχεις
σοὶ ξυμπονῆσαι καὶ ταχὺν προσαρκέσαι,
βραδὺν δ', Ἀχαιοῖς εἰ διαβληθήσομαι.
Εκ. φεῦ.
οὐκ ἔστι θνητῶν ὅστις ἔστ' ἐλεύθερος·
ἢ χρημάτων γὰρ δοῦλός ἐστιν ἢ τύχης,   865
ἢ πλῆθος αὐτὸν πόλεος ἢ νόμων γραφαὶ
εἴργουσι χρῆσθαι μὴ κατὰ γνώμην τρόποις.
ἐπεὶ δὲ ταρβεῖς τῷ τ' ὄχλῳ πλέον νέμεις,
ἐγώ σε θήσω τοῦδ' ἐλεύθερον φόβου,
σύνισθι μὲν γάρ, ἤν τι βουλεύσω κακὸν   870
τῷ τόνδ' ἀποκτείναντι, συνδράσῃς δὲ μή.

ἦν δ' ἐξ 'Αχαιῶν θόρυβος ἢ 'πικουρία
πάσχοντος ἀνδρὸς Θρῃκὸς οἷα πείσεται
φανῇ τις, εἶργε μὴ δοκῶν ἐμὴν χάριν.
τὰ δ' ἄλλα—θάρσει—πάντ' ἐγὼ θήσω καλῶς.   875
Αγ. πῶς οὖν; τί δράσεις; πότερα φάσγανον χερὶ
λαβοῦσα γραία φῶτα βάρβαρον κτενεῖς,
ἢ φαρμάκοισιν ἢ 'πικουρίᾳ τινί;
τίς σοι ξυνέσται χείρ; πόθεν κτήσῃ φίλους;
Εκ. στέγαι κεκεύθασ' αἵδε Τρωάδων ὄχλον.   880
Αγ. τὰς αἰχμαλώτους εἶπας, Ἑλλήνων ἄγραν;
Εκ. σὺν ταῖσδε τὸν ἐμὸν φονέα τιμωρήσομαι.
Αγ. καὶ πῶς γυναιξὶν ἀρσένων ἔσται κράτος;
Εκ. δεινὸν τὸ πλῆθος σὺν δόλῳ τε δύσμαχον.
Αγ. δεινόν· τὸ μέντοι θῆλυ μέμφομαι γένος.   885
Εκ. τί δ'; οὐ γυναῖκες εἷλον Αἰγύπτου τέκνα
καὶ Λῆμνον ἄρδην ἀρσένων ἐξῴκισαν;
ἀλλ' ὡς γενέσθω· τόνδε μὲν μέθες λογον,
πέμψον δέ μοι τήνδ' ἀσφαλῶς διὰ στρατοῦ
γυναῖκα.—καὶ σὺ Θρῃκὶ πλαθεῖσα ξένῳ   890
λέξον· Καλεῖ σ' ἄνασσα δή ποτ' Ἰλίου
Ἑκάβη, σὸν οὐκ ἔλασσον ἢ κείνης χρέος,
καὶ παῖδας· ὡς δεῖ καὶ τέκν' εἰδέναι λόγους
τοὺς ἐξ ἐκείνης.—τὸν δὲ τῆς νεοσφαγοῦς
Πολυξένης ἐπίσχες, Ἀγάμεμνον, τάφον,   895
ὡς τώδ' ἀδελφὼ πλησίον μιᾷ φλογί,
δισσὴ μέριμνα μητρί, κρυφθῆτον χθονί.
Αγ. ἔσται τάδ' οὕτω· καὶ γὰρ εἰ μὲν ἦν στρατῷ
πλοῦς, οὐκ ἂν εἶχον τήνδε σοι δοῦναι χάριν·
νῦν δ', οὐ γὰρ ἵησ' οὐρίους πνοὰς θεός,   900
μένειν ἀνάγκη πλοῦν ὁρῶντ' ἐς ἥσυχον.
γένοιτο δ' εὖ πως· πᾶσι γὰρ κοινὸν τόδε,
ἰδίᾳ θ' ἑκάστῳ καὶ πόλει, τὸν μὲν κακὸν
κακόν τι πάσχειν, τὸν δὲ χρηστὸν εὐτυχεῖν.

Χο.　σὺ μέν, ὦ πατρὶς Ἰλιάς,   [στρ. α
　　τῶν ἀπορθήτων πόλις οὐκέτι λέξῃ·   906
　　τοῖον Ἑλλάνων νέφος ἀμφί σε κρύπτει
　　δορὶ δὴ δορὶ πέρσαν.
　　ἀπὸ δὲ στεφάναν κέκαρ-   910
　　σαι πύργων, κατὰ δ' αἰθάλου
　　κηλῖδ' οἰκτροτάταν κέχρω-
　　σαι· τάλαιν',
　　οὐκέτι σ' ἐμβατεύσω.

　　μεσονύκτιος ὠλλύμαν,   [ἀντ. α
　　ἦμος ἐκ δείπνων ὕπνος ἡδὺς ἐπ' ὄσσοις 915
　　σκίδναται, μολπᾶν δ' ἄπο καὶ χοροποιῶν
　　　θυσιᾶν καταλύσας
　　πόσις ἐν θαλάμοις ἔκει-
　　το, ξυστὸν δ' ἐπὶ πασσάλῳ,   920
　　ναύταν οὐκέθ' ὁρῶν ὅμι-
　　λον Τροίαν
　　Ἰλιάδ' ἐμβεβῶτα.

　　ἐγὼ δὲ πλόκαμον ἀναδέτοις   [στρ. β
　　μίτραισιν ἐρρυθμιζόμαν
　　χρυσέων ἐνόπτρων λεύσ-   925
　　σουσ' ἀτέρμονας εἰς αὐγάς,
　　ἐπιδέμνιος ὡς πέσοιμ' ἐς εὐνάν.
　　ἀνὰ δὲ κέλαδος ἔμολε πόλιν·
　　κέλευσμα δ' ἦν κατ' ἄστυ Τροί-
　　ας τόδ'· Ὠ
　　παῖδες Ἑλλάνων, πότε δὴ πότε τὰν   930
　　Ἰλιάδα σκοπιὰν
　　πέρσαντες ἥξετ' οἴκους;

　　λέχη δὲ φίλια μονόπεπλος   [ἀντ. β
　　λιποῦσα, Δωρὶς ὡς κόρα,

σεμνὰν προσίζουσ' οὐκ 935
ἤνυσ' "Αρτεμιν ἁ τλάμων·
ἄγομαι δὲ θανόντ' ἰδοῦσ' ἀκοίταν
τὸν ἐμὸν ἅλιον ἐπὶ πέλαγος,.
πόλιν τ' ἀποσκοποῦσ', ἐπεὶ
νόστιμον
ναῦς ἐκίνησεν πόδα καί μ' ἀπὸ γᾶς 940
ὥρισεν Ἰλιάδος·
τάλαιν', ἀπεῖπον ἄλγει,

τὰν τοῖν Διοσκούροιν Ἑλέναν κάσιν [ἐπῳδ.
Ἰδαῖόν τε βούταν
αἰνόπαριν κατάρᾳ 945
διδοῦσ', ἐπεί με γᾶς ἐκ
πατρῴας ἀπώλεσεν
ἐξῴκισέν τ' οἴκων γάμος, οὐ γάμος ἀλλ' ἀ-
λάστορός τις οἰζύς·
ἂν μήτε πέλαγος ἅλιον ἀπαγάγοι πάλιν, 950
μήτε πα-
τρῷον ἵκοιτ' ἐς οἶκον.

ΠΟΛΥΜΗΣΤΩΡ

ὦ φίλτατ' ἀνδρῶν Πρίαμε, φιλτάτη δὲ σύ,
Ἑκάβη, δακρύω σ' εἰσορῶν πόλιν τε σὴν
τήν τ' ἀρτίως θανοῦσαν ἔκγονον σέθεν. 955
φεῦ·
οὐκ ἔστι πιστὸν οὐδέν, οὔτ' εὐδοξία
οὔτ' αὖ καλῶς πράσσοντα μὴ πράξειν κακῶς.
φύρουσι δ' αὐτοὶ θεοὶ πάλιν τε καὶ πρόσω
ταραγμὸν ἐντιθέντες, ὡς ἀγνωσίᾳ
σέβωμεν αὐτούς. ἀλλὰ ταῦτα μὲν τί δεῖ 960
θρηνεῖν, προκόπτοντ' οὐδὲν ἐς πρόσθεν κακῶν;
σὺ δ', εἴ τι μέμφῃ τῆς ἐμῆς ἀπουσίας,
σχές· τυγχάνω γὰρ ἐν μέσοις Θρῄκης ὅροις

ἀπών, ὅτ᾽ ἦλθες δεῦρ᾽· ἐπεὶ δ᾽ ἀφικόμην,
ἤδη πόδ᾽ ἔξω δωμάτων αἴροντί μοι   965
ἐς ταὐτὸν ἤδε συμπίτνει δμωὶς σέθεν
λέγουσα μύθους, ὧν κλύων ἀφικόμην.
Εκ. αἰσχύνομαί σε προσβλέπειν ἐναντίον,
Πολυμῆστορ, ἐν τοιοῖσδε κειμένη κακοῖς.
ὅτῳ γὰρ ὤφθην εὐτυχοῦσ᾽, αἰδώς μ᾽ ἔχει   970
ἐν τῷδε πότμῳ τυγχάνουσ᾽ ἵν᾽ εἰμὶ νῦν
κοὐκ ἂν δυναίμην προσβλέπειν ὀρθαῖς κόραις.
ἀλλ᾽ αὐτὸ μὴ δύσνοιαν ἡγήσῃ σέθεν,
Πολυμῆστορ· ἄλλως δ᾽ αἴτιόν τι καὶ νόμος,
γυναῖκας ἀνδρῶν μὴ βλέπειν ἐναντίον.   975
Πλ. καὶ θαῦμά γ᾽ οὐδέν. ἀλλὰ τίς χρεία σ᾽ ἐμοῦ ;
τί χρῆμ᾽ ἐπέμψω τὸν ἐμὸν ἐκ δόμων πόδα·
Εκ. ἴδιον ἐμαυτῆς δή τι πρὸς σὲ βούλομαι
καὶ παῖδας εἰπεῖν σούς· ὀπάονας δέ μοι
χωρὶς κέλευσον τῶνδ᾽ ἀποστῆναι δόμων.   980
Πλ. χωρεῖτ᾽· ἐν ἀσφαλεῖ γὰρ ἤδ᾽ ἐρημία.
φίλη μὲν εἶ σύ, προσφιλὲς δέ μοι τόδε
στράτευμ᾽ Ἀχαιῶν. ἀλλὰ σημαίνειν σέ χρῆν·
τί χρὴ τὸν εὖ πράσσοντα μὴ πράσσουσιν εὖ
φίλοις ἐπαρκεῖν ; ὡς ἕτοιμός εἰμ᾽ ἐγώ.   985
Εκ. πρῶτον μὲν εἰπὲ παῖδ᾽ ὃν ἐξ ἐμῆς χερὸς
Πολύδωρον ἔκ τε πατρὸς ἐν δόμοις ἔχεις,
εἰ ζῇ· τὰ δ᾽ ἄλλα δεύτερόν σ᾽ ἐρήσομαι.
Πλ. μάλιστα· τοὐκείνου μὲν εὐτυχεῖς μέρος.
Εκ. ὦ φίλταθ᾽, ὡς εὖ κἀξίως λέγεις σέθεν.   990
Πλ. τί δῆτα βούλῃ δεύτερον μαθεῖν ἐμοῦ ;
Εκ. εἰ τῆς τεκούσης τῆσδε ... μέμνηταί τί μου ;
Πλ. καὶ δεῦρό γ᾽ ὡς σὲ κρύφιος ἐζήτει μολεῖν.
Εκ. χρυσὸς δὲ σῶς ὃν ἦλθεν ἐκ Τροίας ἔχων ;
Πλ. σῶς, ἐν δόμοις γε τοῖς ἐμοῖς φρουρούμενος.
Εκ. σῶσόν νυν αὐτὸν μηδ᾽ ἔρα τῶν πλησίον.
Πλ. ἥκιστ᾽· ὀναίμην τοῦ παρόντος, ὦ γύναι.

Εκ. οἶσθ' οὖν ἃ λέξαι σοί τε καὶ παισὶν θέλω ;
Πλ. οὐκ οἶδα· τῷ σῷ τοῦτο σημανεῖς λόγῳ.
Εκ. ἔστ', ὦ φιληθεὶς ὡς σὺ νῦν ἐμοὶ φιλῇ ... 1000
Πλ. τί χρῆμ' ὃ κἀμὲ καὶ τέκν' εἰδέναι χρεών ;
Εκ. χρυσοῦ παλαιαὶ Πριαμιδῶν κατώρυχες.
Πλ. ταῦτ' ἔσθ' ἃ βούλῃ παιδὶ σημῆναι σέθεν ;
Εκ. μάλιστα, διὰ σοῦ γ'· εἰ γὰρ εὐσεβὴς ἀνήρ.
Πλ. τί δῆτα τέκνων τῶνδε δεῖ παρουσίας ; 1005
Εκ. ἄμεινον, ἢν σὺ κατθάνῃς, τούσδ' εἰδέναι.
Πλ. καλῶς ἔλεξας· τῇδε καὶ σοφώτερον.
Εκ. οἶσθ' οὖν Ἀθάνας Ἰλίας ἵνα στέγαι ;
Πλ. ἐνταῦθ' ὁ χρυσός ἐστι ; σημεῖον δὲ τί ;
Εκ. μέλαινα πέτρα γῆς ὑπερτέλλουσ' ἄνω. 1010
Πλ. ἔτ' οὖν τι βούλῃ τῶν ἐκεῖ φράζειν ἐμοί ;
Εκ. σῶσαί σε χρήμαθ' οἷς συνεξῆλθον θέλω.
Πλ. ποῦ δῆτα ; πέπλων ἐντὸς ἢ κρύψασ' ἔχεις ;
Εκ. σκύλων ἐν ὄχλῳ ταῖσδε σῴζεται στέγαις.
Πλ. ποῦ δ' ; αἵδ' Ἀχαιῶν ναύλοχοι περιπτυχαί. 1015
Εκ. ἰδίᾳ γυναικῶν αἰχμαλωτίδων στέγαι.
Πλ. τἄνδον δὲ πιστὰ κἀρσένων ἐρημία ;
Εκ. οὐδεὶς Ἀχαιῶν ἔνδον, ἀλλ' ἡμεῖς μόναι.
ἀλλ' ἕρπ' ἐς οἴκους· καὶ γὰρ Ἀργεῖοι νεῶν
λῦσαι ποθοῦσιν οἴκαδ' ἐκ Τροίας πόδα· 1020
ὡς πάντα πράξας ὧν σε δεῖ στείχῃς πάλιν
ξὺν παισὶν οὗπερ τὸν ἐμὸν ᾤκισας γόνον.
Χο. οὔπω δέδωκας, ἀλλ' ἴσως δώσεις δίκην·
ἀλίμενόν τις ὡς εἰς ἄντλον πεσών 1025
† λέχριος ἐκπεσῇ φίλας καρδίας,
ἀμέρσας βίοτον. τὸ γὰρ ὑπέγγυον
Δίκᾳ καὶ θεοῖσιν οὐ συμπίτνει·
ὀλέθριον ὀλέθριον κακόν.† 1030
ψεύσει σ' ὁδοῦ τῆσδ' ἐλπὶς ἥ σ' ἐπήγαγεν
θανάσιμον πρὸς Ἅιδαν, ἰὼ τάλας·
ἀπολέμῳ δὲ χειρὶ λείψεις βίον.

Πλ. ⟨ἔσωθεν⟩
    ὤμοι, τυφλοῦμαι φέγγος ὀμμάτων τάλας.   1035
Χο. — ἠκούσατ' ἀνδρὸς Θρηκὸς οἰμωγήν, φίλαι ;
Πλ.   ὤμοι μάλ' αὖθις, τέκνα, δυστήνου σφαγῆς.
Χο. — φίλαι, πέπρακται καίν' ἔσω δόμων κακά.
Πλ.   ἀλλ' οὔτι μὴ φύγητε λαιψηρῷ ποδί·
    βάλλων γὰρ οἴκων τῶνδ' ἀναρρήξω μυχούς.   1040
Χο. — ἰδού, βαρείας χειρὸς ὁρμᾶται βέλος.
    — βούλεσθ' ἐπεσπέσωμεν ; ὡς ἀκμὴ καλεῖ
    Ἑκάβη παρεῖναι Τρωάσιν τε συμμάχους.
Εκ. ἄρασσε, φείδου μηδέν, ἐκβάλλων πύλας·
    οὐ γάρ ποτ' ὄμμα λαμπρὸν ἐνθήσεις κόραις,   1045
    οὐ παῖδας ὄψῃ ζῶντας οὓς ἔκτειν' ἐγώ.
Χο. ἦ γὰρ καθεῖλες Θρῆκα, καὶ κρατεῖς, ξένον,
    δέσποινα, καὶ δέδρακας οἷάπερ λέγεις ;
Εκ. ὄψῃ νιν αὐτίκ' ὄντα δωμάτων πάρος
    τυφλὸν τυφλῷ στείχοντα παραφόρῳ ποδί,   1050
    παίδων τε δισσῶν σώμαθ', οὓς ἔκτειν' ἐγὼ
    σὺν ταῖς ἀρίσταις Τρωάσιν· δίκην δέ μοι
    δέδωκε. χωρεῖ δ', ὡς ὁρᾷς, ὅδ' ἐκ δόμων.
    ἀλλ' ἐκποδὼν ἄπειμι κἀποστήσομαι
    θυμῷ ῥέοντι Θρηκὶ δυσμαχωτάτῳ.   1055

Πλ.   ὤμοι ἐγώ, πᾷ βῶ,
    πᾷ στῶ, πᾷ κέλσω ;
    τετράποδος βάσιν θηρὸς ὀρεστέρου
    τιθέμενος ἐπίχειρα κατ' ἴχνος ; ποίαν
    ἢ ταύταν ἢ τάνδ' ἐξαλλάξω, τὰς   1060
    ἀνδροφόνους μάρψαι χρῄζων Ἰλιάδας,
    αἵ με διώλεσαν ;
    τάλαιναι κόραι τάλαιναι Φρυγῶν,
    ὦ κατάρατοι,   1065
    ποῖ καί με φυγᾷ πτώσσουσι μυχῶν ;
    εἴθε μοι ὀμμάτων αἱματόεν βλέφαρον

ἀκέσαι' ἀκέσαιο τυφλόν, Ἅλιε,
φέγγος ἐπαλλάξας.
  ἃ ἅ,
  σίγα· κρυπτὰν βάσιν αἰσθάνομαι 1070
  τάνδε γυναικῶν, πᾷ πόδ' ἐπᾴξας
  σαρκῶν ὀστέων τ' ἐμπλησθῶ,
  θοίναν ἀγρίων θηρῶν τιθέμενος,
  ἀρνύμενος λώβαν
  λύμας ἀντίποιν' ἐμᾶς; ὦ τάλας. 1075
  ποῖ πᾷ φέρομαι τέκν' ἔρημα λιπὼν
  Βάκχαις Ἅιδου διαμοιρᾶσαι,
  σφακτά, κυσίν τε φοινίαν δαῖτ' ἀνή-
  μερον τ' οὐρείαν ἐκβολάν;
  πᾷ στῶ, πᾷ κάμψω, [πᾷ βῶ,] 1080
  ναῦς ὅπως ποντίοις πείσμασιν, λινόκροκον
  φᾶρος στέλλων, ἐπὶ τάνδε συθεὶς
  τέκνων ἐμῶν φύλαξ ὀλέθριον κοίταν;
Χο. ὦ τλῆμον, ὡς σοι δύσφορ' εἴργασται κακά· 1085
  δράσαντι δ' αἰσχρὰ δεινὰ τἀπιτίμια.
  [δαίμων ἔδωκεν ὅστις ἐστί σοι βαρύς.]
Πλ. αἰαῖ, ἰὼ Θρήκης λογχοφόρον ἔνο-
  πλον εὔιππον Ἄρει κάτοχον γένος. 1090

Ἰὼ Ἀχαιοί.—Ἰὼ Ἀτρεῖδαι.—βοὰν βοὰν αὐτῶ, βοάν.
ὦ ἴτε· μόλετε πρὸς θεῶν.

κλύει τις ἢ οὐδεὶς ἀρκέσει; τί μέλλετε;

γυναῖκες ὤλεσάν με, γυναῖκες αἰχμαλωτίδες· δεινὰ
δεινὰ πεπόνθαμεν. 1095

  ὤμοι ἐμᾶς λώβας.
  ποῖ τράπωμαι, ποῖ πορευθῶ;
  ἀμπτάμενος οὐράνιον 1100
  ὑψιπετὲς ἐς μέλαθρον,
  Ὠαρίων ἢ Σείριος ἔνθα πυρὸς φλογέας ἀφίη-
  σιν ὄσσων αὐγάς, ἢ τὸν ἐς Ἀΐδα 1105
  μελάγχρωτα πορθμὸν ᾄξω τάλας;

Χο. συγγνώσθ', ὅταν τις κρείσσον' ἢ φέρειν κακὰ
πάθῃ, ταλαίνης ἐξαπαλλάξαι ζόης.

Αγ. κραυγῆς ἀκούσας ἦλθον· οὐ γὰρ ἥσυχος
πέτρας ὀρείας παῖς λέλακ' ἀνὰ στρατὸν   1110
Ἠχὼ διδοῦσα θόρυβον· εἰ δὲ μὴ Φρυγῶν
πύργους πεσόντας ᾖσμεν Ἑλλήνων δορί,
φόβον παρέσχεν οὐ μέσως ὅδε κτύπος.

Πλ. ὦ φίλτατ'· ᾐσθόμην γάρ, Ἀγάμεμνον, σέθεν
φωνῆς ἀκούσας· εἰσορᾷς ἃ πάσχομεν;   1115

Αγ. ἔα·
Πολυμῆστορ· ὦ δύστηνε, τίς σ' ἀπώλεσεν;
τίς ὄμμ' ἔθηκε τυφλὸν αἱμάξας κόρας,
παῖδάς τε τούσδ' ἔκτεινεν; ἢ μέγαν χόλον
σοὶ καὶ τέκνοισιν εἶχεν ὅστις ἦν ἄρα.

Πλ. Ἑκάβη με σὺν γυναιξὶν αἰχμαλωτίσιν   1120
ἀπώλεσ'—οὐκ ἀπώλεσ', ἀλλὰ μειζόνως.

Αγ. τί φής; σὺ τοὔργον εἴργασαι τόδ', ὡς λέγει;
σὺ τόλμαν, Ἑκάβη, τήνδ' ἔτλης ἀμήχανον;

Πλ. ὤμοι, τί λέξεις; ἦ γὰρ ἐγγύς ἐστί που;
σήμηνον, εἰπὲ ποῦ 'σθ', ἵν' ἁρπάσας χεροῖν   1125
διασπάσωμαι καὶ καθαιμάξω χρόα.

Αγ. οὗτος, τί πάσχεις;   Πλ.   πρὸς θεῶν σε λίσσομαι,
μέθες μ' ἐφεῖναι τῇδε μαργῶσαν χέρα.

Αγ. ἴσχ'· ἐκβαλὼν δὲ καρδίας τὸ βάρβαρον
λέγ', ὡς ἀκούσας σοῦ τε τῆσδέ τ' ἐν μέρει   1130
κρίνω δικαίως ἀνθ' ὅτου πάσχεις τάδε.

Πλ. λέγοιμ' ἄν.   ἦν τις Πριαμιδῶν νεώτατος,
Πολύδωρος, Ἑκάβης παῖς, ὃν ἐκ Τροίας ἐμοὶ
πατὴρ δίδωσι Πρίαμος ἐν δόμοις τρέφειν,
ὕποπτος ὢν δὴ Τρωικῆς ἁλώσεως.   1135
τοῦτον κατέκτειν'· ἀνθ' ὅτου δ' ἔκτεινά νιν,
ἄκουσον, ὡς εὖ καὶ σοφῇ προμηθίᾳ.
ἔδεισα μὴ σοὶ πολέμιος λειφθεὶς ὁ παῖς
Τροίαν ἀθροίσῃ καὶ ξυνοικίσῃ πάλιν,

γνόντες δ' 'Αχαιοὶ ζῶντα Πριαμιδῶν τινα 1140
Φρυγῶν ἐς αἶαν αὖθις ἄρειαν στόλον,
κἄπειτα Θρήκης πεδία τρίβοιεν τάδε
λεηλατοῦντες, γείτοσιν δ' εἴη κακὸν
Τρώων, ἐν ᾧπερ νῦν, ἄναξ, ἐκάμνομεν.
'Εκάβη δὲ παιδὸς γνοῦσα θανάσιμον μόρον 1145
λόγῳ με τοιῷδ' ἤγαγ', ὡς κεκρυμμένας
θήκας φράσουσα Πριαμιδῶν ἐν 'Ιλίῳ
χρυσοῦ· μόνον δὲ σὺν τέκνοισί μ' εἰσάγει
δόμους, ἵν' ἄλλος μή τις εἰδείη τάδε.
ἵζω δὲ κλίνης ἐν μέσῳ κάμψας γόνυ· 1150
πολλαὶ δὲ χεῖρες, αἱ μὲν ἐξ ἀριστερᾶς,
αἱ δ' ἔνθεν, ὡς δὴ παρὰ φίλῳ, Τρώων κόραι
θάκους ἔχουσαι, κερκίδ' 'Ηδωνῆς χερὸς
ᾔνουν, ὑπ' αὐγὰς τούσδε λεύσσουσαι πέπλους·
ἄλλαι δὲ κάμακα Θρηκίαν θεώμεναι 1155
γυμνόν μ' ἔθηκαν διπτύχου στολίσματος.
ὅσαι δὲ τοκάδες ἦσαν, ἐκπαγλούμεναι
τέκν' ἐν χεροῖν ἔπαλλον, ὡς πρόσω πατρὸς
γένοιντο, διαδοχαῖς ἀμείβουσαι χερῶν·
κᾆτ' ἐκ γαληνῶν—πῶς δοκεῖς;—προσφθεγμάτων 1160
εὐθὺς λαβοῦσαι φάσγαν' ἐκ πέπλων ποθὲν
κεντοῦσι παῖδας, αἱ δὲ πολεμίων δίκην
ξυναρπάσασαι τὰς ἐμὰς εἶχον χέρας
καὶ κῶλα· παισὶ δ' ἀρκέσαι χρήζων ἐμοῖς,
εἰ μὲν πρόσωπον ἐξανισταίην ἐμόν, 1165
κόμης κατεῖχον, εἰ δὲ κινοίην χέρας,
πλήθει γυναικῶν οὐδὲν ἤνυον τάλας.
τὸ λοίσθιον δέ, πῆμα πήματος πλέον,
ἐξειργάσαντο δείν'· ἐμῶν γὰρ ὀμμάτων,
πόρπας λαβοῦσαι, τὰς ταλαιπώρους κόρας 1170
κεντοῦσιν, αἱμάσσουσιν· εἶτ' ἀνὰ στέγας
φυγάδες ἔβησαν· ἐκ δὲ πηδήσας ἐγὼ
θὴρ ὣς διώκω τὰς μιαιφόνους κύνας,

ἅπαντ' ἐρευνῶν † τοῖχον ὡς κυνηγέτης †
βάλλων ἀράσσων.   τοιάδε σπεύδων χάριν   1175
πέπονθα τὴν σὴν πολέμιόν τε σὸν κτανών,
Ἀγάμεμνον.   ὡς δὲ μὴ μακροὺς τείνω λόγους,
εἴ τις γυναῖκας τῶν πρὶν εἴρηκεν κακῶς
ἢ νῦν λέγων ἔστιν τις ἢ μέλλει λέγειν,
ἅπαντα ταῦτα συντεμὼν ἐγὼ φράσω·   1180
γένος γὰρ οὔτε πόντος οὔτε γῆ τρέφει
τοιόνδ'· ὁ δ' αἰεὶ ξυντυχὼν ἐπίσταται.
Χο. μηδὲν θρασύνου μηδὲ τοῖς σαυτοῦ κακοῖς
τὸ θῆλυ συνθεὶς ὧδε πᾶν μέμψῃ γένος.
[πολλαὶ γὰρ ἡμῶν, αἱ μέν εἰσ' ἐπίφθονοι,   1185
αἱ δ' εἰς ἀριθμὸν τῶν κακῶν πεφύκαμεν.]
Εκ. Ἀγάμεμνον, ἀνθρώποισιν οὐκ ἐχρῆν ποτε
τῶν πραγμάτων τὴν γλῶσσαν ἰσχύειν πλέον·
ἀλλ', εἴτε χρήστ' ἔδρασε, χρήστ' ἔδει λέγειν,
εἴτ' αὖ πονηρά, τοὺς λόγους εἶναι σαθρούς,   1190
καὶ μὴ δύνασθαι τἄδικ' εὖ λέγειν ποτέ.
σοφοὶ μὲν οὖν εἰσ' οἱ τάδ' ἠκριβωκότες,
ἀλλ' οὐ δύνανται διὰ τέλους εἶναι σοφοί,
κακῶς δ' ἀπώλοντ'· οὔτις ἐξήλυξέ πω.
   καί μοι τὸ μὲν σὸν ὧδε φροιμίοις ἔχει·   1195
πρὸς τόνδε δ' εἶμι καὶ λόγοις ἀμείψομαι·
ὃς φῂς Ἀχαιῶν πόνον ἀπαλλάσσων διπλοῦν
Ἀγαμέμνονός θ' ἕκατι παῖδ' ἐμὸν κτανεῖν.
ἀλλ', ὦ κάκιστε, πρῶτον οὔποτ' ἂν φίλον
τὸ βάρβαρον γένοιτ' ἂν Ἕλλησιν ·γένος   1200
οὐδ' ἂν δύναιτο.   τίνα δὲ καὶ σπεύδων χάριν
πρόθυμος ἦσθα ;   πότερα κηδεύσων τινὰ
ἢ συγγενὴς ὤν, ἢ τίν' αἰτίαν ἔχων ;
ἢ σῆς ἔμελλον γῆς τεμεῖν βλαστήματα
πλεύσαντες αὖθις ;   τίνα δοκεῖς πείσειν τάδε ;   1205
ὁ χρυσός, εἰ βούλοιο τἀληθῆ λέγειν,
ἔκτεινε τὸν ἐμὸν παῖδα, καὶ κέρδη τὰ σά.

ἐπεὶ δίδαξον τοῦτο· πῶς, ὅτ' εὐτύχει
Τροία, πέριξ δὲ πύργος εἶχ' ἔτι πτόλιν,
ἔ3η τε Πρίαμος Ἕκτορός τ' ἤνθει δόρυ,   1210
τί δ' οὐ τότ', εἴπερ τῷδ' ἐβουλήθης χάριν
θέσθαι, τρέφων τὸν παῖδα κἀν δόμοις ἔχων
ἔκτεινας ἢ 3ῶντ' ἦλθες Ἀργείοις ἄγων;
ἀλλ' ἡνίχ' ἡμεῖς οὐκέτ' ἐσμὲν ἐν φάει—
καπνῷ δ' ἐσήμην' ἄστυ—πολεμίων ὕπο,   1215
ξένον κατέκτας σὴν μολόντ' ἐφ' ἑστίαν.
    πρὸς τοῖσδε νῦν ἄκουσον, ὡς φανῇς κακός.
χρῆν σ', εἴπερ ἦσθα τοῖς Ἀχαιοῖσιν φίλος,
τὸν χρυσὸν ὃν φὴς οὐ σὸν ἀλλὰ τοῦδ' ἔχειν
δοῦναι φέροντα πενομένοις τε καὶ χρόνον   1220
πολὺν πατρῴας γῆς ἀπεξενωμένοις·
σὺ δ' οὐδὲ νῦν πω σῆς ἀπαλλάξαι χερὸς
τολμᾷς, ἔχων δὲ καρτερεῖς ἔτ' ἐν δόμοις.
καὶ μὴν τρέφων μὲν ὥς σε παῖδ' ἐχρῆν τρέφειν
σώσας τε τὸν ἐμόν, εἶχες ἂν καλὸν κλέος·   1225
ἐν τοῖς κακοῖς γὰρ ἀγαθοὶ σαφέστατοι
φίλοι· τὰ χρηστὰ δ' αὔθ' ἕκαστ' ἔχει φίλους.
εἰ δ' ἐσπάνι3ες χρημάτων, ὃ δ' εὐτύχει,
θησαυρὸς ἄν σοι παῖς ὑπῆρχ' οὑμὸς μέγας·
νῦν δ' οὔτ' ἐκεῖνον ἄνδρ' ἔχεις σαυτῷ φίλον,   1230
χρυσοῦ τ' ὄνησις οἴχεται παῖδές τε σοί,
αὐτός τε πράσσεις ὧδε.   σοὶ δ' ἐγὼ λέγω,
Ἀγάμεμνον, εἰ τῷδ' ἀρκέσεις, κακὸς φανῇ·
οὔτ' εὐσεβῆ γὰρ οὔτε πιστὸν οἷς ἐχρῆν,
οὐχ ὅσιον, οὐ δίκαιον εὖ δράσεις ξένον·   1235
αὐτὸν δὲ χαίρειν τοῖς κακοῖς σὲ φήσομεν
τοιοῦτον ὄντα . . . δεσπότας δ' οὐ λοιδορῶ.
Χο. φεῦ φεῦ· βροτοῖσιν ὡς τὰ χρηστὰ πράγματα
      χρηστῶν ἀφορμὰς ἐνδίδωσ' ἀεὶ λόγων.
Αγ. ἀχθεινὰ μέν μοι τἀλλότρια κρίνειν κακά,   1240
      ὅμως δ' ἀνάγκη· καὶ γὰρ αἰσχύνην φέρει,

πρᾶγμ᾽ ἐς χέρας λαβόντ᾽ ἀπώσασθαι τόδε.
ἐμοὶ δ᾽, ἵν᾽ εἰδῇς, οὔτ᾽ ἐμὴν δοκεῖς χάριν
οὔτ᾽ οὖν Ἀχαιῶν ἄνδρ᾽ ἀποκτεῖναι ξένον,
ἀλλ᾽ ὡς ἔχῃς τὸν χρυσὸν ἐν δόμοισι σοῖς.   1245
λέγεις δὲ σαυτῷ πρόσφορ᾽ ἐν κακοῖσιν ὤν·
τάχ᾽ οὖν παρ᾽ ὑμῖν ῥᾴδιον ξενοκτονεῖν·
ἡμῖν δέ γ᾽ αἰσχρὸν τοῖσιν Ἕλλησιν τόδε.
πῶς οὖν σε κρίνας μὴ ἀδικεῖν φύγω ψόγον;
οὐκ ἂν δυναίμην. ἀλλ᾽ ἐπεὶ τὰ μὴ καλά   1250
πράσσειν ἐτόλμας, τλῆθι καὶ τὰ μὴ φίλα.
Πλ. οἴμοι, γυναικός, ὡς ἔοιχ᾽, ἡσσώμενος
δούλης ὑφέξω τοῖς κακίοσιν δίκην.
Αγ. οὔκουν δικαίως, εἴπερ εἰργάσω κακά;
Πλ. οἴμοι τέκνων τῶνδ᾽ ὀμμάτων τ᾽ ἐμῶν, τάλας.   1255
Εκ. ἀλγεῖς· τί δ᾽; ἢ ᾽μὲ παιδὸς οὐκ ἀλγεῖν δοκεῖς;
Πλ. χαίρεις ὑβρίζουσ᾽ εἰς ἔμ᾽, ὦ πανοῦργε σύ;
Εκ. οὐ γάρ με χαίρειν χρή σε τιμωρουμένην;
Πλ. ἀλλ᾽ οὐ τάχ᾽, ἡνίκ᾽ ἄν σε ποντία νοτὶς —
Εκ. μῶν ναυστολήσῃ γῆς ὅρους Ἑλληνίδος;   1260
Πλ. κρύψῃ μὲν οὖν πεσοῦσαν ἐκ καρχησίων.
Εκ. πρὸς τοῦ βιαίων τυγχάνουσαν ἁλμάτων;
Πλ. αὐτὴ πρὸς ἱστὸν ναὸς ἀμβήσῃ ποδί.
Εκ. ὑποπτέροις νώτοισιν ἢ ποίῳ τρόπῳ;
Πλ. κύων γενήσῃ πύρσ᾽ ἔχουσα δέργματα.   1265
Εκ. πῶς δ᾽ οἶσθα μορφῆς τῆς ἐμῆς μετάστασιν;
Πλ. ὁ Θρῃξὶ μάντις εἶπε Διόνυσος τάδε.
Εκ. σοὶ δ᾽ οὐκ ἔχρησεν οὐδὲν ὧν ἔχεις κακῶν;
Πλ. οὐ γάρ ποτ᾽ ἄν σύ μ᾽ εἷλες ὧδε σὺν δόλῳ.
Εκ. θανοῦσα δ᾽ ἢ ζῶσ᾽ ἐνθάδ᾽· ἐκπλήσω βίον;   1270
Πλ. θανοῦσα· τύμβῳ δ᾽ ὄνομα σῷ κεκλήσεται . . .
Εκ. μορφῆς ἐπῳδόν, ἢ τί, τῆς ἐμῆς ἐρεῖς;
Πλ. κυνὸς ταλαίνης σῆμα, ναυτίλοις τέκμαρ.
Εκ. οὐδὲν μέλει μοι σοῦ γέ μοι δόντος δίκην.
Πλ. καὶ σήν γ᾽ ἀνάγκη παῖδα Κασάνδραν θανεῖν.   1275

Εκ. ἀπέπτυσ'· αὐτῷ ταῦτα σοὶ δίδωμ' ἔχειν.
Πλ. κτενεῖ νιν ἡ τοῦδ' ἄλοχος, οἰκουρὸς πικρά.
Εκ. μήπω μανείη Τυνδαρὶς τοσόνδε παῖς.
Πλ. καὐτόν γε τοῦτον, πέλεκυν ἐξάρασ' ἄνω.
Αγ. οὗτος σύ, μαίνῃ καὶ κακῶν ἐρᾷς τυχεῖν ;   1280
Πλ. κτεῖν', ὡς ἐν "Αργει φόνια λουτρά σ' ἀμμένει.
Αγ. οὐχ ἕλξετ' αὐτόν, δμῶες, ἐκποδὼν βίᾳ ;
Πλ. ἀλγεῖς ἀκούων ;   Αγ. οὐκ ἐφέξετε στόμα ;
Πλ. ἐγκλῄετ'· εἴρηται γάρ.   Αγ. οὐχ ὅσον τάχος
νήσων ἐρήμων αὐτὸν ἐκβαλεῖτέ που,   1285
ἐπείπερ οὕτω καὶ λίαν θρασυστομεῖ ;
'Εκάβη, σὺ δ', ὦ τάλαινα, διπτύχους νεκροὺς
στείχουσα θάπτε· δεσποτῶν δ' ὑμᾶς χρεὼν
σκηναῖς πελάζειν, Τρῳάδες· καὶ γὰρ πνοὰς
πρὸς οἶκον ἤδη τάσδε πομπίμους ὁρῶ.   1290
εὖ δ' ἐς πάτραν πλεύσαιμεν, εὖ δὲ τὰν δόμοις
ἔχοντ' ἴδοιμεν τῶνδ' ἀφειμένοι πόνων.

Χο.   ἴτε πρὸς λιμένας σκηνάς τε, φίλαι,
τῶν δεσποσύνων πειρασόμεναι
μόχθων· στερρὰ γὰρ ἀνάγκη.   1295

NOTES

1–58. **Prologue.** Aristotle defines the Prologue as that part of a tragedy which precedes the entrance of the Chorus. In Euripides it is regularly a monologue in which a person (generally not a character in the play, and frequently a god) gives the audience an outline of the plot. This was necessary, because while E. was normally re-handling material already used by his predecessors, he very often made drastic changes in the traditional stories.

Hecuba is unique in having its prologue spoken by a ghost. Aeschylus had introduced the ghost of Darius into *The Persae* and the ghost of Klytaemnestra into *The Eumenides*, and we know that a whole series of ghosts must have appeared in his lost play, *The Psychagogoi*, which dealt with the visit of Odysseus to the underworld. The example of Sophocles was still closer. In his *Polyxena*, which covered the same ground as the first half of *Hecuba*, the ghost of Achilles played an important part, but we have no evidence that it spoke the prologue. Euripides skilfully combines his own invention, the ghost of Polydorus, with the Sophoclean ghost of Achilles, by making the former narrate (37–41) how the latter had appeared to hold back the Greek host when it was ready to sail home. We thus get the arresting effect of a ghost-story within a ghost-story. Polydorus does not, of course, appear again ; but his prologue helps to strengthen the dramatic unity which is endangered by the " diptych " structure of the play.

The ghost was probably represented as hovering in the air (αἰωρούμενος, 32) over the huts where the Trojan captives are lodged, which form the background. This was done by means of a device called μηχανή (Latin *machina*, whence *deus ex machina*) or αἰώρημα. The tent of Agamemnon stands to one side, and the action takes place before it, not on a stage (which did not exist in the fifth century B.C.) but perhaps on a wooden platform, very slightly higher than the level of the orchestra, the circular dancing-floor of the chorus.

1. Compare opening line of *Bacchae:* ἥκω Διὸς παῖς . . .

43

νεκρῶν κευθμῶνα : "hiding-place of the dead." Cp. κεῦθος νεκύων, Soph., *Antigone*, 818.

σκότου πύλας : "gates of darkness." σκότος is practically a synonym for θάνατος, as φάος is for βίος. There is also a neuter n. σκότος, -ους.

2. ˝Αιδης : one of the names of the god of the dead. He is "invisible" (ἀ-ϝιδ) as lord of the realm of darkness.

3. Κισσέως : ἡ Κισσέως, "daughter of Kisseus," is Hecuba. In Homer, her father is Dymas, and the mother of Polydorus is Laothoe. γεγώς : contr. for γεγαώς, participle of γέγονα, as μεμαώς of μέμονα.

4. Φρυγῶν πόλιν : Troy. In Trag. the Trojans are regularly called Φρύγες, name of a people akin to the Thracians, who in historical times occupied the interior of Asia Minor. In Aesch., *Choeph.* 346, they are similarly called Λύκιοι, "Lycians."

5. Ἑλληνικῷ : Another frequent anachronism. In Homer, only the inhabitants of part of Peleus' kingdom in Thessaly are Ἕλληνες ; the sackers of Troy have several names : most common, Ἀχαιοί.

6. ὑπεξέπεμψε : The double prefix ὑπεκ- implies *secret escape*. Cp. ὑπεξελών, Soph., *O.T.*, 227.

8. Χερσονησίαν : Χερσόνησος means " peninsula " and is applied to other places besides Gallipoli, e.g. the Crimea, known as Tauric Chersonese. πλάκα : lit. "flat place, plateau." Irish *leac.* English *flag* (-stone).

9. εὐθύνων : from εὐθύς, "straight," hence "directing, ruling." He was a warrior ruler (δορί) over a people noted for cavalry (φίλιππον λαόν). Note λᾶός is origin of English *lay, laity.*

13. ὃ καί με γῆς : The neuter rel. is best taken as acc. of respect expressing cause, an old use seen in Homeric ὅτε, ὅτι. "Wherefore he sent me secretly away." The subject of ὑπεξέπεμψεν is Πρίαμος understood from Πριαμιδῶν.

15. βραχίονι : Note that Latin *bracchium* is a borrowing of this word, whose origin is unknown.

16. ὁρίσματα : not equivalent to πύργοι as Schol. takes

it, but simply "boundaries," marked presumably by *standing stones* (ὄρθα). ἔκειτο : "were in their place " as often.

17. πύργοι : obscurely related to German *Burg*, "fortress."

18. Ἕκτωρ : Priam's son, chief defender of Troy. His name seems to indicate his function, hence Prof. J. A. Scott believes he was invented by Homer.

20. ὥς τις πτόρθος : "like a plant." Cp. frequent Homeric phrase ὁ δ' ἀνέδραμεν ἔρνεῖ ἶσος.

22. ψυχή : lit. "breath" like Latin *anima*, hence "life" in Homer and Trag. The meaning "soul" was first given it by Pythagoras (late sixth century). ἑστία : also deified as goddess of family hearth.

23. αὐτός : "he himself," ref. to πατρῷα as implying πατήρ. The word often means "the master " as in Pythagorean αὐτὸς ἔφα Latin *ipse dixit*. θεοδμήτῳ "built *for* the gods."

24. ἐκ : poet. equivalent of ὑπό, as often.

26. ξένος πατρῷος : ξένος, like Latin *hospes*, meant both "host " and "guest." To the Greeks, the relation of "guest-friendship " was peculiarly sacred and was under the protection of Ζεὺς Ξένιος. Its violation was one of the gravest crimes ; hence these words are strongly ironic.

29. διαύλοις κυμάτων : "Ebb and flow of the waves," compared rather oddly to the two "laps " (in Greek αὔλοί, "pipes ") of a racecourse, in which the runner turned at a post (τέρμα, νύσσα, καμπτήρ, Latin *meta*) and came back to his starting-place. There is no question of the tide, which is practically unfelt in the Mediterranean.

30. ἄκλαυστος, ἄταφος : To the Greek mind the solemn mourning (cf. Irish *caoine*) was as much part of the funeral service as the actual burial, and in many cities professional mourners (forbidden in Athens by a law of Solon) were employed for it. The soul could not find its proper resting-place till the body was duly buried. Cp. Virgil, *Aen.* vi, 327-8 : *Nec ripas datur horrendas et rauca fluenta | transportare prius quam sedibus ossa quierunt.*

30-1. ὑπὲρ μητρὸς ... ἀΐσσω : to be taken literally. The

ghost hovers above the camp where his mother is. As the spectators see him in one aspect, so she sees him in another, more symbolical one. (90). ἀίσσω : Schol. ὁρμῶμαι, "appear suddenly."

32. τριταῖον here means τρίτον. Normally it is used with verbs to agree with subj.: τριταῖος ἦλθον, "I came on the second day." Note that the Greeks counted inclusively. Méridier translates correctly "voici deux jours."

αἰωρούμενος : The vb. is connected with the n. αἰώρα, "swing." See introductory note on Prologue, above.

34. πάρα : frequent as contraction for πάρεστι. Note accent.

37-41. These lines summarise part of the Polyxena of Soph.

39. εὐθύνοντας : "directing." See n. 9, above.

πλάτην : "oar-blade," lit. "flat of oar." Cp. πλάτος, English flat, Irish leathan.

41. φίλον : because according to one account (Schol.) she had been affianced to him. πρόσφαγμα : "sacrifice on others' behalf." The idea of human sacrifice was not entirely remote from Euripidean Athens. Themistocles, before the battle of Salamis, had sacrificed three noble Persian youths to Dionysus Omestes. (Plutarch, Themistocles, 13.)

43. ἡ πεπρωμένη : to be construed w. μοῖρα understood : "her appointed doom." Defective vb. only occurring in aor. act. ἔπορον, pf. pass. πέπρωμαι, meaning "to furnish, appoint."

45. δυοῖν . . . δύο : Note balance of clauses, a device borrowed from rhetoric.

47. ὡς . . . τύχω : It should be noted that ὡς final is normally confined to poetry ; prose ἵνα, ὅπως.

52. γεραιᾷ : dativus commodi used as well as gen. w. ἐκποδών, which is simply ἐκ ποδῶν.

53. περᾷ πόδα : Acc. almost cognate here. ὑπό : "from under."

54. φάντασμα : She also has been seeing the ghost, in a symbolic dream. Cp. 90.

55. ἐκ : "after" ; ἦμαρ . . . ἐκ χείματος, "day after storm," Aeschylus, Agamemnon, l. 900.

57. ἀντισηκώσας : ἀντιστσθμήσας, "weighing her an equivalent," Schol. The god is giving her an amount of ruin equal to her former grandeur. σηκός, from which comes σηκόω, means "pen, enclosure," but its root idea seems to imply "pressure." It is akin to σάττω, "press down, pack," but the transition to the meaning "weight" is obscure. εὐπραξίας, gen. of price or equivalence.

59–215. Parodos.

Aristotle defines the Parodos as the whole first utterance of the Chorus. In earlier Tragedy (e.g. Aesch., *Supp.*, *Pers.*, *Ag.* ; Soph., *Ajax*), it frequently began with a song in anapaestic rhythm, sung while the Chorus marched into its place in the orchestra, and ended with an ode of regular strophic structure, all sung by the Chorus, and often giving a lyrical account of events antecedent to the play—a kind of lyrical prologue. Later it became fashionable to introduce the Chorus as taking part in a dirge shared in by one or more of the characters. Such a parodos is called *kommatic*, from κομμός, the regular name for a dirge in Tragedy (its ordinary name being θρῆνος). The usual place for the κομμός is after the dénouement. *Hecuba* shares with Sophocles' *Electra* and with E.'s own *Tauric Iphigenia* the peculiarity that its parodos is kommatic, and with the latter the further peculiarity that it is entirely in anapaestic rhythm. Hecuba is the "leader" in this dirge as she is in the Iliad (xxiv, 747 : ἀδινοῦ ἐξῆρχε γόοιο).

Though all anapaestic, this parodos is by no means as simple in structure as anapaestic songs usually are. It falls into three distinct parts or movements. First comes a song in which Hecuba describes her dream (59–97) ; next a song in which the Chorus confirm its message by the news that her daughter is to be sacrificed (98–153) ; and finally, an *amoibaion*, or part-song, between Hecuba and Polyxena, whom she calls out of the tent (154–215). While the first t parts are in ordinary anapaests, the third is in anapaests of a special kind, suited to the dirge. In these a spondee is very frequently substituted for an anapaest (— — for ◡◡ —),   is giving an effect of slowness and desolation. Furthermore, the third part has a strophic structure like a regular choral ode. It consists of a strophe (154–74, Hecuba's song) a mesode (177–96, part-song of Hecuba and Polyxena) and an antistrophe (197–2 5, Polyxena's song) in exact rhythmic correspondence with the strophe. This structure was first recognised by G. Hermann, and its recognition has led to the exclusion as interpolations of 175-6 and the marking of a lacuna in the text at 207.

59. δόμων : the camp.

62. μου : gen. w. προσλαζύμεναι, regular w. vbs. of taking hold.

64. γεραιᾶς : scan as anapaest ; αι short before vowel. προσλαζύμεναι : λάζυμαι : tragic for epic λάζομαι, cognate w. λαμβάνω.

65. σκίπωνι : cp. σκῆπτρον, Latin *scipio*, English *shaft*.

67. ἤλυσιν : "gait," cp. ἤλυθον, ἦλθον. The word seems peculiar to Eur. A late variant is ἔλευσις "Advent." *Acts of Apostles*, 7; 52.

68. στεροπά : normally of lightning, "flash"; here, "dazzling light" as also in Soph. The time is early dawn. Note that sun's light belongs to *Zeus*; cp. 706. There was no worship of the sun as a god, except in Rhodes.

69. αἴρομαι : "am distracted"; ἤρθην φόβῳ, Aesch., *Seven*, 214. ἔννυχος : note two terminations.

70. φάσμα : "ghost" (φαίνω). Menander wrote a play called Φάσμα. Cp. Plautus' *Mostellaria*. πότνια : fem. with peculiar ending -νιἄ, from πόσις; cp. Latin *potis sum*. δέσποινα, "house-mistress" is cognate word. χθών : a rare synonym for Γῆ as earth-*goddess*.

71. Dreams are "dark-winged" because children of night.

72. ἀποπέμπομαι : middle voice, "avert, exorcise."

74-5. Two dactylic hexameters; rhythm repeated 90-1. Like the run of short syllables at 62, this gives variety and excitement to H.'s song.

76. ἐδάην : only Epic and Trag. Obsolete δάω, "teach," in passive, "know." Cp. Homeric δαίφρων. The words in brackets were deleted by Hartung as redundant : ἔμαθον : prob. gloss on ἐδάην.

79. χθόνιοι θεοί : Plouton and Kore-Persephone. As children of night, dreams are also denizens of the underworld. Cp. Virgil, *Aeneid*, VI, 894, f. They are thus subject to χθόνιοι θεοί.

80. ἄγκυρ' ἔτ' ἐμῶν : note long ῠ. This is reading of the late MSS. for earlier ἄγκυρα τ' ἐμῶν, and needs no emendation.

81. χιονώδη : Prob. Ionic prose-word, only here in Trag.

Θρήκην : Ionic for Attic Θράκην.

κατέχει : here "dwells in." Often "hold, occupy," used of gods, Soph., *Ant.*, 609, Aristoph., *Clouds*, 603 ; of dead holding graves, Aesch., *Ag.*, 454.

83. νέον : "untoward." In questions, τί νέον always implies that *bad* news expected.

84. μέλος γοερόν : almost synonym for θρῆνος, "dirge," for which another word was γόος, whence γόης "professional mourner," then "charlatan."

85. ἀλίαστος : negative verbal adj. from λιάζομαι, "turn aside, quail," hence "unabating." Cp. 98. πόλεμος ἀλίαστος Homer, "ceaseless war."

87. Ἑλένου ψυχάν : simply "Helenus" on model of βίη Ἡρακλείη, or perhaps "dear Helenus." He is θεῖος because, like Cassandra, he has gift of prophecy. In *Iliad*, VII, 44, he is already a soothsayer. In Soph., *Philoct.*, 604 f, we hear how he prophesied fall of Troy. Cp. Virgil, *Aen.*, III, 333 f.

88. The true reading here is Κασάνδρας (Weil, Méridier), to be construed w. ψυχάν. The acc. is due to a commentator who supposed ψυχάν to mean ghost. εἶπε δὲ τὸ ψυχήν Ἑλένου, ἐπειδὴ τεθνηκὼς ἦν, Scholiast. But other scholia point out that this is not so. The great literary presentation of Cassandra is of course Aesch., *Ag.*, 1072 ff.

ἐσίδω : deliberative subj.

90. αἵμονι χαλᾷ : the lexicon of Hesychius (fifth century A.D. ?) explains χαλᾷ here as equivalent to γνάθος, "jaw." Normally, however, it means "talon, claw," sometimes "hoof," Attic χηλή. Here "bloodstained *claw*" seems to suit best.

92. τόδε : "what follows," as regularly.

94. Ἀχιλέως : trisyllabic by synizesis (two vowels, such as -εω- here, scanned as one.)

ᾔτει : note tense : " kept asking."

95. τινά : This is in apparent contradiction with 40, where Polydorus explicitly mentions Polyxena. The contradiction has led some scholars to excise 92–7, 104–43, 187–96, and 267–70 as interpolations. Two less radical solutions are, however, possible. One is that of the Scholiast, who says : οὐ γὰρ ἰδικῶς τὴν Πολυξένην ᾐτήσατο, ἀλλὰ μίαν τῶν αἰχμαλωτίδων κάλλει ὑπερφέρουσαν. This implies that the choice of P. was so obvious to the Greeks as to need no further motivation. See, however, on 390. A still simpler solution is provided by supposing that Hecuba has not yet heard more than a vague report.

98. ἐλιάσθην : " hastened to you." Only occurrence in Trag. of epic λιάζομαι. Cp. 85.

99. δεσποσύνους : " tents of our masters." This adj. (two terminations) is chiefly poetical.

σκηνάς : note that Latin scena, Eng. scene, are from the booth or wooden structure which was the normal background of a play.

102. ἵν'. ἐκληρώθην : " to which I was assigned by lot." For this use of ἵνα, cp. Soph., O. T., 687 : ὁρᾷς ἵν' ἥκεις.

110. δόξαι : technical term, " decrees."

111. θέσθαι : note middle voice. τίθημι is cognate w. Latin facio, as well as with Latin do, Eng. do, and from Homer down often means " make," e.g. Od. V, 136, θήσειν ἀθάνατον. In the middle voice it means " make for oneself." Cp. phrases like. θέσθαι ἄκοιτιν.

109. τύμβου δ' ἐπιβάς : gen. regular w. ἐπιβαίνειν, " mount."

110. χρυσέοις : dissyllable, by synizesis.

111. ἔσχε : " held back." ἔχω is cognate w. Gaulish sego- (Segomārus, " greatly victorious "), German Sieg, " victory," and often means " master, control, restrain."

σχεδίας : poet. for " ships " ; lit. " rafts."

112. ἐπερειδομένας : " staying their sails with ropes," L. and S. The phrase may mean either " furling their sails," or

more probably, " though their sails were straining at the stays," lit. " pressing their sails against the stays—*en train d' appuyer les voiles sur les cordages* " (Mér.).

113. θωύσσων : lit. "barking." θωύσσω also means "call on dogs," *Bacch.*, 871. Probably onomatopoeic. (Boisacq.).

114. ποῖ δή : construe w. στέλλεσθ' : "whither are you setting forth ?"

117. ἐχώρει : regular of *rumours* ; cp. ἡ φάτις κεχώρηκε, Hdt., I, 122.

119. δοκοῦν : common accus. absol., with certain intrans. verbs like δοκεῖ, ἔξεστι. Construe : τοῖς μὲν διδόναι δοκοῦν, τοῖς δ' οὐχί.

120. ἦν δ' ὁ τὸ μὲν σὸν : "and A. was the one who defended your interests."

121. βάκχης : Bacchus was a god of prophecy ; cp. *infra*, 1207, *Bacch.*, 298. The word means thus simply " possessed."

ἀνέχων : "maintaining, remaining constant to."

123. Θησείδα : (dual). The Schol. names T's sons Akamas and Demophon. They had come to Troy, not as leaders of a contingent, but to bring back their grandmother, Aithra, whom the Dioscuri had carried off and given to Helen. They were first mentioned in the lost " Cyclic " epic, *Iliou Persis*.

124. δισσῶν : simply "two." Cp. Aesch., *Ag.*, 123, δισσούς Ἀτρείδας. Here used for antithesis w. γνώμῃ μιᾷ in next line.

126. στεφανοῦν : "that it should be crowned." Note Greek preference for active const., where English prefers passive.

127. χλωρῷ : νέας παιδὸς αἵματι, Schol. ; "fresh, young " ; lit. " green."

128-9. οὐκ ἐφάτην . . . θήσειν : "declared they would never put." Note fresh antithesis in τὰ Κασάνδρας λέκτρα and τῆς Ἀχιλείας λόγχης.

130. σπουδαὶ : "zeal," equal on both sides.

132. πρὶν : "until," w. indic in past time after affirmative ; not frequently found.

κόπις : "talker" apparently an Attic colloquialism, not to be confused w. κοπίς, "knife," though both are akin to κόπτω, and though κοπίς is also used of a speaker (Phocion, whom Demosthenes called ἡ τῶν ἐμῶν λόγων κοπίς, Plut., *Phocion,* 5; "pruner of my periods." As Weil points out, Phocion, though a κοπὶς λόγων, was exactly the opposite of a κόπις.).

135. εἶνεκ' : reading of the best MSS. as against οὕνεκ' of others. The confusion is as old as the fifth century B.C. Cp. L. and S. *s. v.* οὕνεκα.

δούλων σφαγίων : "sacrifice of a slave"; noun in apposition used for adjective.

136. Φερσεφόνη : This curious compromise form (Hom. Περσεφόνη, Attic Φερρέφαττα) occurs in Pindar (*Ol.,* 14, 21).

137. φθιμένων : with τιν' in previous line. "None of the dead." Note how skilfully O. turns the demand of Achilles into a demand of *all* the dead.

139. οἰχομένοις : a pathetic word, "dead and gone." Cp. Soph., *Ant.,* 841. Note full equivalence of Ἕλληνες and Δαναοί here; cp. n. on l. 5.

141. ὅσον οὐκ ἤδη : Lit. "almost at once."

142. πῶλον : very common in Tragedy for "child." Cp. *Hipp.,* 546, *Andr.,* 621, and in a simile, *Bacch.,* 166.

143. ὁρμήσων : active, less common than middle, which means "start, begin."

144. πρός to be supplied w. ναούς, by anticipation.

145. γονάτων : obj. gen. w. ἱκέτις.

146-7. οὐρανίδας . . . ὑπὸ γᾶν : This is the familiar distinction between Ὀλύμπιοι and χθόνιοι θεοί. It should be noted that the distinction was not felt by the Greeks as one between an *earlier* and *later* set of gods, but was one of *function* merely.

148. λιταί : cp. λίσσομαι, λιτανεύω, Eng. *litany.*

150. τύμβου προπετῆ : "fallen before the tomb," as if the second word were part of προπεσεῖν.

153. νασμῷ : from νάω, "flow." μελαναυγεῖ, "dark-gleaming," only here in classical Greek. It is suggested prob. by Hom. μελάνυδρος, a common epithet of springs. The application of such an epithet to *blood* has an effect of horror.

154. The heavily spondaic rhythm of Hecuba's reply emphasises her desolation. ἀπύσω : Doric for ἠπύσω, "say," as ἀχώ in next line is for ἠχώ, Eng. *echo*.

156. γήρως : gen. of cause.

158. φερτᾶς : adj. unique for normal φιστός.

159. γέννα : metrically irregular because of final ᾰ. Porson conjectured γενέα.

160. φροῦδος : from προ-όδός w. metathesis of aspirate. " On the way," hence " gone." For form, cp. φρουρά from προ-όρά.

163. στείχω : Cp. Irish *teighim*, "go," German *steigen*, "mount."

ποῖ δ' ᾖσω is difficult without object, and Reiske's conjecture, πόδα for ποῦ, is generally approved.

164. δαιμόνων : metrically wrong, and the awkward distinction from θεῶν is an argument even against the sing. δαίμων. Furthermore. τίς θεῶν ἢ δαίμων would involve a strange ellipse of the pronoun. Nauck's θεός ἢ δαίμων gets rid of this, but leaves the first difficulty unsolved. Perhaps δαιμόνων is an intrusion which has displaced some entirely different word. Cp. n. on 206.

167. ἀπωλέσατ' ὠλέσατ' : When a compound verb is repeated, the prefix is omitted without affecting the sense. Cp. *Bacch.*, 1065: κατῆγεν, ἦγεν, ἦγεν. Note dactyls here and at 209.

169-76. Page (*Actors' Interpolations in Greek Tragedy*) thinks this passage may be " melodramatic interpolation." Cp., however, note on 171.

171. αὐλάν : lit. " courtyard," here " tent," later " royal court." The history of the word is curiously similar to that of French *cour*, English *court*, German *Hof*.

ὦ τέκνον, ὦ παῖ : Obviously parodied by Aristophanes, *Clouds*, 1165 ; ὦ τέκνον, ὦ παῖ, ἔξελθ' οἴκων, ἄιε σοῦ πατρός. The parody, as well as providing a *terminus ante quem* for *Hecuba*, also seems to prove the genuineness of this passage against Page's suspicion. Cp. Introduction.

174. ἄιε : trisyllabic, by diaeresis.

177. (Polyxena comes out of the tent.)

ἰώ : an exclamation, *extra metrum*.

τί νέον : cp. 83.

178. καρύξασ' : We should expect fut. part. καρύξουσ', expressing purpose ; but Hecuba *has* announced a misfortune, without explaining what it is.

ὥστ' : Epic for ὥσπερ.

179. ἐξέπταξας : from ἐκπτήσσω, only here. πτήσσω normally intrans., "cower," but trans., "scare," in *Iliad* XIV, 40, Theognis, 1015.

181. δυσφημεῖς : "address with unlucky words." Note that εὐφημεῖν, from meaning the opposite, has developed a secondary meaning, "be silent," Latin *favere linguis*. εὐφημεῖσθαι later came to mean "be called by a nice name," hence Eng. *euphemism*.

φροίμια : from πρό and a form of οἶμος, "way" with initial aspirate. Boisacq distinguishes οἴμη, "song," from οἶμος, "way."

183. ἐξαύδα : Homeric echo. *Iliad*, I, 363 : ἐξαύδα, μὴ κεῦθε νόῳ.

δαρόν : Ionic δηρός, adj. ; here acc. of time, w. χρόνον understood. Cp. *Bacch.*, 889 : δαρὸν χρόνου πόδα.

189. συντείνει : "tends to" a euphemism for "has decided."

190. Πηλείᾳ is Paley's correction of MSS. Πηλεῖδα, gen. of Πηλείδης (Homeric) which would give phrase meaning "son of Achilles."

191. πῶς : "on what authority ? "

192. ἀμέγαρτα : ἀφθόνητα Schol. ; "unenviable," from μεγαίρω, "grudge." For gen. κακῶν, cp. phrase κακὰ κακῶν.

196. περί μοι ψυχᾶς : μοι is *ethical* dat., not to be construed w. ἀγγέλλουσ'. It has no literal English equivalent, and hence can only be paraphrased. "Your darling life." σᾶς ψυχᾶς governed by περί.

200. ἀρρήταν : usually has only two terminations, like all compound adjs. This form is unique. "Unspeakable."

202. ἄδ' : ὅδε is often used in reference to the speaker. Cp. Soph., *O.T.*, 815 : τίς τοῦδε γ' ἀνδρὸς νῦν ἔτ' ἀθλιώτερος ; In Latin *hic* is similarly used : huic homini verbera, Terence, *Haut.*, 356.

205. Construe σκύμνον with μ', and οὐριθρέπταν with μόσχον.

206. The lacuna marked in the text (Murray) makes Polyxena's song correspond strophically with Hecuba's, 154-74. It may be significant that the text of the latter seems defective at exactly the corresponding place ; cp. n. on 163-4.

207. ἀναρπαστάν : The verbal adj. in -τός is here used, as often in poetry, like the Latin perf. part. pass., of which it is the etymological equivalent.

208. τε joins λαιμότομον w. ἀναρπαστάν. Ἀΐδα : dat. of indirect obj. ; "to Hades, down to the darkness of the earth."

209. σκότον : acc. of motion, or "internal" acc. w. ὑποπεμπομέναν.

215. It is very rare for an anapaestic sequence to end in a full dimeter without catalexis ; the paroemiac (e.g. 153) is normal. Exceptions, however, do occur, and no emendation is called for here. Perhaps the reason for the exception here is that these are *lyric* anapaests, with strophic correspondence. Cp. 174.

216-443. First Epeisodion.

Aristotle defines an Epeisodion (English *episode*) as "All that comes between two whole songs of the Chorus." The word is obviously a compound of ἐπί, εἰς, and ὁδός, and meant originally "parenthesis, addition." Thus it is probably an old name for part of a tragedy, as it emphasises the secondary nature of the dialogue in the early period, when the Chorus was all-important. By the end of the fifth century, this relation had been entirely reversed. Agathon, the pupil of Euripides, actually wrote tragedies in which the choral songs had nothing at all to do with the play (ἐμβόλιμα, "interludes," a name curiously similar in meaning to ἐπεισόδια.) It was Aeschylus, we are told by Aristotle, who "reduced the importance of the Chorus." Euripides carried the process a long way further, and in some of his late plays (e.g. *Iphigenia*, *Helen*) the choral songs are often largely irrelevant to the action. The regular division of a tragedy into *stasima* and *epeisodia* was the distant origin of the division into *acts* with which we are familiar.

This is the liveliest act in the play except the last. As there, all three actors are on the stage together ; in the second and third acts, only two are needed. Notice the formal structure of this Epeisodion, which is characteristic of all Tragedy. It opens with a brief speech by Odysseus, who brutally announces his mission. He is answered in a slightly briefer speech by Hecuba ; then comes a short dialogue in which they speak line for line. This kind of dialogue is called στιχομυθία, "conversation in alternate lines." It is followed by a great speech of Hecuba's, in which she begs Odysseus to save her daughter. After three lines spoken by the Coryphaeus (leader of the Chorus) Odysseus replies in a speech of almost equal length, justifying his refusal by specious arguments. After a piteous appeal by her mother, Polyxena, in a speech almost as long as the other two, boldly refuses to beg for mercy, and declares herself ready to die. Hecuba now offers herself in her daughter's place ; but Odysseus refuses even to let her share Polyxena's fate. There is then another passage of στιχομυθία, broken by a last speech of Polyxena, and ending with her attempting to console her mother by the illusory reminder that Polydorus still lives. Two brief speeches by Polyxena and Hecuba complete the act, and Polyxena is led away.

216. καὶ μὴν : regular formula to announce new entry.

218. γύναι : " Lady." Beware of translating " woman," which gives the word a derogatory sense. For μέν followed by ἀλλ' ὅμως cp. Soph., *El.*, 450 : σμικρὰ μὲν τάδ', ἀλλ' ὅμως | ἄχω, δὸς αὐτῷ.

219. κρανθεῖσαν : from κραίνω, often of voting : " cast." Cp. Aesch., *Supp.*, 943 : κέκρανται ψῆφος.

221. σφάξαι : note sense of *urgency* conveyed by aor. inf. The present is more normal w. δόκει.

223. ἐπιστάτης : from ἐφιστάναι. Common to poetry and prose ; " superintendent, overseer."

224. ἔπεσται : Nauck's correction of MSS. ἐπέστη, which

he holds is wrong tense, besides being too close an echo of ἐπιστάτης. The tense, however, is intelligible if ἐπέστη be understood as meaning "has been appointed," and the repetition would not have offended a Greek ear. Weil and Méridier keep ἐπέστη.

παῖς 'Αχιλλέως : Neoptolemus, to whom late Epic and Tragedy assigned a chief part in the capture of Troy. He is a principal character in Soph., *Philoctetes.*.

225. οἶσθ' οὖν ὃ δρᾶσον : An obvious colloquial blend of question and command. Cp. Soph., *O. T.*, 543, w. Jebb's note, which lists a dozen exx. fronf Tragedy and Comedy. An extreme form of this colloquialism is seen in Eur., *I. T.*, 1203, οἶσθα νῦν ἅ μοι γενέσθω, and Ar., *Ach.*, 1064, οἶσθ' ὡς ποιείτω. Usually explained as a "transposition" for δρᾶσον, οἶσθ' ὅ, "do, do you know what?" but this is unnecessarily logical. An English parallel will illustrate how easily such colloquialisms occur in all languages : "I'll tell you what let's do" (Hulbert Footner, *Queen of Clubs*, p. 158). Cp. French phrases like *voilà-t-il pas*?

227. Note constant sharp distinction between present imperative (durative or inceptive aspect) and aorist (instantaneous).

These two lines (227-8) express in elaborate language a common Greek precept, more succinctly put at *Heracleidae*, 706 : χρή γνωσιμαχεῖν ("recognise one's strength").

228. ἃ δεῖ φρονεῖν : "to think as one ought," i.e. yield to superior force. Cp. στέργειν τὰ παρόντα. O. speaks throughout as the representative of Greek *Realpolitik* as opposed to barbarian passion.

ΤΟΙ : "as you know."

230. The apparent tautology of this line is in keeping with the slow, rhetorical style of the whole scene. "Full of groans and tears."

231. ἄρ' : "after all" as often.

232. ΤΡέφει : "keeps me alive." The word has a much wider meaning than English "nurse" by which it is sometimes translated. Cp. γηροτροφεῖν, etc.

235. μή : not with ἐξιστορῆσαι but with λυπρά. "To ask questions that are not painful nor heart-wounding." δηκτήρια : from δάκνω, "bite."

236–7. "You ought to answer this question, and I ought to hear your answer." Construe σοί as dative of agent with εἰρῆσθαι (passive): "this (τάδε) ought to be told once for all by you." Some edd. make ἡμᾶς object of ἀκοῦσαι, but this is unparalleled; ἡμᾶς and τάδε are the subjects of the two infinitives. Note gender of τοὺς ἐρωτῶντας. A woman regularly uses the masculine when speaking of herself in the plural. Cp. 512.

238. ἔξεστ' : note the stern abruptness. ἐρώτα: inceptive pres.: "go on, put your question."

239. ἡνίκ' : probably the conjunction is deliberately used to imply that *she* remembers the *exact* time. πηνίκα, its correlative, means "at what time of day ?" πηνίκα μάλιστα, "What o'clock ?"

240. The story of how O. entered Troy is told in *Od.*, IV, 244 f, and was probably given more fully in the *Little Iliad*. In the Epics Helen was the only one to recognise him. His recognition by Hecuba is a detail invented by Eur. himself for the purpose of this scene, and is a good instance of how poets freely handled their material.

241. The φόνου σταλαγμοί were due to the severe whipping he had given himself (αὐτόν μιν πληγῇσιν ἀεικελίῃσι δαμάσσας, *Od., l.c.*).

γένυν : Latin *gena*, German *Kinn*, English *chin*. Cognate also w. γνάθος, γναθμός, "jaw." It often means "cheek," and even "blade of an axe."

242. ἄκρας καρδίας : "the surface of my heart." Cp. Aesch., *Ag.*, 805, ἀπ' ἄκρας φρενός. ψαύειν, like θιγγάνειν, ἅπτεσθαι ("touch") takes gen. Cp. 245.

243. This is Eur.'s device for linking his new story with Homer's old one.

245. ταπεινὸς ὤν : where English would use an adverb, "humbly," Greek feeling calls for adj. and participle.

246. ἐνθανεῖν : νεκρωθῆναι, Schol., "grow numb." A rare word, unique in this sense.

γε : "Yes, to such an extent that," with ὥστε. One of the commonest uses of γε. Cp. 248.

249–50. Some late MSS. put these lines before 247-8, and were followed by Porson. This puts *events* in their correct order. Weil remarks, however, that O.'s answers have up to this point been all that H. can desire ; it is only when she comes to the essential point that he grows evasive, suggesting that whatever he said to escape death had no real validity. H. is thus forced to cease her cross-examination and turn to direct appeal. Line 250 is exactly in keeping with the realism displayed by O. throughout, and should not be excised or altered.

251. οὔκουν : thus accented, asks a question expecting the answer " yes." οὐκοῦν means " therefore." The meaning depends upon the accent.

κακύνῃ : " become wicked, act badly."

252. ἐξ ἐμοῦ : for ὑπ' ἐμοῦ, " at my hands."

253. δύνῃ : Ionic 2 sing., pres. ind. ; Attic δύνασαι. Porson's reading here, δυνᾷ, is a Doric form, unsuited to dialogue.

254. Eur. puts into H.'s mouth a very topical criticism of democratic politicians. It is obviously entirely anachronistic as applied to the Homeric Odysseus. None the less, Eur. gives him the traits of a contemporary Athenian politician. Cp. 131–2 : ποικιλόφρων, κόπις, ἡδυλόγος, δημοχαριστής. The Scholiast's remark is apt : ταῦτα εἰς τὴν κατ' αὐτὸν πολιτείαν λέγει. καὶ ἔστι τοιοῦτος ὁ Εὐριπίδης, περιάπτων τὰ καθ' ἑαυτὸν τοῖς ἥρωσι καὶ τοὺς χρόνους συγχέων.

255. μηδέ γιγνώσκοισθέ | · : Passive opt., expressing a wish. " Would you were unknown to me ! "

257. ἢν : Attic for ἐάν. τοῖσι : Homeric.

258. σόφισμα : " clever trick, piece of policy." From σοφίζομαι, " practise cleverness." Cp. σοφιστής, " teacher of cleverness." Eur. may be thinking of the close connection between Sophistic rhetoric and politics, as seen for instance in Cleon's speeches in Thucydides, III.

259. ψῆφον ὥρισαν : synonym for ἐψηφίσαντο.

260. τὸ χρῆν : This is a unique phrase. Nauck conjectures τὸ χρή. as in Herakles, 828 (where χρῆν is a marginal substitute). The word χρή was originally a fem. noun, which when contracted w. parts of εἰμί gave such forms as χρῆναι, χρείη, χρῆν (imperfect : ἐχρῆν is an analogical form, rare in classical poetry), χρῆσται (future). If χρῆν be kept here, it might still be construed as

imperf., made into a substantive by article ; " was it your so-called necessity (lit. " the it-was-necessary ") that led them on ? " It is generally taken as inf., but this assumes, as Wilamowitz declares (note on *Herakles,* 311) that " Eur. understood his own language as little as did all grammarians before H. L. Ahrens." Another conjecture is χρεών (with synizesis).

σφ' : for σφε, Epic enclitic acc. (sing. and pl.) of 3 pers. pron. σφείς. The original starting-point of all these forms was σφί, σφίν, cognate w. Latin *sibi*, where -bi was the case-ending. In σφί, σ-was all that remained of the original stem. But σφ- was felt as a stem, and given case-endings, σφείς like ἡμείς, σφέ like μέ, etc.

263. τείνει : " aims," metaphor from archery.

265. νιν : Doric equivalent of Homeric μιν, which is Aeolic 3rd person, all genders, sing. and pl. Both forms occur in Tragedy. They seem to contain an old pronoun found in Cypriot ίν, Latin *is* (old acc. *im*) but the initial nasal is obscure.

Eur.'s frequent denunciations of Helen follow a fashion set by Aesch. Cp. Aesch., *Ag.*, 681 f, Eur., *I. T.*, 439 f. They may, perhaps, be explained by the fact that she was a Spartan goddess. Eur.'s *Helena* is in a sense a palinode.

266. ὤλεσεν . . . ἄγει : note combination of aorist and historic pres.

269. ἡ Τυνδαρὶς : Helen and Klytaimnestra were daughters of Tyndareus and sisters of the " Heavenly Twins," Kastor and Polydeukes. For Helen's beauty, the *locus classicus* is, of course, *Iliad*, III, 145-60.

271. τῷ μὲν δικαίῳ : " on the score of justice," instrumental dat. ἀμιλλῶμαι is intrans., and τόνδε λόγον is equivalent to τήνδ' ἄμιλλαν λόγου, a cognate acc.

274. γραίας : Valckenaer's correction of unmetrical γεραιᾶς of the MSS.

275. τῶν αὐτῶν : hands and face. σοῦ depends on τῶν αὐτῶν.

276. χάριν τὴν τόθ' : " (requital for) the favour I did you then." χάρις means both " benefit " and " thanks."

ἀπαιτῶ : " ask in return."

279. Line deleted by Hartung, because repeated in *Orestes*, 664 ταύτη γέγηθι, κ.τ.λ. Page (*l.c.*) condemns it as an actor's interpolation.

280. παραψυχή : " consolation." This is earliest occurrence of the word. Cp. παραμυθεῖσθαι, παρηγορεῖν.

281. Porson compares frag. 858 :

ἀλλ᾽ ἥδε μ᾽ ἐξέσωσεν, ἥδε μοι τροφός,
μήτηρ, ἀδελφή, δμωΐς, ἄγκυρα, στέγη.

Both passages are evidently modelled on Andromache's words to Hector, *Iliad*, VI, 429 f.

282. ἃ μὴ χρεών : acc. of respect. χρεών : indeclinable noun. μὴ : generic use.

283. δοκεῖν : " to think " ; personal.

εὖ πράξειν : " be prosperous."

284. ῇ : supply εὐτυχής from εὐτυχοῦντας, 283.

286. ὦ φίλον γένειον : ἁπτομένη τοῦ γενείου τοῦτό φησιν. Schol.

γένειον : from γένυς, means both "chin" and "beard," as here.

αἰδέσθητί με : from Hom. αἴδομαι, Attic αἰδοῦμαι. Lit. "show αἰδώς," the noun meaning " respect, reverence, pity."

288. παρηγόρησον : aorist for urgency. The verb here has its primary sense, " advise to *change*." It also meant " console, comfort," whence English *paregoric*.

φθόνος : with ἐστί understood ; " act likely to cause jealousy " (of the gods) or *nemesis*.

ὡς : equivalent to γάρ.

289. τὸ πρῶτον : " on your first victory."

291. νόμος δ᾽ ἐν ὑμῖν : She is speaking of *Athenian* law, as O. has the qualities of an Athenian politician. In Athens, if a slave was killed, his master could take action against his slayer as if he were a free relation. Cp. Antiphon, *Herodes*, 48, Demosth., *In Midiam*, 529.

293. λέγῃ is certainly the correct reading, and ἀξίωμα must be its subject, as it is of πείσει. κακῶς must mean " looked on as

bad, unpopular," H. pays a last compliment to O.: "your authority, even if your cause is unpopular, will win them over."

ἀξίωμα: his standing as leader and orator. The next two lines repeat this: "the same plea has not the same strength in the mouth of a man of standing and in that of a man of no standing."

ἀδοξούντων: from ἀδοξέω (derivative from ἄδοξος), used only here in poetry. τῶν δοκούντων (εἶναί τι), lit., "those who seem to be something."

296. στερρός: Attic form of στερεός, "hard," English *stern*, German *starr*.

299. τῷ θυμουμένῳ: part. for more usual infin., "in your anger." Both inf. and part. w. article are common as abstract nouns in Thuc.

300. φρενός: The MSS. have φρενί, which may be construed w. ποιοῦ: "make for yourself *in your mind* an enemy of one who gives good advice." Murray's φρενός is an inference from the Schol., who explains it as depending on τῷ θυμουμένῳ: τῷ θυμουμένῳ μέρει τῆς ψυχῆς, τούτεστι τῷ θυμοειδεῖ. This, however, is an obvious piece of Platonic psychology, and may not imply the reading φρενός at all. We must not suppose Eur. to have anticipated Plato in such detail. φρενί should be kept.

301. σωμ᾽: "your person," a mere expansion of σέ.

302. ἄλλως: as often, "in vain." He means "what I say, I do."

303. ἃ δ᾽ εἶπον: He is referring to his speech before the assembly.

305. δοῦναι: O. O. for an imperative: "I bade them give."

306. κάμνουσιν: "go wrong"; lit. "are weary, sick." (νοσοῦσι.)

308. φέρηται: "wins for himself." μηδέν: μή w. subj. in all constructions; Goodwin, Gr. Gram., 1610.

τῶν κακιόνων: "the base."

310. ὑπὲρ γῆς Ἑλλάδος: a phrase only appropriate in the fifth century, after Persian Wars.

311. οὔκουν : cp. on 251.

βλέποντι : "living." Cp. on σκότος, line 1, and Aesch., *Eum.*, 321-2, ἀλαοῖσι καὶ δεδορκόσιν, "dead and living."

φίλῳ : prob. to be taken as predicate w. χρώμεσθ' in both clauses ; "treat him (Achilles) as a friend," a regular use of χρῶμαι.

313. ἢν τις αὖ φάνῃ : The vb. is simply equivalent to ᾗ (from εἰμί) : "if there be another hosting."

314. ἀγωνία : here synonym for ἀγών, as often. Like many nouns in -ία (ναυτία, etc.) the word properly denotes a pathological condition, "anxiety about a contest," whence *agony*.

315. μαχούμεθ' : not "are we to fight ?" which would require deliberative subj., but "are we *likely* to fight or play the coward ?" O. is thinking of how a man like himself would react if Achilles were neglected.

φιλοψυχεῖν : lit. "be fond of life."

317. καθ' ἡμέραν : to be taken with κεἰ σμίκρ' ἔχοιμι, "if I should have enough from day to day." Cp. *infra*, 627, and *Bacch.*, 910-11 : τὸ δὲ κατ' ἦμαρ ὅτῳ βίοτος εὐδαίμων, μακαρίζω, "him I count blest, whose life from day to day is happy." This has been strangely mistranslated by Murray : "But whoe'er can know, as the long days go, that to live is happy, hath found his heaven." The Greek is a commonplace of pessimism ; Murray has made it into a declaration of belief in the Shavian "Life Force."

320. διὰ μακροῦ : "lasting." This sentiment would be very topical when *Hecuba* was first produced, and as the Funeral Speech of Pericles (Thuc. II, 35 and 43) shows, the Athenians were careful to honour their dead in war with much ceremony. Cp. also the monument to those fallen at Potidaea, Hicks-Hill, *Greek Historical Inscriptions*, No. 54, p. 93-4. O. is perverting a very normal desire of the citizen-soldier into a brutal demand for human sacrifice.

323. ἠδέ : Homeric conjunction, common in Lyric and Tragedy. Originally it was preceded by ἠμέν. ἤ is the ordinary particle "or," Latin -ue in neue, etc.

πρεσβῦται : Prose form for πρέσβεις, used less often in Trag. Distinguish πρέσβυς from πρεσβευτής, "ambassador" (a derivative of πρεσβεύω, itself from πρέσβυς), and note that πρέσβεις is used as plural of the latter. πρεσβύτερος (comparative of πρέσβυς) is used in papyri of Hellenistic period to mean "elder, alderman." The original meaning of πρέσβυς was "leader," hence πρεσβεύειν often means "be best, take precedence."

σέθεν : for genitive, w. ἧσσον ἄθλιαι.

325. Ἰδαία κόνις : O. speaks as if the host were still on Trojan soil. Ida is the mountain near Troy. The phrase is pathetic ; cp. Aesch., *Ag.*, 452, f. :

οἱ δ' αὐτοῦ περὶ τεῖχος
θήκας Ἰλιάδος γᾶς
εὔμορφοι κατέχουσιν, ἐχ-
θρὰ δ' ἔχοντας ἔκρυψεν.

326. τόλμα : Imperative (note pres.) "be resigned." Cognate w. Latin *tollo, tuli, tolerare*, English *thole*.

νομίζομεν : "are accustomed."

327. ὀφλήσομεν : ὀφλισκάνω, cognate w. ὀφείλω, "owe," means "become liable to pay" ; hence δίκην ὀφλεῖν "lose one's case," then "deserve, bring on oneself" : γέλωτ' ὀφλισκάνειν, and finally, as here, "get reputation for, incur charge of," μωρίαν, δειλίαν, ἀδικίαν ὀφλισκάνειν.

328. οἱ βάρβαροι δέ : nom. sometimes used for voc. in commands ; cp. Ar. *Aves*, 665, ἡ Πρόκνη ἔκβαινε. Here it has an ironical sound ; the contrast is sarcastic.

330. ὡς ἄν : Note that ὡς is the commonest final particle in Trag. In prose only Xenophon uses it thus. ἄν is sometimes used with it and with ὅπως (not with ἵνα) followed by subj., with no effect on the meaning.

It need hardly be said that this confrontation of Greeks and Barbarians is characteristic of the late fifth century, and of Athens, where the idea of παιδεία as the distinguishing mark of Greeks had been propagated by the Sophists from about 460 on. O. speaks here almost as a pupil of the Sophists, and is skill in representing as a token of higher civilisation what was in fact a savage crime cannot fail to remind us of Cleon's speeches in Thuc.

333. τολμᾷ : " puts up with."

334. οὑμοὶ : crasis for οἱ ἐμοὶ (adj.).

335. ῥιφέντες : metaphor from archery. Cp. Homeric τῇ δ' ἄπτερος ἔπλετο μῦθος.

337. σπούδαζε : with μὴ στερηθῆναι βίου.

ὥστ' ἀηδόνος στόμα : ὥστε for ὥσπερ is Homeric and Tragic. ἀηδόνος στόμα : best taken as in apposition w. subject of σπούδαζε, " like the nightingale's tongue." The nightingale was remarked both for the variety of its notes (Od. XIX, 521 : χέει πολυηχέα φωνήν) and for the sadness of its tone (Aesch., Ag., 1146 : λιγείας μόρον ἀηδόνος). The story of Philomela was widely familiar.

338. ἱεῖσα : " uttering," common with φωνήν. Note short first syllable ; usually long in Attic.

340. πεῖθ' : " try to persuade."

πρόφασιν : from προφαίνω, hence " motive or cause alleged, whether true or false," then " false motive, excuse." In Xen., Cyrop., III, 1, 27, πρόφασιν ἔχει means " it is excusable." Here the meaning is " you have something to plead," i.e. the parallel with his own children.

341. ὥστε : sometimes w. πείθω even in prose : cp. Thuc., III, 31.

343. ἔμπαλιν : " back," the spatial sense predominates in the use of πάλιν, especially in Epic.

344. μή : a verb of fearing is understood.

345. Ἱκέσιον Δία : a typically Euripidean phrase of the kind called παρακεκινδυνευμένον (" risky ") in Ar., Ran., 99. Here it stands for τὴν ἐμὴν ἱκετείαν. Zeus, as protector of strangers and guests (supra, 26) was also protector of those seeking help or shelter. His aid was ritually invoked by the gesture of touching the beard, the right hand, or the knees. O. is in no danger, because P. is not going to invoke Zeus in order to escape.

347. εἰ δὲ μὴ βουλήσομαι : the future after εἰ is always emphatic, and often implies a warning.

348. φιλόψυχος : Cp. 315. Compound adj. of two terminations.

350. πρῶτον : literal, w. ἔπειτ' in 351 : " this was the first thing in my life, and then . . . ." Not " this was my chief glory in life," which would have little point.

352. ʒῆλον : " rivalry for my hand " w. γάμων.

353. ἔχουσ' : " causing," equivalent to παρέχουσα. Cp. συγγνώμην ἔχειν, " to pardon."

ὅτου δῶμ' ἑστίαν τ' : an indirect question, w. vivid fut., after ʒῆλον. Cp. 360.

355. This line lacks caesura. Lesser MSS. try to mend the defect by inserting τ' before ἀπόβλεπτος. Weil compares ἀπόβλεπτος w. περίστρεπτος in Aesch., Cho., 350 ; " such as people turn away from others to look at." μετά w. dat. imitates Homeric μετ' ἀνδράσιν, etc.

356. ἴση θεοῖσι : Cp. Homeric ἰσόθεος φώς.

πλὴν τὸ κατθανεῖν : πλὴν is an adverb, τὸ κατθανεῖν acc. of respect. Note Aeolic prefix κατ-, an Epic usage.

The chief distinguishing mark of the gods was their immortality ; they are μάκαρες θεοὶ αἰὲν ἐόντες.

357. νῦν δ' : " but as it is " a common meaning.

τοὔνομα : " the name of slave."

358. τίθησιν : " makes." Cp. 111.

359. ὠμῶν : ὠμός, lit. " raw," Latin amarus, Irish amh, older om.

φρένας : acc. of respect.

360. ἄν : repeated for emphasis.

ὅστις : " someone who." ὠνήσεται, vivid fut.

362-4. Closely paralleled by speech of Hecuba in Troades, 490 f.

362. προσθείς : προστίθημι, lit. " add to," hence " impose on."

ἀνάγκην σιτοποιὸν : " compulsion to bake bread." All these were tasks of household slaves.

365. ποθεν : " who knows whence ? " There is a contrast implied w. 352 ; the whole speech is a careful study in parallel structure.

368. φέγγος : Most expressive Greek word for "light," especially beloved by Pindar ; cp. *Pyth.* 8, 97.

προστιθεῖσ' : Cp. 362. She will become the bride of Hades, like Antigone ; Soph., *Ant.*, 816, 891. "I will put this light away from my eyes while they are free." ἐλευθέρων, Blomfield, for MSS. ἐλεύθερον.

369. διέργασαι : The prefix δια- with verbs indicates *completion*. For sense, cp. διαμοιρᾶσαι, *Hipp.* 1376.

370-1. ἐλπίδος and δόξης depend on θάρσος : "I can see no encouragement to hope or believe that I am destined ever to be happy." του, for τινός, Ionic τεο, τευ.

δόξα : "belief, opinion." παρ' ἡμῖν : with θάρσος : "in my reach."

372. μῆτερ, σὺ δ' : Note word-order, regular when a new person addressed. Cp. 1287.

ἐμποδών : formed by analogy from ἐκποδών. Cp. 52. ἡμῖν : *dativus incommodi.*

373. συμβούλου : from συμβούλομαι : "join me in wishing" ; earliest use of a word later common in prose.

374. πρίν : w. inf., referring to future in affirmative sentence.

377. μᾶλλον εὐτυχέστερος : double comparative, common also in English poetry (Shakespeare).

379. χαρακτήρ : from χαράσσω, "inscribe, engrave, stamp," used of coining.

ἐπίσημος : from σῆμα, "stamp," keeps up the metaphor.

Eur. only partly agrees with Burns that "the rank is but the guinea-stamp," though he does hold that rank is enhanced by virtue. This reverence for rank is a surprising trait of the democratic Athenians at their finest hour.

380-1. "The name of nobility has increased force (ἐπὶ μεῖζον ἔρχεται) for those who are worthy," as Polyxena is. Note that ἀρετή originally meant "capacity," like Latin *virtus*; it was an aristocratic quality.

382. εἶπας : Common in Attic as 2 pers. of εἶπον, for which

Ionic prose used εἶπα. The confusion is due to a tendency to assimilate archaic second aorist to first. Cp. Irish simplification in Connacht *ni rinne* for *ni dhearna*, Munster *do dheineas* for *do rinne*. For antithetical sentiment,' " well said—but how sad ! " cp. Sappho's ᾽Ερος, γλυκύπικρον ὄρπετον, " bitter-sweet love."

383–4. H. concedes O.'s arguments, but only in order to make a new proposal.

385. μὴ κτείνετε : " do not go on to kill " ; it does not follow that P. is the proper victim.

386. πυράν : with long ᾱ; Homeric πυρή, distinct from πυρά used as pl. of πῦρ, which has short ᾰ. English *pyre* comes from the former. Here used metaphorically to mean " tomb."

387. κεντεῖτε : from κεντέω, whose noun κέντρον gave Latin *centrum*, English *centre*. As mother of Paris, whose slaying of Achilles formed part of the lost " Cyclic " epic, *Aithiopis*, H. is a more fitting victim than her daughter. The death of Achilles at the hands of Paris and Apollo is prophesied by Hector, *Iliad*, XXII, 359 f.

390. Cp. note on 95. These plain words seem to show that the ghost, as Polydorus also explicitly says (40), asked for the sacrifice of Polyxena. At 95 therefore we must suppose that H. has not heard the full news.

391. ἀλλὰ : highly emphatic, as often. H., in despair, tries at least to share in her daughter's death.

393. γαίᾳ : This hardly implies that the *goddess* Gê required libations of blood. In order to give the blood to the dead warrior, it had to be poured into the earth through an opening in the tomb, which is thought of as an ἐσχάρα or hero-altar.

395. μηδὲ τόνδ᾽ ὠφείλομεν : ὠφείλομεν is imperf. of ὀφείλω (aor. ὤφελον) which corresponds to Epic ὀφέλλω, ὤφελλον, ὤφελον. Both imperf. and aor. can be used (neg. μή) to express an unattained wish. Here, therefore, some verb like φέρειν, διδόναι, is to be understood. " I wish we did not have to offer this death." The imperf., as in certain conditional sentences, here applies to *present* time. Note that O. here rather departs from his earlier *Realpolitik* and betrays momentary compunction.

396. γ᾽ : emphatic ; " indeed."

397. πῶς : the abrupt question shows that O. is offended. He resents the suggestion that he has any master, implied in πολλή γ᾽ ἀνάγκη.

398. The correct punctuation is surely ὁποῖα κισσός, δρυὸς ὅπως, τῆσδ᾽ ἕξομαι : " I will cling to her like ivy, as (it clings) to the oak," with ellipse of ἔχεται after ὅπως. Thus ὁποῖα (neut. pl. used as adverb) is in antithesis to ὅπως, but it is an artificial antithesis, which, as Weil says, splits a simple simile in two. Murray's comma after δρυὸς makes ὅπως ἕξομαι mean " let me cling to her." He compares Troades, 146–7, Ar. Eccl., 297. But such a command by H. to herself is surely forced. ἔχομαι, " cling to," like vbs. of touching, takes gen. For simile of clinging ivy. cp. Soph. Ant., 826–7.

400. ὡς . . . μεθήσομαι : ὡς is here emphatic, implying perhaps an ellipse of ἴσθι : " know that." Cp. Medea, 609.

401. ἀλλὰ . . . μὴν : go together, " but neither will I go and leave her here."

403. χάλα : Imper. of χαλάω, " slacken," used intransitively ; " yield to."

τοκεῦσιν : pl. generically for sing. So also with κρατοῦσι in next line.

θυμουμένοις : from θυμόω " to make angry."

406. γέροντα χρῶτα : For γέρων as adj. cp. Herakles, 26 : γέρων λόγος.

407. ἀσχημονῆσαι : " behave disgracefully " ; here " be put to shame," unique in Trag. It is evidently colloquial. ἐκ for ὑπό, as often.

408. ἃ πείσῃ : " which will happen to you " (πάσχω).

μὴ σύ γ᾽ : again prob. colloquial ; often used in entreaties.

410. δὸς : governs both χέρα and προσβαλεῖν (zeugma).

411–12. Also in Alcestis, 207–8, where edd. have bracketed the second line.

415. ἐν φάει : " among the living."

4—1683

416. Cp. Soph., *Ant.*, 876 : ἄκλαυτος, ἄφιλος, ἀνυμέναιος ὤν μ᾽ ἐχρῆν τυχεῖν. Relative has for antecedent ὑμεναίων understood ; genitive of privation.

417. ἀθλία : stronger than οἰκτρά. The living are more miserable than the dead.

418. ἐκεῖ : often used as euphemism for Hades ; here along with it.

419. ποῖ : stands for normal εἰς τί with τελευτῶ.

421. In Homer, while Priam has fifty sons (four daughters only are named in *Iliad*, of whom Polyxena is not one) only nineteen are from one mother, presumably Hecuba (*Iliad*, XXIV, 495). Eur. is vague here in order to increase the pathos of the situation.

ἄμμοροι : Homeric for ἄμοιροι " without share in, bereft of."

422. σοί : ethical dative. εἴπω : deliberative subj. This idea of greeting among the dead is given a grisly turn in Aesch., *Ag.*, 1555 f., where the murderous queen imagines her victim being greeted beside Acheron by the daughter he himself has sacrificed.

424. στέρνα : " bosom."

425. ἀώρου : " dead before her time." The Greeks thought that the souls of those who had died πρίν μοῖραν ἐξήκειν βίου (Soph., *Ant.*, 896) are peculiarly likely to appear as ghosts. So also with those who, like Polydorus, had died a violent death (βιαιοθάνατοι). Such ghosts wandered in the company of Hecate, and there is frequent reference on tombstones to untimely or violent death as something specially lamentable. In popular belief, the deaths of ἄωροι were ascribed to Gello, herself one who παρθένος ἀώρως ἐτελεύτησε. The whole subject is dealt with by Rohde, *Psyche*, English trans., p. 593 f.

428. The mention of Polydorus has of course an " ironic " effect. κάσις : common in Trag., not in Homer, who uses longer form, κασίγνητος.

429. H.'s ἀπιστῶ is once more " ironical." These hints serve to link together the two parts of the play. Note γ᾽ : " yes, if . . ."

430. θανούσης : agrees w. genitive implied in τὸ σόν.

432. κόμιζ᾽ : " come, take me."

433. ὡς: given reason for κόμιζε: she has mourned enough.

434. ἐκτήκω: " am causing her to melt in lamentation."

435. Cp. Cassandra's last prayer, Aesch., *Ag*., 1323–4, also addressed to the Sun's light: ἡλίου δ' ἐπεύχομαι πρὸς ὕστατον φῶς.

436. μέτεστι: " you belong to me."

437. μεταξύ: usually explained by taking ξίφους closely with πυρᾶς as together giving only one of the two points between which she will still live, the other being the moment of her words. There is a parallel of sorts in Soph., *O. C*., 290 : τὰ δὲ μεταξὺ τούτου μηδαμῶς γίγνου κακός, " meanwhile, show no baseness." The present passage would, according to this interpretation, mean " between this spot and the sword and pyre of Achilles." Weil, however, is surely right in preferring the obvious meaning " between the pyre of Achilles and the sword," with an easy *hysteron proteron*. This is much more vivid and expressive, and the only objection to it is the pedantically literal one that it is an exaggeration.

438. προλείπω: " I swoon."

441-3. Attributed to the Chorus by Hermann ; deleted by Hartung on the prosaic ground that H., having said at 438 that she is swooning, is not in a fit condition to utter the lines. Yet they are admirably in character, and their outburst of hatred for Helen is so appropriate both to Hecuba (cp. 265–6) and to Eur. (cp. *I. T*., 439 f.) as well as being much more forcible than the general run of actors' interpolations, that they must surely be retained. Page (*l.c.*) thinks the case for interpolation " very weak." H., of course, does not fall in a dead faint.

441. ὡς: " even so," Epic. Cp. Aesch., *Ag*., 930.

Διοσκόροιν: cp. n. on 269. Kastor and Polydeukes, like Helen herself, were divinities, worshipped all over Greece as " Saviours," especially from dangers in battle and on sea. Their intervention at Lake Regillus was a famous incident in early Roman saga. Note the Attic form of their name. Διὸς κοῦροι meant of course " sons of Zeus," and was accounted for by a well-known legend.

442-3. Note pun in Ἑλένην . . . εἷλε, in imitation of course of Aesch., *Ag*., 681 f, and repeated *Troades*, 890 f. Belief in magic significance of names, for good or ill, is universal. Cp. *Bacchae*, 367 : Πενθεὺς δ' ὅπως μὴ πένθος εἰσοίσει δόμοις.

καλῶν ὀμμάτων : literally *beaux yeux.*

αἴσχιστα : In antithesis both with **καλῶν** and with **εὐδαίμονα.**

444–483. First Stasimon.

A stasimon is defined by Aristotle as a song of the Chorus without anapaests or trochees. By "trochees" he obviously means not lyric trochees, which are quite frequent in stasima, but the trochaic tetrameter, which is rather a recitative than a song rhythm. The stasimon represents, in a highly stylised form, greatly influenced by the Choral Lyric of Stesichorus and others, the original ritual kernel of Tragedy, and the history of Tragedy is in one aspect that of the gradual extrusion of the choral part in favour of the dialogue, as the latter's dramatic possibilities came to be realised. In early Tragedy, and in certain late examples like the *Oedipus* of Sophocles and the *Bacchae*, the ritual element in the choral part is still strong. Even in Aeschylus, however, the normal choral ode has become at most a lyric presentation of certain aspects of the plot, placed side by side with the dramatic presentation in the dialogue. The three stasima of this play show a slight development on Aeschylean practice. All are shorter than the normal Aeschylean ode, but there are instructive variations in their form. The first consists of a pair of strophes with their antistrophes, the second of strophe, antistrophe, and epode, and the third and longest of the same elements as the first with the addition of an epode. All three deal with aspects of the fall of Troy.

The first stasimon has a distinct kinship with a type of choral ode known as "escape-prayer," examples of which are *Bacchae*, 402–16 (ἱκοίμαν ποτὶ Κύπρον), *Helena*, 1478–86 (δι' ἀέρος εἴθε ποτανοὶ) and *Hippolytus*, 732–51 (ἠλιβάτοις ὑπὸ κευθμῶσι γενοίμαν). This "escape-prayer" is very probably a development of an old ritual hymn in which the votaries of Dionysus, Maenads, Bassarai, Lenai or Thyiades, expressed their longing to fly with their god to the mountains. In the present ode, the Chorus are captives, as Dionysiac votaries often were in the ritual, and their song has become rather a series of speculations on what will befall them in their new homes beyond the sea than a prayer to escape. The effect, however, is a similarly " romantic " one ; it is to bring the audience in imagination first to the Dorian lands, next to Delos, and finally home to Athens. At Delos and Athens the captives imagine themselves as taking part in two famous festivals, and we may be sure that a reference to these was part of the poet's purpose, while his silence about Dorian festivals is deliberate. He would not thus glorify enemy institutions during a war. The ode ends with a single strophe of lamentation. It is instructive to compare the closely similar song, *Troädes* 197–234, where the Chorus explicitly pray that they may not go to Sparta, and where the reference to Italy and Sicily was very topical at the date of the play.

This stasimon is an excellent example both of the poet's peculiar power to evoke emotion by imagined movement from one hallowed place to another, and of his metrical art at its simplest and strongest. The student should read the fine translation by T. F. Higham in the *Oxford Book of Greek Verse in Translation* (No. 365).

Metrical Scheme. *Aeolic Rhythm.*

1. Strophe α'.
   444. — ⏑ — ⏑ — ⏑ — ⏑   Pherecratic. .
   445. — ⏑ — ⏑ ⏑ — ⏑ ⏑ —   Glyconic.
        — ⏑ — ⏑ ⏑ — ⏑ ⏑ — — Hendecasyllabic (Phalaecian).
        — ⏑ — ⏑ ⏑ — ⏑ ⏑ —   Glyconic.
        — — — ⏑ ⏑ — ⏑ —   Glyconic.
        — — — ⏑ — ⏑ ⏑ —   Choriambic Dimeter.
   450. — ⏑ ⏑ — ⏑ — — —   *Versus Aristophanicus.*
        — — ⏑ ⏑ — ⏑ —   Telesillean.
        — — — — ⏑ ⏑ — ⏑ ⏑ ⏑ Glyconic (resolved).
        ⏑ ⏑ — ⏑ ⏑ — ⏑ ⏑ ⏑ — — Hendecasyllabic (resolved).

2. Strophe β'.
   466. — — ⏑ ⏑ — ⏑ —   Telesillean.
        — — ⏑ ⏑ — ⏑ —   Telesillean.
        — ⏑ — ⏑ ⏑ — ⏑ —   Glyconic.
        — ⏑ ⏑ — ⏑ — — —   Choriambic Dimeter.
   470. — ⏑ ⏑ — ⏑ — — —   Choriambic Dimeter.
        — ⏑ ⏑ — ⏑ — — —   Choriambic Dimeter.
        — ⏑ — ⏑ ⏑ —   Choriambic Dimeter, Acephalous.
        — — — ⏑ ⏑ — — —   Glyconic.
        — — — ⏑ ⏑ —   Choriambic Dimeter, Acephalous.

Each strophe falls into three Periods of approximately equal length, the end of each being marked by a change in the form of the colon. Thus in Strophe α' the first period ends with the Hendecasyllabic, the second with the *Versus Aristophanicus*, and the third with a special form of the Hendecasyllabic, which has twelve syllables by resolution of the last syllable of its Glyconic. In Strophe β' the first period consists of two Telesilleans followed by a Glyconic, the second of three Choriambic Dimeters of identical rhythm, and the third of two acephalous Choriambic Dimeters with a Glyconic between them.

444. The Chorus apostrophise the sea-breeze that will blow them to Greece, and inquire of it their exact destination. They have been already allotted to their masters (l. 100) but there is here no " negligence " on the poet's part ; they are not booking places on a steamer, but singing a song.

ποντιάς : only here in Trag. ; also in Pindar (gen. ποντιάδος).

445. ποντοπόρους : " faring over the open sea."

446. ἀκάτους : ordinarily " light vessel, small boat." Here ποντοπόρους implies that it is used metaphorically to mean " ships."

οἶδμα λίμνας : " swell of the sea." λίμνη in Attic normally means " lake " ; in Homer, " sea " as here.

448. τῷ : for τίνι, which is rarer in poetry. Ethical dat. w. πρὸς οἶκον, for gen.

δουλόσυνος : synonym for δοῦλος. A unique word, modelled on δεσπόσυνος (99).

449. κτηθεῖσ' : a rare passive, elsewhere found only in Thuc. and late prose : " got by purchase." The Chorus seems to be thinking, not of its present masters, but of possible new ones. Cp. Méridier's note.

450. Δωρίδος . . . αἴας : plainly the Peloponnese ; an anachronism, as there were no Dorians there when Troy fell. But the references to Delos and Athens in this ode are equally anachronistic. Note that the Peloponnese is Agamemnon's dominion, Thessaly that of Achilles ; the order of precedence may be a concession to Epic.

451. Φθιάδος : Phthia and Hellas are the dominions of Achilles in the *Iliad.* Hellas is the Spercheus valley, S. of Mt. Othrys, Phthia the Apidanos valley, N. of it.

454. 'Απιδανὸν : flows N. from Mt. Othrys, is joined by the Enipeus, then flows into the Peneus, which drains all Thessaly and reaches the sea through the Vale of Tempe in the N.-E.

πατέρα : common epithet of rivers, and more applicable to the Peneus than to its tributary. Cp. *Bacchae*, 572, where the epithet is applied to the Lydias, the river of Aegae in Macedon.

λιπαίνειν : from λίπα. "Makes fat, fertilises." Thessaly has the richest pasture-land in Greece.

455–65. Delos was one of the two great centres of Apollo's worship, the other being Delphi. As the latter was under Spartan influence, the Athenians magnified Delos as much as possible. From ancient times it had been the seat of a festival, " where the long-robed Ionians gather with their lady wives " (*Hymn to Apollo*). This took place, like the Olympic and Delphic festivals, every fourth year, and the contests included both athletic and musical competitions. In the winter of 426–5 the Athenians purified the island (Thuc., III, 104) by removing all graves from it and forbidding birth or death on it for the future ; they also re-established the festival. It was long ago suggested that this antistrophe is a graceful reference to that event. This gives us a valuable indication of the play's date (see Introduction). A similar reference occurs in *Herakles*, 681. The last three lines of the antistrophe evidently refer to a ritual in honour of Apollo's twin-sister, Artemis, in which the girls of Delos played a part. In many Greek communities, including Sparta and Athens, young girls were enrolled in cult-associations dedicated to Artemis. Cp. 936. Whereas it is probable that the Delphic Apollo came there by sea from Crete (*Hymn. Apoll.*, 388 f), the Delians believed that the god and his sister were born on their island. Perhaps the most sacred object in Delos was the πρωτόγονος φοίνιξ of 458, the sacred date-palm, to which Leto, mother of the twin divinities, was said to have clung at their birth. It was still shown in Cicero's day (*palmam . . . hodie monstrant eandem*, De legibus, I, 1, 2). Eur. seems to be alone in joining with it the laurel (δάφνη) the sacred tree of Apollo. He mentions this also *Ion*, 920; and in a chorus, *I. T.*, 1100, which contains a phrase clearly modelled on one in this ode (Λατοῦς ὠδῖνα φίλαν) he also mentions the olive. It is perhaps worth noting that in the latter passage the mention of Delos forms part of a regular "escape-prayer." The island had, of course, nothing to do with the Trojan War. Its mention is a pure topical allusion, in the art of which Eur. is almost as skilful as Dante.

455. νάσων : best taken, like Δωρίδος αἴας and Φθιάδος in the strophe, as dependent on ὅρμον (450) "a haven of the island." It may also be construed as partitive gen. w. ἔνθα (458) "among the islands, where," or w. ποῖ (447) "where among the islands?" but both are less probable.

ἁλιήρει : (ἁλί, ἐρέσσω) "sweeping the sea (with oars)."

457. οἴκοις : locative dat., "in a house (in Delos) where." This is the proper antecedent to ἔνθα.

458. πρωτόγονος : "first that ever grew," like the olive in the Erechtheum at Athens. The date-palm does not grow in Greece.

460. φίλος is not a common epithet for a god; indeed, Aristotle denies the possibility of φιλία at such a distance (E. N., 1158b, 35, and M. M., 1208b, 30) : ἄτοπον γὰρ ἂν εἴη εἰ τις φαίη φιλεῖν τὸν Δία. It is probably best explained here as due to some ritual use. The only classical parallel appears to be Theognis, 373 : Ζεῦ φίλε, θαυμάζω σε, where Harrison "detects a note of flippant earnestness."

461. ἄγαλμα : in apposition w. πτόρθους. "In honour of."

Δίας : fem. gen. of Δῖος, adj., "of Zeus." Cp. Δίου πυρός, Bacchae, 8.

462. κούραις : Ionic form ; Attic κόραις. Cp. 485.

465. ἄμπυκα : "head-band, fillet," always on statues of Artemis.

εὐλογήσω : "sing hymns in praise of." The girls' choirs sang hymns in which the well-known attributes of the goddess naturally received mention, and the older women joined in the singing.

466. The next step in their imaginary destiny is Athens, and here again the poet associates their captivity with a great festival, a πεντετηρίς like the Delia, celebrated in Hecatombaion (August) every fourth year. This was the Panathenaia, in honour of Athena Polias, tutelary goddess and almost the personification of the Athenian State. The chief ritual event of the four-day festival was the solemn presentation to Athena of a new robe (πέπλος) which was carried in solemn procession from the Ceramicus to the Propylaea, and there handed to the Archon Basileus to be put on the ancient wooden statue (ξόανον) in the Erechtheum. It was splendidly embroidered with pictures showing Athena's part in the war of Gods and Titans. This work was put in hands six months before the festival. It was done under the direction of priestesses, and the women employed on it were called ἐργαστῖναι. The procession, of which we possess a splendid sculptural representation in the Parthenon frieze, included all the principal citizens.

467. καλλιδίφρους is the reading of MS. Marcianus, adopted by Murray. All other MSS. have καλλιδίφρου, which requires something like Nauck's correction of 'Αθαναίας to θεᾶς ναίουσ'. With Murray's reading, 'Αθαναιάς and καλλιδίφρους qualify πώλους. καλλιδίφρους occurs only here.

'Αθαναίας : acc. pl. of fem. adj., Doric form of Αθηναίας. The official title of the goddess was 'Αθηναία, later contracted to 'Αθηνᾶ. The Doric form was 'Αθάνα, Homeric 'Αθήνη. Note accents.

469. ζεύξομαι : " embroider the yoking of," w. ποικίλλουσ'.

471. πήναις : " woof, web." ἀνθοκρόκοισι : from κρέκω : " worked with flowers."

472. Τιτάνων γενεάν : " race of Titans," enemies of Athena.

474. ἀμφιπύρῳ φλογμῷ : " blaze (of lightning) flaming at both ends." ἀμφί always " on both sides of " not " around." Cp. Hipp. 559, βροντᾷ ἀμφιπύρῳ.

τὰν Ζεὺς κοιμίζει : τὰν, Doric for τὴν, relative. The present refers to the embroidered picture. English prefers a participial construction : " the race of Titans being put to sleep (i.e. slain) by Zeus."

475. ΤΕΚΈΩΝ : gen. of exclamation.

478. Ἀργείων : gen. w. δορίκτητος, " spear-won (prize) of the Greeks."

482. The reading θεραπνᾶν (gen. pl.) is due to Wilamowitz. " Having exchanged the chambers of Hades (i.e. death : Ἀιδα gen.) for the dwellings of Europe." They might have been slain at Troy ; instead, they go to Greece. θεράπνη is common in pl. as a place-name, and always means " dwelling " in Eur., though in *Hymn. Apoll.*, 157, it means " handmaid," which accounts for the reading θεράπαιναν here. Both words are cognate w. θρᾶνος, θρῆνυς, " plank, footstool," Latin *fretus, fere, firmus*, Sanskrit *dhármah*, " custom, law," θρησκεία, " cult of a god." Their root-meaning appears to be " fixed, settled." With the reading θεράπναν the sense would be " having left Asia and taken in exchange an abode in Europe, (which is to me) the chamber of Hades." It has also been taken to mean " having left Asia, the slave of Europe, and having taken in exchange the equivalent of death," i.e. slavery.

484–628. Second Epeisodion.

This scene is all filled with the news of how Polyxena died, told by the Spartan herald, Talthybius, and with Hecuba's forlorn reply to his speech. The narrative of Talthybius, which begins at 518, is called a ῥῆσις. There is at least one such narrative in every tragedy. It is used to convey to the audience news of an event which cannot be represented dramatically, such as the tragic πάθος normally is. As there are two such πάθη in this play, so there is a second ῥῆσις (1132–82), that of Polymestor, parallel to this. In the present scene, the tragic effect of the first part of the play reaches its climax.

484. δή ποτ' : " lately."

485. ἂν ἐξεύροιμι : opt. used as polite future.

κόραι : Attic form. Cp. 462 for Ionic dat. pl.

487. ξυγκεκλημένη : " close wrapped," stronger, as Weil remarks, than συγκεκαλυμμένη, to indicate her desolation.

488. λέξω : delib. subj., " what am I to say ? "

πότερά σ' ἀνθρώπους ὁρᾶν ; : " that you *watch over* men," not " that you *see* " simply. Both the tense and the root-meaning of ὁρᾶν imply duration.

489-90. Nauck has rightly excised 490, because it spoils the syntax and is difficult to construe, and above all because its only possible construction makes Talthybius doubt, not the *providence* of the gods (489), but their *existence*. If 490 be kept, δοκοῦντας must have ἀνθρώπους for subject, δόξαν must mean "opinion," and δοκοῦντας "thinking." The alternative is to make the subject ὑμᾶς understood from σέ in 488. The meaning will then be "you have vainly got yourselves a false repute, seeming to be a race of gods," which either denies the existence of the gods or makes nonsense. With 490 excised, κεκτῆσθαι has σέ for subject, and the meaning is clear : "Am I to say that you watch over men, or that you (Zeus) have got this reputation (of so watching) for nothing, that it is false, and that Chance is what watches over all human affairs ? "

Eur. is here playing with an idea which, whatever its origin, is as old as Aesch. It is condemned in *Ag.* 369–72 : οὐκ ἔφα τις θεοὺς βροτῶν ἀξιοῦσθαι μέλειν . . . ὁ δ' οὐκ εὐσεβής. This view is practically identical with modern Deism. It was strongly condemned also by Plato, but became one of the chief doctrines of Epicureanism, from which, through the medium of writers like Montaigne, it was transmitted to modern Europe. Its essence lies in admitting the existence of a Divinity, while denying Divine Providence. Originally τύχη was identified w. ἀνάγκη, and we get the phrase ἀναγκαία τύχη in Sophocles, *El.*, 48. This passage of *Hecuba* is the first in which we meet it in its later sense, that of a στέρησις τέχνης (cp. Stewart on Aristotle, *E.N.* 1112 a, 27), *i.e.* an absence of all determination, mere blind chance. In the Comedy of Menander, where it plays a great part, τύχη is the synonym of ταὐτόματον, " fluke." Cp. Figaro on *le hasard*, Mariage de Figaro, iv, 1.

Whereas in *Hecuba* Eur. merely plays with the idea of Chance as the governing power in human life, *Herakles* (perhaps produced at the same time : see Introd.) is really a whole play on this theme. Though thinly disguised by a mythological motif and presented with the help of ancient ritual machinery (for the figure of Lyssa, " Madness," seems to come from the *Lykourgeia* of Aesch.), the plot of *Herakles* depends on a purely capricious reversal, and the hero puts it in a correct light when he says at the end (1357) : νῦν δ', ὡς ἔοικε, τῇ τύχῃ δουλευτέον. Most of Eur.'s later plays depend on Chance as their motive-force. This is why they are not, strictly speaking, tragedies at all, but forerunners of New Comedy, in which not Aristotle's τὸ εἰκὸς καὶ τὸ ἀνάγκαιον, but τύχη, κυβερνᾷ πάντα (Menander).

491. ἐπισκοπεῖν : same meaning as ὁρᾶν above ; common in prose and verse for " guard," both of divine and human agents. The noun ἐπίσκοπος meant " superintendent."

492. Φρυγῶν : the Trojans ; cp. 4.

πολύχρυσος is Homer's epithet for Mycenae.

493. μέγ' ὀλβίου : note μέγα common as adverb.

494. ἀνέστηκεν : intrans., as perf. of ἵστημι always is. In prose ἀνίστημι means " transplant, uproot," and is applied to a country ; cp. Herod. v, 29, χώρα ἀνεστηκυῖα. The phrase ἀνάστατον ποιεῖν, " devastate," is common.

495. αὐτή : the reading of Vaticanus, much better than αὕτη of other MSS. In antithesis to πόλις μέν : " her city . . . she herself."

497. ὅμως δέ : ellipse. " I am old (and have little more misfortune to fear), but yet . . ."

498. αἰσχρᾷ : " ignominious, vile," lit. " ugly."

περιπεσεῖν : " fall upon, encounter," mostly of disaster.

499. μετάρσιον : Ionic for Attic μετέωρον, (μεταίρω) " raised from the ground," here " up."

500. πλευράν : part for whole ; " your body."

501. For ἐᾷ, late MSS. have ἐᾷς, which is often (wrongly) printed.

503. Talthybius is here, as in the Iliad, Agamemnon's herald. In post-Homeric times he became associated with Sparta, where he was worshipped as a hero, and his descendants, the Talthybiadae, were hereditary heralds. Herod. vii, 134.

504. μέτα : by tmesis w. πέμψαντος, from μεταπέμπω, " send for."

505. H. is overjoyed at her first thought that she also is to be sacrificed. ἆρα for Epic and Lyric ἦ ρα, " indeed."

506. δοκοῦν : Acc. absol. of impersonal vb.

507. ἐγκονῶμεν.: " make haste " ; cp. διᾱκον·

ἡγοῦ : come, guide me." She rises hastily.

511. τί λέξεις : " What are you going to say ? " Future, to express her incredulity, a common idiom in Eur. Cp. 712 and *Hipp.*, 353, with Weil's note.

θανουμένους : for gender, cp. 237.

514. τοὐπὶ σ' : Ironical ; she is thinking of Polydorus. (Crasis for τὸ ἐπί σε).

515. ἐξεπράξατ' : Cp. Aesch., *Ag.*, 1275 : καὶ νῦν ὁ μάντις μάντιν ἐκπράξας ἐμέ.

αἰδούμενοι : " did you show any compassion ? "

516. πρὸς τὸ δεινὸν ἤλθετε ; : " did you go to the extreme of cruelty ? "

518. δάκρυα κερδᾶναι : Oxymoron. κερδαίνω, from κέρδος " gain." Cp. κέρδη, 1207. Irish *ceard*, " craft. work for gain."

520. Supply ἔτεγξα. Common ellipse.

523. χερός : gen. w. vb. of " taking " or " holding."

524. ἔστησ' : Transitive ; " placed her."

ἐγώ w. ἔστην, understood.

526. μόσχου : Cp. 206.

527-8. There is a good deal of repetition here : ἐν χεροῖν 527, χειρὶ 528. Cp. πλήρης 522, πλῆρες 527.

529. χοάς : in apposition w. δέπας. The cup *contained* the offering to be poured (χοαί from χέω). Some MSS. give ἔρρει, from ῥέω, but this transitive use (" let flow ") would be unique. The χοαί used in libations to the dead consisted of honey, milk, wine and water. *Od.* x, 519-20 :

πρῶτα μελικρήτῳ, μετέπειτα δὲ ἡδέϊ οἴνῳ
τὸ τρίτον αὖθ' ὕδατι,

where μελίκρητον means " honey mixed with milk."

532. σῖγα : Adverb. Cp. Ar.. *Ach.*, 238 : σῖγα πᾶς.

533. σίγα: Imperative of σιγάω, as σιώπα of σιωπάω.

ἔστησα: "I made stand still." νήνεμον, predicative.

535. κηλητηρίους: from κηλεῖν. "Soothing."

536. νεκρῶν ἀγωγούς: "that bring up the dead," *i.e.* to drink them.

537. ἀκραιφνὲς αἷμ᾿: "fresh blood."

539. χαλινωτήρια: "mooring-cables." Pindar calls the Argo's anchor its "rein"; θοᾶς Ἀργοῦς χαλινόν *Pyth.* 4, 25. The construction is: δὸς ἡμῖν λῦσαι πρύμνας . . . νεῶν.

540. πρευμενοῦς is suspect after πρευμενής in 538, but the repetition may well be emphatic. Construe w. νόστου and τυχόντας: "having got a favourable voyage home."

541. τυχόντας: acc., because not to be taken closely w. ἡμῖν, but as part of infin. clause.

542. ἐπηύξατο: "joined in prayer." Prefix has same force as in ἐπερρόθησαν (553) and Homeric ἐπευφημεῖν.

543. ἀμφίχρυσον: "gilt on both sides," presumably of hilt; a unique word. Transferred epithet.

κώπης: gen, like χερός, 523.

546. ἐφράσθη: pass. for Homeric mid., ἐφράσσατο. "Noticed it."

551. μεθέντες: with ἐλευθέραν, "leave."

553. ἐπερρόθησαν: Hesychius explains as equivalent to ἐπήχησαν, ἐπεβόησαν, "applauded loudly."

ῥόθος: "noise of waves," then "any confused noise."

555-6. All edd. now agree with Jacobs in rejecting these two lines, which merely spoil the sequence without adding anything. The second is pure circumlocution. "Possibly a Byzantine interpolation," Page.

558. ἐπωμίδος: ἐπωμίς can mean either the point of the shoulder or that part of the χιτών where the pin was put in. The first is better here.

560. ἀγάλματος : "statue," lit. "thing of joy." The comparison, typical of the Greek attitude to art, may be suggested by Aesch., *Ag.*, 242 f., but, as Weil remarks, the point there is different. For various words for "statue" and their meaning, cp. Webster, *C.Q.* 1939, p. 166.

562. τλημονέστατον : "heroic" (τλήμων). The meaning "wretched" is secondary in this word, cognate w. Latin *tolerare*. Cp. τόλμα, 326.

566. οὐ θέλων τε καὶ θέλων : Cp. *Iliad* iv., 43, ἑκὼν ἀέκοντί γε θυμῷ. A typical antithesis.

568. πνεύματος διαρροάς : "windpipe," abstract for concrete.

569. κρουνοί : "spouts," a strong word. There was a famous Athenian fountain called Ἐννεάκρουνος, "Nine Spouts."

572. It has been well remarked (Jeffery) that this line indicates the sudden burst of activity after all had been spell-bound by the sacrifice.

574. φύλλοις ἔβαλλον : φυλλοβολεῖται ἡ Πολ. ὥσπερ ἐν ἀγῶνι νικήσασα, Schol. It was customary to pelt victors in the games with flowers. Cp. Pindar, *Pyth.* 9, 131 f.

577-8. The reproaches were for not casting any *offering* on the pyre. Cp. Lucian, *de luctu*, 14 : καὶ ἐσθῆτα καὶ τὸν ἄλλον κόσμον συγκατέφλεξαν ἢ συγκατώρυξαν, Thuc. iii, 58, 4 : οὓς ἀποθανόντας . . . ἐτιμῶμεν κατὰ ἔτος ἕκαστον δημοσίᾳ ἐσθήμασί τε καὶ τοῖς ἄλλοις νομίμοις, Virgil, *Aen.* vi, 221 : *purpureasque super vestes . . . coniciunt.*

579. οὐκ εἶ : from εἶμι, "go." Not to be translated as a question, "will you not go ?" which has too polite an effect. Very common in Greek as a rough command ; cp. Ar., *Av.*, 1032, οὐκ ἀποσοβήσεις; *Nub.*, 1295, οὐκ ἀποδιώξει σαυτόν; etc. "Go and give something !" Cp. also 1282 f., *infra.*

περίσσ' : Attic περιττός "odd," then "unusual." Here adverbial neut. pl.

581-2. Note antithesis once more in εὐτεκνωτάτην . . . δυστυχεστάτην.

583. ἐπέζεσεν : ἀπὸ μεταφορᾶς τοῦ ζέοντος ὕδατος ἐν τοῖς λέβησι, Schol. The metaphor of a pot boiling over is homely, but effective.

Πριαμίδαις . . . πόλει : *Dativi incommodi.*

586. **τινος**: a little awkward w. **τόδε**, where one would expect τοῦδε followed by **τἄλλο**.

588. **διάδοχος κακῶν κακοῖς**: "succeeding to evil by way of evil." κακῶν obj. gen. w. διάδοχος, which is normal for " successor " (cp. *Diadochi*, successors of Alexander the Great).

κακοῖς: instrumental dat.

590. **ἐξαλείψασθαι**: from ἐξαλείφω, lit. " plaster over."

591. **τὸ λίαν**: *sc.* στένειν.

591-2. **ἀγγελθεῖσά μοι γένναιος**: unparalleled without a participle such as οὖσα. Perhaps repeated feminine was felt to lack euphony.

592-602. This philosophical disquisition, which is excused by 591, clearly reflects contemporary debates on the possibility and value of education (παιδεία), such as we find so frequently in Plato's early dialogues. The question is whether men are good or bad φύσει or νόμῳ, that is, whether the aristocratic tradition (reflected, for instance, in Pindar's doctrine of φυά) that everything depends on birth, or the new theory of the Sophists, that goodness is a matter of convention and can be acquired by practice, is correct. The comparison between education and agriculture (from which our word *culture* in fact derives), though first explicitly drawn in Plutarch's treatise on education, is as old as the fifth century B.C. In the present passage there is a possibility of confusion because of the double comparison between good *and* bad in land *and* in the human being. The whole point is that whereas land is affected by external circumstances, so that even bad soil can give a good crop if the weather (καιρός) be good, while good soil can be made to give only a poor crop by bad weather, no such law obtains in the case of the human person. There the bad remains always bad, and the good even under unfavourable conditions (συμφορᾶς ὕπο) never alters his nature (φύσις) for the worse. So far, Eur. is on the side of Pindar ; but he now (599), goes on to put the question " is heredity or education the superior power ? " and answers that undoubtedly (μέντοι) good rearing does impart something of goodness, whereby its recipient can also take the measure of the bad. All through, the poet seems to be musing aloud in the person of Hecuba, and his conclusion is studiously moderate. In his *Suppliant*

Women (911–15), he seems to lean more to the side of education ; but in *Electra* (a much later play), he relapses into complete agnosticism on the subject (367–70) :

> οὐκ ἔστ' ἀκριβὲς οὐδὲν εἰς εὐανδρίαν·
> ἔχουσι γὰρ ταραγμὸν αἱ φύσεις βροτῶν.
> ἤδη γὰρ εἶδον ἄνδρα γενναίου πατρός
> τὸ μηδὲν ὄντα, χρηστὰ δ' ἐκ κακῶν τέκνα.

In any case he never goes so far as to declare with Socrates that goodness *is* knowledge. Indeed, in *Hippolytus* (earlier than *Hecuba*) this is expressly denied in a famous passage (380–1) :

> τὰ χρήστ' ἐπιστάμεσθα καὶ γιγνώσκομεν
> οὐκ ἐκπονοῦμεν δέ.

In all such disquisitions as this, Eur. was not of course working out a philosophical or moral question in the Platonic manner, but " seasoning " his drama to suit the taste of his audience. This tendency to follow the current fashion for sophistical debate is one of his most original characteristics, and one which differentiates him sharply from his contemporary, Sophocles.

593. καιροῦ : here almost equivalent to ὥρα, "(favourable) season." θεόθεν because Zeus, the Sky-god, controlled the weather. εὖ w. φέρει, " bears its crop successfully."

597. οὐδὲ : after εἰ (592) is irregular ; but this is strictly a *statement* : δεινόν (ἐστιν) is equivalent to a verb like θαυμάζω, after which εἰ takes the place of ὅτι in indirect discourse. In indirect questions οὐ may follow εἰ.

598. διέφθειρ' : gnomic aorist.

599. διαφέρουσιν : " are superior."

600. ἔχει : w. δίδαξιν, a deliberately vague phrase. " Is capable of teaching." δίδαξις, as compared w. διδαχή, emphasises the *action* of the verb. It does not occur again till Aristotle.

602. τό γ' αἰσχρόν : γε emphasises αἰσχρόν, but has normal position after article. Its use here has been called in question : Cobet corrected to δίοιδε τᾀσχρόν, Weil prints ὅδ' οἶδε τᾀσχρόν.

603. " Euripides, having so developed a critical sense, was the first to see that this digression (592–602) was out of place," Weil, who quotes Theon, the rhetorician (1st or 2nd cent., A.D.) : τὸν δὲ Εὐρ. καταμεμφόμεθα, ὅτι παρὰ καιρὸν αὐτῷ Ἑκάβη φιλοσοφεῖ.

μὲν δή is the equivalent of a shrug. Many particles were the accompaniment or verbal expression of gestures.

ἐτόξευσεν : cp. *Supp.*, 456, καὶ ταῦτα μὲν δὴ πρὸς τάδ' ἐξηκόντισα, and Aesch., *Supp.*, 446, καὶ γλῶσσα τοξεύσασα μὴ τὰ καίρια.

605. μοι : *dativus commodi* ; its effect best rendered by Eng. " please."

606-8. Page (*Interpolations*) finds it hard to believe in the authenticity of these three lines. He thinks they were inserted to make 605 more explicit, by an actor who remembered Herod. ii, 89. 608 recalls also Thuc. iii, 82 (the famous diagnosis of στάσις), especially § 4 f : καὶ τὴν εἰωθυῖαν ἀξίωσιν τῶν ὀνομάτων εἰς τὰ ἔργα ἀντήλλαξαν τῇ δικαιώσει. τόλμα μὲν γὰρ ἀλόγιστος ἀνδρεία φιλέταιρος ἐνομίσθη . . . ἁπλῶς δὲ ὁ φθάσας τὸν μέλλοντα κακόν τι δρᾶν ἐπηνεῖτο. Cp. 831-2. Page is very probably right in his suspicion ; κρείσσων πυρός may well be a reminiscence of Soph., *O.T.*, 177, and ναυτική τ' ἀναρχία of *Iph. Aul.*, 914.

609. ἀρχαία λάτρι : this is the old servant who returns at 658 with the body of Polydorus. λάτρις (masc. and fem.) is cognate w. Latin *latro*, " robber," which probably first meant " mercenary," and may derive from λάτρος, glossed as μισθός by Hesychius. (Manu Leumann, *Gnomon*, 1937, p. 30.)

610. ποντίας ἁλός : part. gen. after βάψας ἔνεγκε.

612. " bride without spouse, virgin no longer virgin." The double oxymoron refers to the sacrifice which made her the bride of Hades. An alternative explanation is that she has through it been offered as his part of the booty to the dead Achilles.

613. προθῶμαι : πρόθεσις meant the " laying-out " of the body for the ἐκφορά (" funeral "). The vase kept for the nuptial bath (λουτροφόρος) was set up over the grave of an unmarried girl. There is also a class of vases called " πρόθεσις-vases " because they have on them pictures of this ceremony.

ἀξία : refers to Polyxena ; " as she deserves."

614. οὐκ ἂν δυναίμην : note that this negative apodosis provides a very emphatic form of denial.

τί γὰρ πάθω ; : naturally means " what is to become of me ? " as in *Od.* xi, 404, ὤμοι ἐγώ, τί πάθω ; Here it seems better to understand an ellipse of some such phrase as ἄλλως ποιῶν. The whole sentence would be equivalent to τί παθὼν ἄλλως ποιοῖμ' ἄν ; " how could I do otherwise ? " For τί παθών, cp. L. and S. *s.v.* πάσχω.

615. ἀγείρασ' : normal meaning, " having collected." From this comes ἀγύρτης " beggar."

618. κλέμμα : " n'implique pas nécessairement l'idée d' un vol," Weil. This is unnecessarily prudish. Hadley rightly notes the bitter irony of H.'s suggestion that one of the captives has " stolen " some of her own property.

619. ὦ σχήματ' οἴκων : " O splendid house ! " The word σχήματα is only apt if it refers to the *beauty* of the house's form ; but this is a secondary and prosaic sense of the word.

620. ὦ πλεῖστ' ἔχων : κτήματα ἢ τέκνα, Schol. The simplest construction of πλεῖστ' ἔχων κάλλιστά τε is " owner of the fairest wealth." Porson and most modern edd. take κάλλιστα with εὐτεκνώτατε, and Weil goes even further, construing ὦ Πρίαμε εὐτεκνώτατε, πλεῖστα κάλλιστά τ' ἔχων (τέκνα), and making the whole series of adjs. refer entirely to Priam's *children.* Both interpretations seem unnecessarily forced ; there is no reason why Priam's wealth should not be referred to. The real difficulty is in the tense of ἔχων, which seems to require some complement such as ποτέ. Murray suggests κάλλη ποτ' for κάλλιστα.

622. ἐς τὸ μηδὲν : Cp. Soph., *El.*, 1,000, ἐπὶ μηδὲν ἔρχεται.

φρονήματος : " pride."

623. στερέντες : frequent in Eur. for normal στερηθέντες.

ὀγκούμεθα : pass. of ὀγκόω, from ὄγκος, " bulk," hence " puffed up, conceited." ὄγκος became later a critical term, " bombast " in style.

626. οὐδὲν ἄλλως : Cp. *Troades*, 476, οὐκ ἀριθμὸν ἄλλως, and *supra*, 489.

φροντίδων βουλεύματα : almost literally " wishful thinking."

627-8. Muretus compared Ennius, quoted by Cicero, *de Finibus* ii, 13 : *nimium boni est cui nil est [in diem] mali* (supplement by Ribbeck). See note 317, *supra*.

629–656. **Second Stasimon.**

This is the shortest and structurally simplest ode in the play, consisting of a single strophe, antistrophe, and epode. Its theme is exactly that of the Second Stasimon in Aesch., *Ag.* (681–781) : the woe brought by Helen on Troy. Eur., however, following his habit, traces the story back to its origin in the fatal judgment of Paris, a theme not touched by Aesch., but elaborated in the First Stasimon of *Andromache* (274–308).

Metrical Scheme.

Strophe-Antistrophe : Aeolic-Iambic.

Epode : Dactylic-Iambic-Aeolic.

1. *Strophe-Antistrophe* :

629. ⏑— — — —⏑——   Bacchius, Cretic.
630. ⏑— — —⏑— ⏑— —   Bacchius, Cretic, Bacchius.
      — — —⏑⏑— ⏑— —   Hipponacteum.
      ⏑——⏑ — ⏑⏑——   Choriambic Dimeter.
      ⏑⏑⏑ ⏑⏑⏑ —⏑— ⏑— —   Three Iambic Metra.
635. ⏑⏑ — ⏑⏑ — ⏑ —   Glyconic.
      — — —⏑ —⏑⏑—   Choriambic Dimeter.
      —⏑⏑— — —   Choriambic Dimeter Catalectic.

2. *Epode.*

648. ⏑⏑ ⏑⏑— ⏑ —⏑⏑ —⏑⏑— — —   Iambelegus, Spondee.
650. ⏑— ⏑— — ⏑⏑ —⏑⏑ — — —   Iambelegus, Spondee.
      ⏑— ⏑⏑⏑ ⏑— ⏑— ⏑— ⏑—   Iambic Trimeter.
      ⏑⏑ —⏑⏑ ⏑ — —   Hipponacteum.
      ⏑— ⏑— —⏑⏑—   Choriambic Dimeter.
655. ⏑⏑— ⏑ — ⏑⏑— —   Anapaest, Reizianum.
      ⏑— ⏑⏑⏑ ⏑⏑ ⏑ — ⏑— —   Iambic Dimeter, Bacchius.

The division into periods is uncertain. The simplest procedure is to divide the Strophe-antistrophe into three (2 cola, 3 cola, 3 cola). Wilamowitz thinks the final colon may be Iambic, but as it comes at the end of an Aeolic sequence, it is best treated as a "hypercatalectic" Choriambic Dimeter. (Cp. *Ion*, 148-9). The Epode seems to consist only of two periods, the first ending with the Hipponacteum.

629. χρῆν : Imperfect. Cp. 260. "It became my lot, when . . ." εἱμαρμένον ἦν, Schol.

633. Ἀλέξανδρος : Greek name of Paris, possibly a translation.

634. ἐτάμεθ' : for ἐτάμετο, aor. middle ; "cut." For reference to ship, cp. *Medea*, 3, *Helena*, 229.

ἅλιον : from ἅλς. "Briny."

635. τάν : article (old demonstrative) for relative.

636. καλλίσταν : a title of Artemis (cp. *Hippol.*, 66), with whom the Spartan Helen was closely akin.

640. ἀνάγκαι : "a doom more harsh (κρείσσονες) than the sorrows of war (πόνοι)."

κυκλοῦνται : "have made a circle (round us)."

641. ἐξ ἰδίας ἀνοίας : "from the folly of one man (Paris)."

642. τᾷ Σιμουντίδι γᾷ : "the land of the Simois," one of the two rivers of Troy, the other being the Scamander.

643. ὀλέθριον : adj. w. κακόν, "evil of destruction."

συμφορά τ' ἀπ' ἄλλων : Wilamowitz (*Griech. Verskunst*, p. 547, n. 1), calls this "a platitude, which we rightly feel to be too colourless," attributing the "disaster" to the vengeance of the Achaeans, or to Trojan submissiveness towards Paris. It becomes more forcible if by ἄλλων is understood, not any human agency, but Hera, Athena, and Aphrodite (Scholiast, cited by Méridier). The word would be a deliberate euphemistic obscurity.

644-5. ἄν . . . κρίνει . . . παῖδας : the double acc. is normal w. verbs of judging, indicting, condemning, etc. ἄν is really cognate acc. The whole force of the sentence depends on a contrast of *aspect* in the same verb : ἐκρίθη ἔρις ἄν . . . κρίνει, "the strife, which Paris *sought to decide* by his judgment (historic pres.

for imperf.) between the three daughters of the gods, *was finally decided* (aorist) in war and blood and the ruin of my home." ἐπί with dat. of *purpose*.

645. τρισσὰς μακάρων παῖδας : Aphrodite, Hera, and Athena. The earliest reference to the famous Judgment is in *Iliad* xxiv, 29–30, lines generally condemned as spurious. K. Reinhardt (*Das Parisurteil*, 1938) has, however, recently shown that the germ at least of the story is older than has been thought. Cp. Rose, *C.R.*, 1938, p. 196.

646. ἀνὴρ βούτας : Paris. Cp. *inf.*, 941, *Andromache* 280 : σταθμοὺς ἐπὶ βούτα, and for βούτας as adj. *v.* . 337 : βούταν φόνον.

649. Such continuity of phrase is common in Aesch. from strophe to antistrophe ; it never occurs in Soph., and is rare in Eur., the examples occurring only in epodes. (Kranz, *Stasimon*, p. 177.)

650. εὔροον Εὐρώταν : a typical play on words. The Eurotas is the famous river of Sparta ; the fury of war strikes both vanquished and victors. Some edd. see an allusion to the Spartan disaster at Sphacteria in 425.

651. πολυδάκρῦτος : elsewhere passive, " lamented," here active, " tearful."

653. πολιὸν is the reading of Wilamowitz and Weil, and is preferable to πολιάν, read by Murray and Méridier, which is meaningless with χέρα and can scarcely be taken with παρειάν.

655. The metre seems to require τε after δρύπτεται, as in some MSS. Wilamowitz omits τίθεται χέρα as a "doublet " on τιθεμένα, and alters the sequence to read :

> πολιόν τ' ἐπὶ κρᾶτα μάτηρ
> δίαιμον ὄνυχα τιθεμένα σπαραγμοῖς
> τέκνων θανόντων δρύπτεται παρειάν.

This, however, if τιθεμένα means " making,"·with δίαιμον as predicate, leaves πολιόν τ' ἐπὶ κρᾶτα in the air. The change in meaning from τίθεται, " puts," to τιθεμένα makes the repetition less intolerable.

For the *meiosis* or *litotes* in τίθεται, cp. Aesch., *Choeph.* 426, τὰ χερὸς ὀρέγματα, for the *blows* self-inflicted by the keening-woman.

" The mother, for her children dead, strikes her grey head and tears her cheek, making her nail bloody with the tearing."

656. δίαιμον: elsewhere a prose word, and a medical term Cp. δίαιμον ἀναπτύειν, "spit blood," Plut., *Aratus*, 52.

658-904. Third Epeisodion.

Here the second part of the play really begins. It is concerned with Hecuba's revenge on Polymestor, murderer of her son Polydorus. The present act shows how the body of Polydorus was discovered, and how the queen, after a long debate which has the quality of a rhetorical ἀγών, succeeds in securing the benevolent neutrality of Agamemnon. A remarkable feature of the act is the number of *asides* it contains. There is one at 674-5, where the old servant remarks to herself that the queen does not hear her, and there is a whole series in the passage 736-51, where the queen, deliberating at length with herself, is incomprehensible to Agamemnon. Hecuba's speech, 812-23, is again virtually a soliloquy, if not actually an aside. The use of asides is quite rare in Greek drama (cp. Grube, *Drama of Euripides*, p. 223 and Index), and there is no other example so elaborate and skilful as the dialogue from 736-51 here. Eur.'s technical mastery is shown to great effect in his use of it to represent the combination of doubt, calculation, and revengeful rage in Hecuba's mind. In her handling of Agamemnon, her character rises to its full intellectual height, and this act more than any other part of the play made her a lasting favourite with ancient audiences.

The θεράπαινα is of course the ἀρχαία λάτρις of 609. Her errand to the seashore has had a very different result from what was expected. She enters bringing the corpse of Polydorus, covered with a cloth. We have here a minor instance of what Aristotle calls περιπέτεια, "Reversal of Intention," one of the mainsprings of Tragedy.

658. παναθλία: the crown of her sorrows has now been reached, as is said in so many words at 660. Note the hint at an "ironic" comparison with a victor in the games: ἆθλον is implied in παναθλία, νικῶσα, στέφανον.

659. θῆλυν: this and other adjs. in -υς have often only two terminations in poetry.

660. ἀνθαιρήσεται: unique in this meaning: "dispute, seek to take away."

661. τῆς κακογλώσσου βοῆς : gen. of cause ; cp. *Medea*, 1028, ὦ δυστάλαινα τῆς ἐμῆς αὐθαδίας.

662. εὕδει : "ar still," a metaphor commoner in Greek than in English. ὡς has sense of γάρ.

663. Ἑκάβη : "*for* Hecuba " ; *dativus incommodi.*

664. εὐφημεῖν στόμα : for idiom, cp. 53, περᾷ πόδα. For meaning, see n. on 181.

665. καὶ μὴν : cp. 216.

περῶσα τυγχάνει : " is just coming out."

ὕπερ : can only mean "from beyond," but this is exceedingly doubtful. Most edd. (e.g. Méridier) read ὕπο, " out from."

668. βλέπουσα φῶς : "*though* alive."

670. H. thinks the old servant is talking of *Polyxena's* death. καινὸν : " fresh."

ὠνείδισας : "you offer insults." She is hurt by the old servant's extravagant expressions, of the cause of which she is ignorant ; a subtle touch.

671. ἀτάρ : common to express sudden transition to a new thought or to indicate surprise, as here.

672. τάφος : "burial." She is recalling what Talthybius has told her, 572 ff.

673. σπουδὴν ἔχειν : normally active, " be busy " ; here passive, " be attended to."

674-5 : An aside. Cp. introductory note to Epeisodion, above.

μοι : ethic dative, almost "if you please." Jeffery translates " she bewails *me* Polyxena," in Shakespearian style. The effect of the pron. is pathetic.

ἅπτεται : lit. " touches " ; here " grasps."

676. τὸ βακχεῖον κάρα (τῆς Κασάνδρας) : simply, " the inspired prophetess, Cassandra." With κάρα, cp. ψυχή, 87 ; with βακχεῖον, cp. Βάκχης, 121.

678. λέλακας : from λάσκω (cognate w. Latin *loquor*), "shriek, cry aloud."

τὸν θανόντα δ' οὐ στένεις : "him that *is* dead you do not mourn." The servant here uncovers the corpse.

680. ἐλπίδας : "expectation," as often.

681. δή : "So!"

682. She is quick to attribute the guilt to the real culprit, but this is skilfully indicated as done by instinct.

μοι . . . ἔσωζ' : "was guarding, forsooth." The combination of imperf. and ethic dative has an ironical effect.

684–725 : The remainder of this scene is a κομμός or dirge (cp. introductory note to Parodos). A κομμός is defined by Aristotle as θρῆνος κοινὸς χοροῦ καὶ ἀπὸ σκηνῆς, *i.e.* a dirge in which one of the characters joins with the Chorus. Here there is a reversal of the usual roles in such a dirge : the Chorus speaks in iambic trimeters, Hecuba sings in Dochmiac dimeters. Lines 684–7, 690–2, 694–7, 700, 702–3, 704, 706, 710–11, 715–20, are dochmiac.

685. κατάρχομαι : a technical term in ritual, usually of beginning a sacrifice. The normal word for "leading off" a dirge is ἐξάρχω.

686. βακχεῖον νόμον : "a frenzied chant." The Bacchic rhythm was in fact closely akin to the dochmiac which was normal in the dirge. Cp. Aesch., *Cho.* 423 f. ἐν τε Κισσίας νόμοις ἰηλεμιστρίας, "with the refrain of a Kissian (Asiatic) keening woman." Such dirges were quite certainly a fixed component of the ritual from which Tragedy sprang. Thus βακχεῖον is peculiarly appropriate here.

ἐξ ἀλάστορος : "taught me by a spirit of woe."

687. ἀρτιμαθῆ : "learned just now," because she has just discovered the terrible truth. Dirges were naturally often improvisations. The word is unique in Classical Greek, and doubly so because passive in sense. It ought to be active, like ὀψιμαθής, "late learner."

688. γάρ : "what, then ?" cp. 709.

ὦ δύστηνε σύ : almost colloquial ; cp. Ar., *Nub.*, 398 : ὦ μῶρε σύ. The effect is once more pathetic. It is far-fetched to suppose that ἄτην refers, not to the death of Polydorus, but to the curse of Paris. This is a dirge, not an examination in mythology, and the question in fact hints at Hecuba's knowledge of Polymestor's guilt.

690. κυρεῖ : "follow." κυρεῖ, like πέλεται, is a common substitute for ἐστί, which was felt to be insufficiently emphatic. This weakness of the copula is Indo-European, and explains its reinforcement with other verbs like Latin *fui*, Eng. *was*, Italian *sta*, Irish *tá*, etc.

691. ἐπισχήσει : ambiguous. It can mean either "prevent (from grieving)," or "last out, continue." The first is rather awkward w. ἀστένακτος ἀδάκρυτος, and the second fits in with what she has already said at 628 : no day will henceforth *pass* for her without grief and tears. There is nothing unusual, as Méridier thinks, about this use of ἀμέρα. If this interpretation be right, μ' must either be excised, with Hermann (whom Murray follows), or stand for μοι. Such elision is common in Epic and Lyric, doubtful in Trag., but possible in choral passages.

695. Rhetorical questions like this are the stuff of dirges ; cp. the Irish keener's refrain, "why did you die ? " Hecuba of course knows the answer.

696. κεῖσαι : "are lying dead."

698. The Chorus take the queen's words literally.

κυρῶ : vivid present ; "I found him." This is a common meaning of the word, which normally takes gen.

699. πέσημα : the neuter is pathetic. Cp. *Andromache*, 652 : οὐ πεσήματα | πλεῖσθ' Ἑλλάδος πέπτωκε δοριπετῆ νεκρῶν.

700. λευρᾷ : "smooth." She wishes to be sure that he has been cast up by the sea.

702. The answer of the Chorus at once assures her that her dream was true. ἔμαθον : "I was right about."

704. παρέβα : "escaped me." She had interpreted her dream aright, after all.

709. γάρ : cp. 688.

ὀνειρόφρων : a unique adj., here used almost as a participle ; " wise in dreams," lit. " dream-minded."

710. ἐμὸς ἐμὸς : the repetition gives an effect of concentrated passion.

ἱππότας : cp. 9.

711. ἵνα : " where," common in poetry, rare in prose.

712. τί λέξεις : cp. 511.

715. For sanctity of strangers, cp. on 26.

716. ἀνδρῶν : cp. 192.

διεμοιράσω : cp. *Hippol.*, 1376.

722. ἔθηκεν : " made " ; cp. 111, 656.

ὅστις ἐστί : " whoever it be that is cruel."

724. ἀλλ᾽ εἰσορῶ γάρ : γάρ parenthetical.

δέμας : cp. κάρα, 676. Here the word is *formal*, not *affectionate*, as κάρα is there.

726. μέλλεις : takes pres. or fut. inf. Here " delay to."

727. ἐφ᾽ οἷσπερ : Rel. attraction for ἐπὶ τούτοις ἅ : " under the conditions which."

731. τἀκεῖθεν : Greek, unlike English, prefers prepositions of *motion* to those of *rest at*. As A. has come from the Greek camp, he speaks as if he had brought with him *from* there the " things " which he says are in good shape. Cp. phrases like οἱ ἐκ τῆς πόλεως ἠμύνοντο, " those *in* the city resisted." In Greek you cannot say " come for a walk *in* the garden."

" On our side, all is well—if anything in this affair is well."

733. ἔα : " Ha ! " expressing surprise.

734-5. Construe : οὐ γὰρ Ἀργεῖον (εἶναι αὐτὸν) ἀγγέλλουσί μοι πέπλοι δέμας περιπτύσσοντες.

736. ἐμαυτὴν γὰρ λέγω : an indication to the audience that this is an aside. The phrase puzzled the great Alexandrian scholar, Didymus : τὸ δὲ δύστηνε ὁ Δίδυμός φησι πρὸς τὸν Πολύδωρον λέγειν τὴν Ἑκάβην, ὦ δύστηνε Πολύδωρε, ἐμαυτὴν γὰρ λέγω, δύστηνον ἀποκαλοῦσα σέ, Schol.

Such indications were rendered necessary by the unfamiliarity of the device, which became banal in the New Comedy and from there was inherited by Renaissance drama. Since Ibsen, it has been rigorously banished as "unreal" from the modern stage.

737. προσπέσω : Deliberative subj. The compound verb, having a meaning which requires an object, is transitive.

738. νῶτον ἐγκλίνασα : "turning your back on." προσώπῳ, like μοι, ethic dat.

742. The double ἄν emphasises her uneasiness.

προσθείμεθ' : "add."

743. οὔ τοι : τοι has the force of "you know."

744. ἐξιστορῆσαι : "search out"; ἱστορέω, "to enquire," ἱστορία, primarily "enquiry," then "history." Cp. 230. Note that a Greek prophet had knowledge of past, present, and future : τά τ' ἐόντα, τά τ' ἐσσόμενα, πρό τ' ἐόντα.

745. ἐκλογίζομαι : "reckon." λογίζομαι, "calculate," λογιστική ⟨τέχνη⟩ "arithmetic."

ἆρα . . . γε : "am I, I wonder (reckoning) ? "

μᾶλλον : "rather, too much."

ὄντος οὐχὶ δυσμενοῦς : w. τουδ', " whereas he is not ill-disposed."

748. εἰς ταὐτὸν ἥκεις : supply ἐμοί. " You agree with me." With κλύειν, supply βούλομαι from βούλῃ.

Agamemnon here turns to go away.

749. τοῦδε : w. ἄτερ, " without this man's help."

τιμωρεῖν takes dat. of person avenged, acc. of object of vengeance. Cp. ἀμύνειν, and note τιμωρεῖσθαι (756), " to punish."

750. τάδε : acc. of respect or adverbial acc.

752. Here H., who has hitherto (cp. 749) been turned away from A., suddenly turns round and throws herself at his knees in supplication. Cp. 286.

754. τί χρῆμα : not merely " what thing ? " but " what in

the world ? " χρῆμα in such questions often adds this *nuance* of astonishment. Cp. Aesch., *Prom.*, 298. The same effect is seen in phrases like μέγα χρῆμα ἀνθρώπου, etc.

μαστεύουσα : Homeric ματεύω. Cp. 779.

755. θέσθαι : " have made free." Pflugk actually thinks A. is here suggesting suicide. The point is, as Weil remarks, that he offers her freedom so that she can be represented as opting for slavery, with revenge.

758. καὶ δή : concessive ; " well then, that being so."

759. ὧν : rel. attraction, with antecedent not suppressed as it usually is.

760. οὗ : simply " on which," gen. of place after καταστάζω.

761. τὸ μέλλον : " what follows."

Here begins a στιχομυθία, which goes on to 785.

765. ἦ γάρ : " indeed."

766. ἀνόνητά γ' : " yes, to my sorrow," from ὀνίνημι. Neut. pl. used as adverb.

Note γε, ' yes," as often. The phrase is an effective understatement.

767. πτόλις : Epicism, *metri gratia*, for πόλις.

768. ὀρρωδῶν : " in terror," a strong word, peculiar, in poetry, to Euripides, and normally absolute. θανεῖν is thus unusual, and the omission of the second νιν almost ambiguous.

769. Construe : μόνον τῶν τότ' ὄντων τέκνων.

771. Πολυμήστωρ : Transferred to rel. clause for emphasis, and thus made nom. case. Cp. 987.

772. πικροτάτου : an effective prolepsis, " which *was to be* his bitter ruin."

774. γ' : exclamatory ; " why, by whom else ? " Both Θρήξ and ξένος are emphasised by their position. The Thracians were noted both for perfidy and savagery. Cp. Thuc. ii, 95-101, Ar., *Ach.*, 134 f, where Thracian ξενία is scoffed at in memory of the

abortive alliance w. Sitalces in 429. Later on a Thracian mercenary force committed a shocking atrocity at Mycalessus in Boeotia (Thuc. vii, 29).

775. ἦ που : "Can it have been that ?" This line undoubtedly alludes to a well-known propensity of Sitalces, of whom Thuc. says (ii, 97, 4) : οὐ γὰρ ἦν πρᾶξαι οὐδὲν μὴ διδόντα δῶρα, "nothing could be done with him unless by means of gifts."

776. τοιαῦτ' : like ταῦτα, Ar., Pax, 275, "just so, exactly so."

ἐπειδή : "as soon as."

780. Cp. 611-13.

782. γ' : "yes." διατεμών : "having disfigured." Cp. διεμοιράσω, 716.

783. πόνων : gen. w. nouns signifying both happiness and the reverse. Cp. Ar., Vesp., 1292, ἰὼ χελῶναι μακάριαι τοῦ δέρματος.

784. οὐδὲν λοιπόν : "nothing left (to befall me)."

786. τὴν τύχην : τὴν δυστυχίαν δηλονότι, Schol. ; "misfortune itself." In Greek, τύχη is neutral, as Fortune is not. Weil suspects this line.

787. The explanations have been only preliminary to the main scene, which now begins.

788. ὅσια : "according to divine law."

789. στέργοιμ' ἄν : "I am willing to put up with it."

τοὐμπαλιν, for τὸ ἔμπαλιν, "the reverse."

790. ἀνδρός . . . ξένου : objective gen.

791. τοὺς γῆς νέρθεν : supply θεούς. "The gods below," χθόνιοι θεοί.

792. The repetition of ἀνοσιωτάτου is rather untidy than emphatic. Weil suggests that in 790 we should read ἀνοσίου, κακοξένου.

793-7. These verses are highly suspect. Nauck rejected them all, earlier edd. having rejected only some of them. There are difficulties in every line : κοινῆς τραπέζης in 793 is vague ("my table" ?), ξενίας in 794 is ambiguous, ἀριθμῷ both ambiguous and unnecessary, τυχὼν δ' ὅσων δεῖ in 795 is a banal repetition, προμηθίαν with λαβὼν is almost unintelligible, and εἰ κτανεῖν ἐβούλετο in 796 is intolerably frigid. We have here a fairly obvious example of the commonplace interpolations made in Greek plays by actors of the Hellenistic and Roman periods. Page (*l.c.*) thinks it may date from as late as 250 A.D.

The least unsatisfactory way to construe the lines is to take ξενίας in 794 closely w. τραπέзης and τυχὼν in the previous line. This will require a comma after ξενίας τ'. The phrase ἀριθμῷ πρῶτ' ἔχων might then mean "having first rank (τὰ πρῶτα would of course be more usual) in number among my friends." προμηθίαν λαβὼν could mean either "having experienced my solicitude" or "having taken charge of," w. παιδός (strangely) understood.

796. εἰ κτανεῖν ἐβούλετο : This can only be construed by a rather violent ellipse "assuming (that there might be some excuse for) his wanting to kill the boy (he might at least have buried him, but) he did not think him worth a grave." The feeling is Greek, the language very peculiar.

797. ἀφῆκε πόντιον : for predicative use of local adj., cp. Soph. *O.T.*, 477-9, φοιτᾷ πετραῖος ὁ ταῦρος (a famous "crux," wrongly emended by Jebb) and *ibid.*, 1411, θαλάσσιον ἐκρίψατε. "cast into the sea."

800. νόμῳ γὰρ, κ. τ. λ. : This often-quoted passage is probably intentionally equivocal. Its obvious meaning is the well-known Sophistic thesis that the gods *exist* by law or custom, not by nature (νόμῳ, οὐ φύσει), a thesis known to have been stated by Protagoras in his book Περὶ θεῶν, which is said to have been publicly read in Eur.'s house. That a similar view was held by Pericles we learn from Plutarch's report of his Funeral Speech after the Samian War (Plut., *Pericles*, 8, 5). It was roundly condemned by Plato (*Laws*, x, 889E) and though it was a "rationalist" inference from the variegated nature of Greek polytheism, it can hardly have been very popular in Athens. Hence the present passage may also be given a different, less unorthodox, sense, similar to the doctrine of Anaxagoras, that the world is ruled by νοῦς (Intelligence) : "It is by reason of (the existence of) Law that we (are led to) believe in the gods, and this Law is what enables us to distinguish wrong

'from right." The Intelligence of Anaxagoras, almos' as suspect
as the *Nomos* of Protagoras, would thus be cleverly identified with
a different *Nomos*, the Natural Law (νόμοι ἄγραφοι) to which
Sophocles makes his Antigone (*Ant.*, 453, f.) and the Chorus in his
Oedipus (*O.T.*, 865, f.) appeal.

There is a good parallel in *Troades*, 884 (Hecuba speal-).

ὦ γῆς ὄχημα κἀπὶ γῆς ἔχων ἔδραν,
ὅστις ποτ' εἶ σύ, δυστόπαστος εἰδέναι
Ζεύς, εἴτ' ἀνάγκη φύσεος εἴτε νοῦς βροτῶν
προσηυξάμην σέ· πάντα γὰρ δι' ἀψόφου
βαίνων κελεύθου κατὰ δίκην τὰ θνήτ' ἄγεις.

Here there is the same ambiguity about the phrase νοῦς βροτῶν as
there is about νόμος in our passage, and the most daring speculations
are prefaced by a devout ritual formula (cp. Aesch., *Ag.*, 160 :
Ζεύς, ὅστις ποτ' ἐστίν). To Hecuba's strange surmises Menelaus
answers in words any Athenian might have echoed :

τί δ' ἐστιν; εὐχὰς ὡς ἐκαίνισας θεῶν.

802. εἰς σ' ἀνελθών : There is a curious anachronism in the
reference to a Homeric king of this fifth-century concept of law.
The δῆμος was the fountain-head of law in a sense in which the
King of course was not.

εἰ διαφθαρήσεται : fut. w. εἰ implying *threat*.

804. φέρειν : the usual phrase is φέρειν καὶ ἄγειν, " plunder."
φώρ, " thief," is cognate w. φέρω.

805. ἴσον : once more an anachronism. Ἰσονομία was the
Athenian democratic ideal of equality before the law, opposed to
the aristocratic εὐνομία. No Homeric queen would demand equality.
Méridier's translation, *équité*, is ambiguous. Radermacher pro-
posed to read ἀνθρώποισι σῶν (" safe ") ; but surely the anachronism
is characteristically Euripidean.

807. γραφεύς: " a painter." If the text is correct, the meaning
is " stand back like a painter and view my plight." But one MS.
has a reading .ρα.ευς (first and fourth letter indecipherable) which
may stand for βραβεύς, " judge, arbiter."

808. ἀνάθρησον : prose word, unique in poetry.

812. (Agamemnon again makes a move to go.)

ὑπεξάγεις: for prefix ὑπεκ-, ep. 6. μ' acc., w. ὑπ. πόδα.

814-820. An apologia for Sophistic παιδεία, the great aim of which was persuasiveness in public speaking. Its first and finest product was the friend of Protagoras, Pericles, of whom we are told that Πειθώ τις ἐπεκάθιζεν ἐπὶ τοῖς χείλεσιν (Eupolis, fr. 94, 5). Protagoras first came to Athens about 460 B.C., so that his concept of παιδεία (for which see Plato's *Protagoras*) was long familiar by the time of this play. It had been recently reinforced by the introduction of the Sicilian art of rhetoric, which for the first time adapted for prose the rules of formal composition (colon, period, balance of equal and contrasting clauses, etc.) hitherto applied only to poetry. Its great exponent at this time was Gorgias of Leontini, who had come to Athens in 427 as envoy of his native city. He lived till about 375, and became the teacher of Isocrates, through whom and his Latin imitator, Cicero, he may be said to have been the father of all European prose regarded as an art. This passage may well have been intended as an advertisement for Gorgias, of whom Eur. was certainly a friend.

Πειθώ was at first a minor goddess, attendant on Aphrodite; her function was to help in winning the consent of reluctant maidens to marriage. In this capacity we often meet her in Hesiod, Sappho, Ibycus, and Pindar. She is given a more general function for the first time in Aesch., *Ag.*, 107, where she is identified with "the power of song." Here she has become the power of *rhetoric*, exactly as in the saying of Eupolis about Pericles, quoted above. Rhetoric has taken over the functions, as well as the attributes and rules, of poetry.

814. μαθήματα: "subjects of learning," prob. first used in this technical sense by the Sophists, among some of whom (notably Hippias of Elis) it already had also the narrower sense of "mathematics," afterwards commonly given it, e.g. by Plato (cp. *Laws*, 817 E, where τὰ τρία μαθήματα are arithmetic, geometry, astronomy).

816. τύραννον ... μόνην: Cp. description of Eros in First Stasimon of *Hippolytus* (538) as τὸν τύραννον ἀνδρῶν. There was, of course, an ancient kinship between Eros and Peitho as agents of Aphrodite, and τύραννος is a natural epithet of the former (cp. Soph., *Ant.*, 785 f). The theme of the *Hippolytus* passage resembles that of this speech: "in vain does Hellas ever increase the slaughter

of her kine beside Alpheus and at the Pythian shrine of Phoebus,
while we give no worship to Eros, the King of men." Cp. also
Hippol., 916 f. (Theseus speaks) :

> ὦ πολλ' ἁμαρτάνοντες ἄνθρωποι μάτην
> τί δὴ τέχνας μὲν μυρίας διδάσκετε . . .
> ἐν δ' οὐκ ἐπίστασθ' οὐδ' ἐθηράσασθέ πω,
> φρονεῖν διδάσκειν οἷσιν οὐκ ἔνεστι νοῦς ;

818. μισθοὺς διδόντες : the taking of fees was the great mark
of the Sophists. At one end of the scale we hear that Protagoras
charged 100 *minae* for a course, at the other that Evenus of Paros
charged 5 (cp. Burnet, *Plato's Apology*, p. 86). The mina was
worth 100 drachmas, and the present-day equivalent of the latter
in purchasing-power would be nearly 10s. (cp. Tod, C.A.H., vol. v,
p. 8, with allowance for depreciation since 1927). There are many
criticisms of the Sophists for this practice in Plato and Xenophon,
whose master, Socrates, derided it.

ἵν' ἦν ποτε : imperf. or aor. indic. w. ἵνα to express *unrealisable*
purpose ; " so that one could persuade (others) of whatever he
wished and so get at once what he wanted." ἅμα : " at one and the
same time."

820. ἐλπίσαι : older form of opt. The later form, ἐλπίσειε,
avoids confusion w. aor. inf.

822. ἐπ' αἰσχροῖς : " under shameful conditions." The
MSS. are divided between αὐτή and αὕτη. Murray, following
Verrall, prints the latter, understanding it of Cassandra, and
puts a stop after αἰχμάλωτος. But the reference to Cassandra
is far-fetched, and the punctuation leaves οἴχομαι almost without meaning. Most edd. print αὐτή, rightly.

824. καὶ μήν : looks forward to 826. "Well, then!" She has
decided to play her last card.

τοῦ λόγου : w. τόδε. "Perhaps *this part of my argument* is
vain." τόδε looks *forward*.

825. προβάλλειν : in apposition to τόδε. Eur. is particularly
fond of ἀλλ' ὅμως, and uses it fifteen times at the end of a
line, a trick parodied by Aristophanes (*Ach.*, 402, 407).

εἰρήσεται : fut. middle for pass. ; Ionic for Attic ῥηθήσεται.

826 f. Eur. was reproached even in antiquity for making H. thus utilise her daughter's wretchedness ; but two points must be kept in mind. The queen, like Medea, is prepared to go to any length for revenge ; and the ugliness of the appeal is greatly softened by the response to it of Ag., who throughout the play acts a moderate part, and here is almost like Hecuba's son-in-law.

831–2. First recognised as an interpolation by Matthiae. A frequently-quoted commonplace. Page thinks it is probably due to the same actor who interpolated 606–8.

834. κηδεστὴν : "linked by a κῆδος," lit. The original meaning of κῆδος seems to have been " care," as in Od., xxii, 254, τῶν ἄλλων οὐ κῆδος. From this it developed in two opposite directions. On the one hand it came to mean " grief," then " funeral," as in Pindar Pyth. 4, 112, κᾶδος ὡσεί τε φθιμένου . . . θηκάμενοι. On the other it came to mean " connection by marriage," as in the phrase κῆδος συνάπτειν, and finally almost " marriage." The verb κηδεύειν similarly meant " take care of," then " bury," then " contract a marriage, make kin by marriage." κηδεστής keeps only one of these meanings, " kin by marriage, son-in-law, father-in-law, brother-in-law." For development of meaning cp. perhaps Hiberno-English " your care," meaning " your family," a translation of Irish do chúram. Cognate w. Eng. hate, German Hass, Irish caiss, " anger."

Here the κηδεστής is of course Polydorus.

835. ἑνός : "one thing." μοι : eth. dat. "I have only one more thing to say."

836. εἴ μοι γένοιτο : εἴ for more usual εἰ γάρ, " would that." Cp. Soph., O.T., 863.

838. Δαιδάλου : Daedalus began as an Attic " culture-hero," like Hephaestus, to whom the invention of moving statues was also attributed (Iliad, xviii, 417). He was at first an inventor, early connected with folklore about Crete (story of Labyrinth), and with Sicily ; then he became a sculptor, who could endow his works with speech and movement (first in this passage). Last of all, he figures as a wonder-working architect (Diodorus Siculus, i, 97, 5). Here there is a certain exaggeration, not free from frigidity, in the

mention of him. Cp. *Electra*, 332 f. The Schol. quotes the lost
Eurystheus

τὰ Δαιδάλεια πάντα κινεῖσθαι δοκεῖ
βλέπειν τ' ἀγάλμαθ'· ὧδ' ἀνὴρ κεῖνος σοφός.

839. ὁμαρτῇ : equivalent to ὁμοῦ, and found in same sense
Hippol., 1195, *Heraclidae*, 138.

841. She shows the extremity of her despairing passion for
revenge by the elaborate epithets here applied to her late enemy
and present master.

843. τιμωρόν : w. χεῖρα, "avenging hand."

844. ἐσθλοῦ γὰρ ἀνδρὸς : predicative gen. "For it is *the
part of* a noble man."

845. Cp. the definition of Justice ascribed to Simonides, Plato,
Rep., i, 332 D : τὸ τοὺς φίλους εὖ ποιεῖν καὶ τοὺς ἐχθροὺς κακῶς, and its
refutation by Socrates, who insists that the good man cannot harm
others.

847. τὰς ἀνάγκας : Hadley corrects to τῆς ἀνάγκης, which goes
smoothly w. οἱ νόμοι, "the laws of necessity," but this runs
counter to the critical maxim, *difficilior lectio potior*. Others suggest
χρόνοι (for νόμοι), "times and seasons," and render τὰς ἀνάγκας as
"relationships, ties." It is best to keep to the MSS. and translate,
with Méridier, "law (or custom) determines our necessities, making
our worst enemies into friends and our former well-wishers into
foes." "Law or custom" is then what enjoins revenge on Hecuba.

διώρισαν : gnomic aor.

852. θεῶν θ' οὕνεκ' : the god in question is Zeus Xenios.

Construe : θεῶν θ' οὕνεκα καὶ τοῦ δικαίου βούλομαι
(τὸν) ἀνόσιον ξένον τήνδε σοι δοῦναι δίκην.

855. μὴ δόξαιμι : We should expect ἐμέ τε μὴ δόξαι, after ὥστε.
The change may be due to attraction to εἴ πως φανείη, which is
best taken, not w. δίκη as by most edd., but impersonally, "if in
any way it should appear possible."

857. ἔστιν γὰρ ἧ : The vagueness shows the king's embar-
rassment.

859. For the MSS. δὲ σοὶ Elmsley reads δ' ἐμοὶ, which gives a

much clearer sense. ὅδ' in 860 then means Polydorus. If we keep δὲ σοί, ὅδ' can only be A. himself (cp. 202). But this is very awkward here, and ὅδε is very rarely used in this meaning without some noun like ἀνήρ. Translate " if this boy is *my* friend, that is a special matter, having nothing to do with the army." The text must be translated "if *I* am *your* friend."

861. πρὸς ταῦτα : "in view of this." Note *present* imper. : " go on and reflect."

862. προσαρκέσαι : There is here a suppressed protasis, "if I can do so without being embroiled with the Greeks." The suppression subtly indicates A.'s delicacy of feeling.

863. εἰ διαβληθήσομαι : fut. after εἰ, implying a *threat*, as often ; " if I am to fall out with, lose favour with."

864. As often in such reflexive passages, there is a slight anachronism ; πλῆθος, for example, suggests the Athenian *demos*, and νόμων γραφαί the law-code of Solon.

867. μὴ κατὰ γνώμην : μὴ should precede χρῆσθαι, and is displaced *metri gratia*. It is the redundant μή after verbs of preventing.

τρόπος : " humour, character," originally perhaps a colloquial word, very frequent in Comedy.

868. τῷ τ' ὄχλῳ : once more a topical phrase.

870. σύνισθι : from σύνοιδα, " be privy to, share knowledge of." Imperative only here. She means " be my passive, not my active, accomplice."

873. ἀνδρὸς Θρηκὸς : Cp. 81. The phrase is contemptuous.

οἷα πείσεται : a sinister euphemism. Cp. Soph., *O.T.*, 1376, βλαστοῦσ' ὅπως ἔβλαστε.

874. μὴ δοκῶν ἐμὴν χάριν : elliptical ; "not seeming *to do so* for my sake." μὴ, not οὐ, because sentence imperative.

ἐμὴν χάριν for χάριν ἐμοῦ.

875. θήσω καλῶς. Cp. 111. Common phrase.

880. Τρωάδων ὄχλον : This is intended to surprise the audience, as it does Ag.

881. ἄγραν : " booty," to emphasise their helplessness.

882. τὸν ἐμὸν φονέα : ἐμὸν should be objective, "murderer *of me*," but it is more probably ironical, " my particular murderer." φονέα normally disyllabic (∪—) by synizesis ; here and at *Electra*, 599, 673, a tribrach.

883. ἀρσένων κράτος : objective gen. " upper hand over a man."

884. τὸ πλῆθος : simply " numbers."

885. μέμφομαι : Schol. φαῦλον ἡγοῦμαι, "I think poorly of," a rare meaning which I cannot find listed in L. and S.

886-7. These two instances of μεγάλα ἔργα done by women are the most suitable for the present purpose out of a long catalogue exemplified by Aesch., *Choeph.*, First Stasimon, (585-638) where the case of the Lemnian Women gets special mention. The murder of the sons of Aegyptus by their wives, the daughters of Danaos, was the subject of the lost *Danaides* of Aesch. ; that of the men of Lemnos of his Λήμνιοι. It also formed the background of the Λήμνιαι of Soph., and of Eur.'s own *Hypsipyle*, of which a large part has been recovered from a papyrus. (*New Chapters in Greek Literature*, 3rd Series, p. 120, f.). The " Lemnian horror " (τὸ Λήμνιον ἔργον) was proverbial. The point of H.'s mention of both cases here is that they showed how numbers could compensate for physical weakness.

ἄρδην : (αἴρω) " altogether."

ἐξῴκισαν : " depopulated."

888. ἀλλ' ὡς γενέσθω : ἀλλά at the end of a speech sums up an appeal. " Come then, let it be so done."

μέθες : " let be, break off."

889. μοι : eth. dat., " pray."

890. (Here H. turns to give instructions to the slave.)

πλαθεῖσα : (irreg. aor. pass. of πελάζω) " having drawn near."

891. δή ποτ' : like *ci-devant* ; " former."

892. χρέος : acc. of respect, " on a matter which concerns you no less than her."

894. ἐκείνης : H. herself. She is giving the slave the exact words she is to use.

900. νῦν δέ : " but as it is," a common phrase.

901. πλοῦν ὁρῶντ' ἐς ἥσυχον : Murray's emendation of MSS. ὁρῶντας ἥσυχον. The preposition is necessary to the sense, " waiting for, looking forward to." ὁρῶντ', w. στρατόν, understood. A ἥσυχος πλοῦς would be one helped by a favourable wind. Méridier, in his note, thinks the two contradictory, but surely a sail without a wind is unthinkable.

903–4. Cp. 845. Ag. accepts H.'s justice.

905–952. **Third Stasimon.**

This is the longest ode in the play, and one of the most beautiful lyrics in Greek. In structure it resembles the First Stasimon (444–83) consisting as it does of two strophes with their corresponding antistrophes, but it is made longer by the addition of an epode (943–52) in an independent rhythm. This may be called the classical structure of a tragic choral ode, the presence or absence of the epode being immaterial (Kranz, Stasimon, p. 175).

The theme of this ode is the fall of Troy, narrated in typical Euripidean fashion. Three points about it should be specially noted : (1) The originality (and " modernity ") of describing the sack of the city as experienced by a luxurious woman. (2) The sharp realism of the detail, which reminds us of the clear outline of a vase-painting, while at the same time looking forward to Hellenistic genre-descriptions ; (3) The violent contrast, skilfully hinted at rather than over-stressed, between the relaxation of the domestic scene and the sudden horror of the surprise-attack. The change comes at 928, where the broken and agitated iambic rhythm (a succession of eleven short syllables), emphasises the startling effect of the unlooked-for din of assault. The picture of the captive woman gazing back on her lost home (938, f.) makes an effective ending to a perfect poetic description, which seems designed to illustrate the Horatian ut pictura poesis. After this perfection, the epode seems a little banal, being merely a fresh recital of the imprecations against Helen which were almost commonplace in Tragedy (cp. 265). There is another lively lyric picture of the sack of Troy in the First Stasimon of *Troades* (511, f.).

Metrical Scheme :

Strophe α'—Antistrophe α' : Aeolic.

Strophe β'—Antistrophe β' : mainly Iambic.

Epode : mainly Iambic.

1. *Strophe α'—Antistrophe α'*.

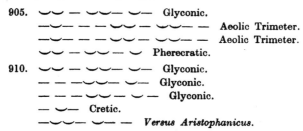

905.   ‿‿ — ‿‿— ‿— Glyconic.
—‿— — — ‿‿ — ‿‿— — Aeolic Trimeter.
—‿— — — ‿‿ — ‿‿— — Aeolic Trimeter.
‿‿ — ‿‿— — ‿ Pherecratic.
910.   ‿‿ — ‿‿— ‿— Glyconic.
— — — —‿‿— ‿— Glyconic.
— — — ‿‿— — ‿ — Glyconic.
— ‿— Cretic.
—‿‿— ‿— — *Versus Aristophanicus.*

Two periods : 905–8, 910–13. The two last cola should be scanned together as a Trimeter, akin to the Alcaic 10–syllable (Horace's *virginibus puerisque canto*) with a cretic instead of a dactyl before the choriamb.

2. *Strophe β'—Antistrophe β'*.

923.   ‿— ‿‿‿ ‿‿‿‿— Iambic Dimeter.
‿— ‿— ‿— ‿— Iambic Dimeter.
925.   ≍ — ‿— — — — Iambic Dimeter Hypercatalectic.
—‿ —‿‿— — — Glyconic.
‿‿— ‿‿— ‿— ‿— — Iambic Trimeter ?
‿‿ ‿‿ ‿‿ ‿‿‿ ‿‿ Iambic Dimeter Catalectic.
‿— ‿— ‿— ‿— Iambic Dimeter.
— ‿— Cretic.
930.   — ‿— — — — ‿‿— ‿‿— Iambic Trimeter ?
—‿‿ —‿‿— Hemiepes.
— — ‿— ‿— — Iambic Dimeter Catalectic.

Again there seem to be two periods : 923–6, 927–31. The first is Iambic, ending in an Aeolic colon, the second Iambic with an

Enoplic colon in the second last place. Note how 930 resembles 927, but in reverse, so to speak ; it is obviously difficult to give names to such cola as these. Wilamowitz suggests that 927 may be scanned as a Phalaecean with ‿‿ instead of — ≅ as its opening syllables. This is tempting, but leaves the kindred 930 unexplained.

3. Epode.

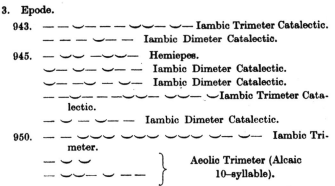

943. — — ‿— — — ‿‿— ‿— Iambic Trimeter Catalectic.
— — — ‿— — Iambic Dimeter Catalectic.
945. — ‿‿ —‿‿— Hemiepes.
‿— ‿— ‿— — Iambic Dimeter Catalectic.
‿— —‿ — ‿— Iambic Dimeter Catalectic.
— —‿— — —‿‿— ‿‿— ‿Iambic Trimeter Catalectic.
— ‿ — ‿— — Iambic Dimeter Catalectic.
950. — — ‿‿‿ ‿‿‿ ‿‿‿ ‿— ‿— Iambic Trimeter.
— ‿ ‿ ⎱ Aeolic Trimeter (Alcaic
— ‿‿— ‿ — — ⎰ 10–syllable).

Three periods : 943–5, 946–9, 950–2. The rhythm is irregular Iambic for the most part, with the third colon Enoplic and the last Aeolic. Wilamowitz, dividing the cola differently, scans as Dactylo-Epitritic down to 950 (*Griech. Versk.*, p. 548). Schroeder (*Eurip. Cantica*, p. 44), has yet another division and a different scansion. Note the close kinship between 951–2 and the last two cola of Strophe α', which opens with a cretic, not a dactyl.

906. λέξῃ : passive, regular in Trag. The fut. pass. λεχθήσομαι is a late formation based on the aor. pass.

907. νέφος : Cp. *Iliad*, xvii, 243, πολέμοιο νέφος περὶ πάντα καλύπτει.

908. δορὶ δὴ δορὶ : διπλασιάζει ἕνεκεν τῆς λύπης, Schol.

910. στεφάναν πύργων : The great Mother-goddess, Cybele, widely worshipped in Asia Minor, is regularly represented with a crown of towers. She is called *turrita* by Virgil and Seneca. For turret-crowned head of Cybele on coins of Hellenistic Smyrna, cp. Head, *Historia Numorum*, p. 592.

κέκαρσαι : perf. pass of κείρω, " shave, shear " ; Latin *caro* (piece of flesh *cut* off), Irish *scaraim*, Eng. *shear*.

911. αἰθάλου: "sooty smoke." The MSS. have αἰθάλου καπνοῦ, the second word being obviously a gloss: correction by Triclinius. Akin to αἴθω, "burn, glow," Latin *aedes, aestus*, Irish *Aed, Aodh*, "red-head."

912. κηλῖδ': "stain," Latin *cālīgo*; cognate acc.

κέχρωσαι: from χρῴζω, "defile," cognate w. χροία, χρῶμα, χρώς, etc.

913. ἐμβατεύσω: This verb, as Hadley remarks, is often used of gods: Soph., *O.T.*, 678, of Dionysus, Aesch. *Pers.*, 449, of Pan.

914. μεσονύκτιος: temporal adj. used adverbially: cp. ἀφῆκε πόντιον, 797, ἐπιδέμνιος, *infra*, 927, where adj. is *local*. The Schol. quotes from *Little Iliad* the following line which fixes the hour of Troy's fall:

νὺξ μὲν ἔην μέσση, λαμπρὴ δ' ἐπέτελλε σελήνη.

Cp. Aesch., *Ag.*, 826, πήδημ' ὀρούσας ἀμφὶ Πλειάδων δύσιν, said of the Wooden Horse. The Pleiads set in Greece in March between 10 and 11 p.m.

ὠλλύμαν: note imperf.; "my ruin began," Jeffery.

915. ἦμος: Only here in Eur.; common in Soph. Correlative w. τῆμος, as ἕως w. τέως.

916. σκίδναται: pass. of σκίδνημι. The MSS. give κίδναται, an equally good form. Both are Epic, not elsewhere used in Trag., but σκίδναμαι occurs in Ionic prose: αἱ κόραι σκίδνανται, "the pupils are dilated," Hippocrates. Cp. ἀποσκίδνασθαι, Thuc. vi, 98.

χοροποιῶν: with ἀπο. Some MSS. have χοροποιὸν θυσίαν, which Wilamowitz takes w. καταλύσας as more idiomatic than our text. καταλύσας is Murray's correction of MSS. καταπαύσας. There seems little reason for any change if χοροποιὸν θυσίαν καταπαύσας be read, as by Méridier.

920. ξυστόν: Only here in Trag. In *Iliad*, xv, 677 it is the "great naval pike" of Ajax. Xenophon, *Cyrop.*, 4, 5, 58, uses it to mean "cavalry lance," and this is its common later meaning. From ξύω, "shave," apparently because of its smooth shaft. The phrase here is parenthetic. The spear hung on the wall was a sign of peace.

922. οὐκέθ' ὁρῶν : must mean "no longer on the watch for." The Greeks had pretended to sail away. Τροίαν 'Ιλιάδ' : "Ilian Troy."

923. ἀναδέτοις : adj. w. μίτραισιν. The word is unique, but the phrase is equivalent to πλεκτή ἀναδέσμη in *Iliad*, xxii, 469.

924. μίτραισιν : μίτρα, Hom. μίτρη, "band." In Homer it meant "a metal guard worn round the waist" (L. and S.). The meaning here, "headband, snood," occurs first in Alcman, 23, 67 : μίτρα Λυδία νεανίδων ἄγαλμα. Its wearing was evidently an Asiatic custom.

ἐρρυθμιζόμαν : "I was arranging."

"Les femmes ne disent pas qu'elles se paraient, ce qui serait fort extraordinaire à cette heure, mais qu' elles faisaient leur toilette de nuit en relevant et fixant leurs cheveux." Weil.

925. ἐνόπτρων : For a fine discussion of some archaic Greek mirrors, and description of a beautiful specimen in the National Museum, Dublin, see Dr. J. D. Beazley's paper, *A Greek Mirror in Dublin*, Proc., R.I.A., 1939. Mirrors were usually of bronze or silver ; the mention of gold here is intended, as Hadley remarks, " to heighten the picture of luxurious ease." Cp. *Troades*, 1107.

χρυσέων : disyllabic, by synizesis.

926. ἀτέρμονας : Schol. explains as meaning περιφερείς or κυκλοτερείς, "circular." This banal explanation, which can hardly apply to αὐγάς, is surprisingly accepted by Méridier and apparently favoured by Weil. Hadley's translation, "looking into the *fathomless* bright depths " is surely better. This was long ago suggested by Boissonade ; Hartung's pedestrian objection, that it could not be said of a mirror hung in a room, is taken seriously by Weil. It was pretty certainly a *hand*-mirror in any case. This is one of the poet's very finest poetic touches.

927. ἐπιδέμνιος : a unique word. Cp. 797, 914. " Before sinking on the cushions of my couch." Porson oddly thought the nom. " otiose " and read ἐπιδέμνιον, which makes the phrase prosy as well. Musgrave went one better by suggesting ἐπιδείπνιος. For πίπτειν, cp. Aesch., *Ag.*, 565–6 :

ἦ θάλπος, εὖτε πόντος ἐν μεσημβριναῖς
κοίταις ἀκύμων νηνέμοις εὕδοι πεσών.

928. The rhythm marks the sudden change from luxurious peace to the din of war.

929. κέλευσμα : "the word of command."

930. παῖδες 'Ελλάνων : An Aeschylean phrase. Cp. *Persae*, 402.

931. σκοπιάν : "hill-top," a Homeric word; here equivalent to πόλιν.

933. μονόπεπλος : clad only in the *chiton*, like a Spartan girl ; hence to be taken closely with Δωρὶς ὡς κόρα. Athenian women wore over the *chiton* the *himation* or *peplos*, a woollen upper-garment.

935-6. Construe : προσίζουσ' "Αρτεμιν οὐκ ἤνυσα, "I besought A. to no avail." προσίζουσ' lit. "sitting as a suppliant," hence "praying to." ἀνύω, "accomplish, succeed."

In the *Iliad*, Artemis is the helper of the Trojans, like her brother Apollo. Both were in historical fact of Asiatic origin. Eur., however, is probably thinking of Athens where Artemis, under various appellations, such as Brauronia, Munichia, Tauropolos, was the great women's goddess. "Αρτεμιν, ἃ γυναικῶν μέγ' ἔχει κράτος, she is called in the Attic skolion (Diehl, no. 3). Every Athenian girl, between the ages of five and ten, was dressed in a yellow robe and consecrated to her at the Brauronia, thus becoming an ἄρκτος ("bear") and being said ἀρκτεύειν. Women in trouble would naturally turn to her. In this case she gives no help : the women's husbands are killed, they themselves enslaved.

940. ναῦς ἐκίνησεν πόδα : a metaphor from running ; "the ship hurried on its way." πόδα w. νόστιμον : "homewards."

941. ὥρισεν : from ὁρίζω, "divide or separate from," used normally of a boundary (ὅρος).

942. ἀπεῖπον : "The aorist denotes a feeling . . . *which began to be just before* the moment of speaking," Hadley. Cp. Soph., *Ajax*, 693 : ἔφριξ' ἔρωτι, περιχαρὴς δ' ἀνεπτάμαν. The normal pres. of ἀπεῖπον is ἀπαγορεύω, its perf. ἀπείρηκα. It means both " succumb, give in," as here, and " forbid."

ἄλγει : instrumental dat., " in my suffering."

944. βούταν : cp. 646.

945. αἰνόπαριν: " wicked Paris " ; cp. *Iliad*, iii, 39, δύσπαρις, Alcman (Diehl 73), δύσπαρις, αἰνόπαρις, and Robertson's brilliant emendation, Aesch., *Ag.*, 713, κικλήσκουσ' ''Απαριν τὸν αἰνόλεκτρον. The same prefix occurs Aesch., *Choeph.*, 315, ὦ πάτερ αἰνόπατερ, but the meaning is different, " unhappy father."

945-6. κατάρᾳ δίδουσ' : a typical Greek phrase. Cp. *Od.*, xix, 167, ἀχέεσί με δώσεις. The word κατάρα (from ἄρη w. Doric final ᾱ) is Ionic and prosaic.

947. ἀπώλεσεν: a pregnant use; "he has driven me to my death from my fatherland."

948. γάμος: Weil, followed by Méridier, on the strength of *Andromache*, 103, takes this as meaning "wife," and as applying to Helen. In the *Andromache* passage, however ('Ἰλίῳ αἰπεινᾷ Πάρις οὐ γάμον ἀλλά τιν' ἄταν/ἠγάγετ' εὐναίαν ἐς θαλάμους 'Ελέναν), the verb ἠγάγετο is clearly used in a double sense : γάμον ἄγεσθαι, "to *celebrate* a marriage," and 'Ελένην ἄγεσθαι, " *to bring home* H. as his bride." The bridal procession was the chief part of a Greek marriage ; the Irish " hauling-home " is probably a very ancient pagan survival of a similar rite.

949. ἀλάστορός τις ὀϊζύς : " Woe sent by a demon." For ἀλάστωρ, cp. 686.

950. ἅν : refers to ὀϊζύς, which is of course Helen personified. In Aesch., *Ag.*, 1461, Helen is called ὀϊζύς.

953-1295 : *Exodos.*

The Exodos is defined by Aristotle as " a complete part of a Tragedy not followed by a song of the Chorus." Strictly interpreted, this definition compels us to classify all the remaining part of this play as an Exodos ; yet, as it is clearly divided into two by a Kommos (1055-1108) and as the two scenes so produced have each a distinct character, it is perhaps more convenient to call the scene 953-1055 the Fourth Epeisodion and that from 1109-1295 the Exodos. Aristotle's definition is only technically violated by this division, because, although the Kommos is not " a song of the Chorus," and is here in fact sung entirely by Polymestor, the Chorus merely replying in Trimeters to his Dochmiacs, it does mark a transition in the action.

The scene from 953-1055 is the most dramatic in the play, and
Eur. has put into it a great deal of the skill in devising tense situations which is more characteristic of his later than of his earlier
work. It is full of the type of Irony which Sophocles had brought
to 'a high degree of perfection and which is perhaps the chief
ingredient of Greek Tragedy. The " ironic " effect is secured, as in
Sophocles, by the contrast between the expressed intention of the
speaker and the spectator's knowledge of the real situation. Here
Polymestor is trying to conceal his crime, while Hecuba is fully
aware of it and in her turn conceals from him her sinister purpose.
We have thus a double deception, of which of course the spectator
is all the time fully aware. There is a similar complexity in the
plot. Hecuba first induces her enemy to dismiss his guards by
saying that she has a secret to discuss with him and his children.
Next, after putting him at his ease by letting him think her entirely
unaware of the fate of Polydorus, she excites his cupidity by hinting
vaguely at " an ancient buried treasure," about which she wishes
her son informed. Polymestor is sharp enough to enquire why
she has requested his children's presence, and she answers (with
perhaps the boldest " irony " of the whole scene) that she wishes
them to know the secret *in case he should die*.[1] In order to get
him into her tent, she mentions almost casually (after purporting
to direct him to the exact spot where the " ancient treasure " lies
hidden), that she wishes him to take care of some valuables *which
she has actually brought with her*. This, coming after the greater
bait, so plausibly offered and so cunningly accepted, is easily swal-
lowed, and the Thracian, after some further suspicious questioning,
goes to his horrible doom among the seemingly helpless women.

We have not so far been explicitly told how Polymestor has
been summoned. He enters, accompanied by his two children and
an armed guard, from the side of the scene to the left of the audience.
This indicates by convention that he has come from a distance ;
and he himself informs us that when Hecuba's messenger came to
him, he was far away in the Thracian mountains. His speech is a
masterpiece of pious hypocrisy.

956.   φεῦ : *extra metrum*, as usual with exclamations.

---

[1] Grube (*Drama of Euripides*, p. 226, n. 1) seems to miss a little of the subtlety here.
This is not said by H. in order to get the children *into the tent*, but rather to motivate
their presence on the scene. This done, they " just follow their father." Polymestor's
question why they were asked to come of course greatly heightens the dramatic
suspense.

οὐκ ἔστι πιστὸν οὐδέν : this "ironic" phrase is almost a keynote for the whole scene.

957. καλῶς πράσσοντα : with μὴ πράξειν. The whole phrase is part of the subject of οὐκ ἔστι, in apposition to εὐδοξία, In prose it would be normal to write τὸ μὴ πράξειν. "Nothing is to be relied upon, neither glory nor the prospect of success derived from present good fortune."

958. φύρουσι : Note quantity of ῡ. Primary meaning, "mix dry with wet," Latin *fermentum*, Eng. *barm*. Secondary meaning, "jumble, confound," first in Aesch., *Prom.*, 450, ἔφυρον εἰκῇ πάντα, used of primitive men. In Plato, *Phaedo*, 97 b, Socrates is made to echo Prometheus in speaking of his own "confused" efforts at reasoning.

αὐτοί : Murray, for MS. αὖθ' οἱ. αὐτά is Hermann's reading.

πάλιν τε καὶ πρόσω : a variant on the usual ἄνω κάτω, for which cp. Aesch., *Eum.*, 650 : (Ζεὺς) τὰ δ' ἄλλα πάντ' ἄνω τε καὶ κάτω/στρέφων τίθησιν. Here the phrase prob. refers to *past and future*, πρόσω καὶ ὀπίσω.

959. ἀγνωσίᾳ : τῇ ἀδηλίᾳ τῶν πραγμάτων τῶν μελλόντων, Schol. This is a "rationalist" view of the origin of worship.

960. A show of manly self-control, whose hollow pretence is as obvious to H. as to the audience.

961. προκόπτοντ' : agrees w. subj. of θρηνεῖν, understood (τινά).

κακῶν : best taken w. ἐς πρόσθεν, "ahead of one's misfortunes."

προκόπτειν is a prose word, obviously metaphorical for the track-making of a pioneer, used commonly in later philosophical Greek in the sense of *moral* progress ; frequent in Eur., but nowhere else in poetry.

962. ἀπουσίας : causal gen. w. μέμφῃ. τι is merely adverbial w. εἰ.

963. σχές : "Hold ! " τυγχάνω : vivid pres.

964. ἀφικόμην : "reached home." Note awkward repetition in 967.

966. ἐς ταὐτόν ... συμπίτνει : "meets me," w. dat. αἴροντι.

967. μύθους : The content of the message is left vague; it becomes sufficiently clear from the action.

968. Hecuba will not look Polymestor in the face. The lines are a deliberate signal to the audience, intended to be emphasised by the actor, so that attention will be concentrated on the subtle play that follows.

971. τυγχάνουσ' : nom. for acc., the construction called κατὰ σύνεσιν (sense-construction) because αἰδώς μ' ἔχει is equivalent to αἰδοῦμαι.

972. ὀρθαῖς κόραις : "with uplifted eyes"; Latin rectis oculis. κόραι, lit. "pupils," because a little image (κόρη, pupillus) is seen in each of them. Cp. King John, ii, 2 : "the shadow of myself formed in her eye."

973. δύσνοιαν : First found here, then Soph., Electra, 654 ; elsewhere only prose.

σέθεν : obj. gen., "against you."

974-5. These two lines, with their irrelevant and anachronistic excuse (such modesty is an Athenian, not a heroic, trait) are perhaps an interpolation due to actors. Page, l.c., says that the objections to 970-5 are not very strong. They are strongest to the last two lines.

Construe : "Apart from this (ἄλλως) another reason for my behaviour is the custom that women should not look men in the face."

976. καὶ θαῦμά γ' οὐδέν : "yes, indeed, and no wonder."

τίς χρεία σ' : understand ἔχει. The phrase is equivalent to Homeric τί δέ σε χρεὼ ἐμεῖο, Iliad, xi, 606.

977. τί χρῆμ' : adverbial, "why in the world ? " ἐπέμψω for more usual μετεπέμψω, "sent for."

979. Note how careful she is to include the children. ὀπάονας : Epic word, equivalent to θεράποντας.

981. ἥδ' ἐρημία : the pronoun is emphatic; "in this case it is all right to be left alone."

982. προσφιλές : διὰ τὸ μὴ συμμαχῆσαι αὐτὸν τοῖς Τρωσί, Schol.

983. He waits a moment while the guards withdraw. ἀλλά: " now," emphatic.

984. τί χρή : "in what way ought ? " He does not purport to question the elementary duty of helping a friend in need. The emphasis is on the τί.

986. εἰπὲ παῖδ' : the well-known Greek idiom by which the subject of a dependent clause becomes the object of the principal clause (ἀντίπτωσις, " exchange of cases ").

989. μάλιστα : " Certainly." Still used in Modern Greek.

τοὐκείνου μέρος : acc. of respect : " as far as he is concerned."

992. Murray is responsible for the pause in the middle of the line, to indicate H.'s emotion. The device is not of ancient date. μοι would be more elegant than μου (Weil).

993. καὶ δεῦρό γ' : " Yes, and he tried to come." Note tense of ἐζήτει.

κρύφιος : without being caught by the Greeks.

995. Here Polymestor is " ironical," but of course Hecuba is not deceived. Indeed no one is, except Polymestor himself ; a subtle Euripidean touch, made more subtle still by the savage undertone in the next line.

996. Note the tenses of the two imperatives : σῶσον expresses urgency, ἔρα (ἐράω) warns against a practice or habit. ἐρᾶν τῶν πλησίον is an almost proverbial phrase ; cp. the Tenth Commandment, Exodus, xx, 17 : οὐκ ἐπιθυμήσεις τὴν οἰκίαν τοῦ πλησίον σου. νυν : Ionic particle ; dist. from νῦν, " now."

997. ὀναίμην τοῦ παρόντος : "may I make the best of (get profit from) what I have," without coveting anyone else's. ὀνίναμαι, middle of ὀνίνημι, " benefit." Cp. στέργειν τὰ παρόντα.

1000. ὦ φιληθείς : note the fierce effect of this extremely " ironical " address.

ἔστ', ὦ is Hermann's convincing correction of MSS. ἔστω.

1001. τί χρῆμ' : Cp. 977. The repetition of the phrase perhaps indicates Polymestor's cupidity.

1002. κατώρυχες: grammatical subj. of ἔστι in l. 1000. This use of plural noun with sing. verb is called σχῆμα Πινδαρικόν. It is perhaps pedantic to apply strict grammar at this high point of dramatic tension. This line is spoken in a loud whisper; the plural Πριαμιδῶν makes the bait more exciting. Note, too, the skilful alliteration. For κατώρυχες, cp. Soph., Ant., 774, where the word means *tomb*.

1004. μάλιστα: here has very emphatic effect: "Yes! Yes!" Note sinister irony in εὐσεβής.

1005. Polymestor is made to ask this dangerous question in order to arouse suspense in the minds of the audience, not because the presence of the children is a "weakness," as Grube thinks. If Eur. had felt it as such, he would certainly not have drawn such explicit attention to it. Hecuba just glides over the danger-point, and her answer, ἢν σὺ κατθάνῃς, is of course delicious "irony." The audience know that Polymestor is doomed, but not yet to what exact fate.

1007. The semi-colon after ἔλεξας, which makes the line perfect, is due to Boissonade. Without it, the last words would be meaningless.

1008. Apparently στέγαι means underground treasuries; perhaps the idea is suggested by the popular belief that such tombs as those at Mycenae were "treasure houses" (Hadley). On the other hand, it may be the existence of real treasuries of the kind that suggested the popular belief. Athena's temple was familiar as the State treasury of Athens.

1011. Polymestor is eager for more information; Hecuba skilfully uses his eagerness to lead him into the tent. Note the intentional vagueness of 1012.

1014. σκύλων ἐν ὄχλῳ: "in a pile of booty."

1015. Polymestor's question is very natural. He waves his arm to indicate that they are surrounded. "This is the circuit of the Greeks' anchorage."

1016. One MS. has ἴδιαι, which is read by Weil and Méridier, and is clearer.

1017. πιστά: "safe." Polymestor is now very nearly caught.

1019. ἀλλ' ἕρπ' ἐς οἴκους : ἀλλά here means simply "please," as often. Cp. 888. Note tense of ἕρπε, " come, move into the house."

1020. πόδα : the sheet, or rope which held the lower edge of the sail. Cp. 940, where the word, in a similar context, has its literal meaning.

1021–2. The " irony " here reaches its height. ὦν : with δεῖ, as *Hipp.*, 23 : οὐ πολλοῦ πόνου με δεῖ.

1024, f. Polymestor now follows Hecuba into the tent, from which his cries can soon be heard as he is seized and blinded. Meanwhile, the Chorus recite a brief song in Dochmiac rhythm to the accompaniment of a jerky, agitated dance. (1024 and 1031 are ordinary Iambic Trimeters.) Cp. 684–725.

1024. δέδωκας : This seems pointless, and Weil may be right in his suggested correction, following Nauck :

οὔτοι δέδωκας ἂν ἴσως δώσεις δίκην.

1025–7. ἁλίμενον ἄντλον : A famous crux. ἄντλον in Homer meant the *hold* of a ship, but its original sense must have been the normal one, " bilge-water," Latin *sentina*. In Pindar, *Ol.* 9, 53, it means simply " flood." In spite of Hadley's protest, there seems no alternative to translating it " water " here, or perhaps " filthy water " would be more precise. Otherwise ἁλίμενον would be meaningless. λέχριος, needlessly suspected by Murray, means " sideways," (πλάγιος, Schol.), and is really quite appropriate to the *sudden, unforeseen* nature of Polymestor's fall. It is to be taken w. πεσών (Weil, Méridier) rather than w. ἐκπέσῃ (Hadley) where it would have to be given a peculiar meaning, " headlong."

φίλας καρδίας : well compared by Hadley w. Creon's words, Soph., *Ant.*, 1105, καρδίας τ' ἐξίσταμαι. Finally, ἀμέρδω means " take, cut off," not " lose."

Translate : " like one fallen sideways into a foul flood from which there is no escape into harbour, you will fall from your heart's desire, having cut off your life (by your act in slaying Polydorus)." καρδίας means, not " life," but " desire, wish," i.e. his eagerness for treasure.

1029. συμπίτνει : should mean " concur, coincide," and this makes plausible the conjecture of Hemsterhuys, οὗ for οὐ, " where a debt to Justice and a debt to the Gods coincide, this means mortal evil ! " On the other hand, no Greek would make a distinction between such debts. According to Schol., Didymus, the great Alexandrian scholar, paraphrased thus : ὑπέγγυον τὸ ἀληθὲς οὔτε παρὰ τῇ Δίκῃ οὔτε παρὰ τοῖς θεοῖς ἐμπεσὸν ἀφανίζεται, giving συμπίτνει apparently the unique meaning " is set aside." The word σύμπτωσις in prose often means " collapse."

1030. With κακόν a verb " to be " is implied.

1031. ὁδοῦ τῆσδ' ἐλπίς : " your expectations from this journey (shall deceive you)."

1032. θανάσιμον : With σέ, not with Ἄιδαν.

1034. ἀπολέμῳ : i.e. the hands of women.

λείψεις βίον : a subtle touch. The Chorus do not know the exact penalty he is to pay (Hadley).

1035. Polymestor is heard crying within. The rule that scenes of violence were not enacted in view of the audience was not universal : Sophocles showed one of Niobe's daughters being killed by Artemis (Pearson, *Soph. Frag.*, ii, pp. 96–7). On the other hand it seems pretty certain that Ajax goes out of sight for his suicide ; the actor Timotheos of Zacynthus, who enacted it before the audience and was therefore called σφαγεύς (Schol., *Ajax*, 864) was a late sensationalist (Schmid, *Gr. Lit.-Gesch.*, i, 2, p. 338) and the Chorus only *hear* the sound of the hero's fall (*Ajax*, 871). Horace's rule is well known (*Ars Poetica*, 185, f.) :

> *Ne pueros coram populo Medea trucidet*
> *Aut humana palam coquat exta nefarius Atreus,*
> *Aut in avem Procne vertatur, Cadmus in anguem,*
> *Quodcumque ostendis mihi sic, incredulus odi.*

Such restraint was of course the normal practice. . There is a close enough resemblance between this scene and that in Aesch., *Ag.*, 1343, f. In both the Chorus divide into two groups.

1037. ὤμοι μάλ' αὖθις : a repetition of Aesch., *Ag.*, 1345.

1038. καίν' : " unheard of."

1039. οὔτι μὴ φύγητε : On this construction with οὐ μή, see now A. Y. Campbell in *C.R.*, 1943, p. 58, f. With the *second person sing.*, fut. ind., οὐ μή expresses a strong *prohibition* ; with *any other person* of the fut. ind., or with *any* person of the aor. subj., a strong *denial*. Campbell shows that the second person aor. subj. is not used in prohibitions, nor the second person fut. ind. in denials. Apparent exceptions are due either to faulty texts or to faulty interpretations. He holds the old view (denied by Goodwin) that the two constructions were originally separate.

1040. βάλλων : " with my javelin." In his rage and anguish he threatens to tear down the flimsy wall of the σκηνή.

1041. Assigned to Polymestor by late MSS. and Scholia, which Hermann, Weil, and Méridier follow. Murray's attribution to the Chorus, which is that of the best MSS., is very much better. The Chorus hear the heavy thud of a javelin striking against something. In 1155, the women have deprived Pol. of his javelin. The Schol. explains that he throws stones, Jeffery that he uses his fists. We are only told what the Chorus think they *hear*.

1042. ἐπεσπέσωμεν : Delib. subj. This construction w. βούλη βούλεσθε, is a favourite one with Plato; an idiomatic combination of two kinds of question.

ἀκμή : equivalent to καιρός. Cp. Aesch., *Ag.*, 1353, τὸ μὴ μέλλειν δ' ἀκμή.

1044. Note tense of imperatives ; " go on, break."

ἐκβάλλων : " burst out." Greek doors opened outward.

1047. ἦ γάρ : "Have you really ? "

1050. τυφλῷ . . . ποδί : A common phrase both in Soph. and Eur.

παραφόρῳ : "stumbling, staggering." L. and S. quote Lucian παράφορον βαδίζειν, of a drunkard's walk.

1055. " The onrush of his Thracian temper, hard to stand against." Cp. *Iliad* v, 87, of Diomedes, rushing like a river, and Ar., *Eq.*, 526, of Cratinus borne on the flood of his popularity.

1055–1108. *Kommos.*

This is simply a long lament, chanted as a solo by the blinded Polymestor. As it is in Dochmiac rhythm, there is no strophic correspondence, but it is broken at 1085 by two Iambic Trimeters recited by the Chorus.

1056. The central doors of the σκηνή are opened, the bodies of the slain children are visible just inside them, and Polymestor himself comes out slowly, feeling his way, his face covered with blood from his blinded eyes.

1057. κέλσω : aor. subj. (delib.) from κέλλω, prose ὀκέλλω, "run to land." The metaphor is common in Greek.

1059. Murray's ἐπίχειρα seems hard to justify for MSS. ἐπί χεῖρα. It can only mean "as punishment" (ἐπίχειρα always "wages," L. and S.) which is far-fetched here. Hadley deletes stop after ἴχνος and takes χεῖρα w. ποίαν : "to which hand will I turn ?" Weil and Méridier read ἐπί ποδί κατ' ἴχνος χέρα, "placing my hand and foot in the track I follow," and explain that Polymestor does not walk on all-fours as Schol. thinks, but simply *asks* rhetorically if he is to do so.

There seems no doubt that Polymestor is intended to fall on hands and feet at one point, and Aesch., *Eum.*, 34 f, offers an interesting parallel, where the Pythia, after her fright, staggers out of the shrine, crying :

· τρέχω δὲ χερσίν, οὐ ποδωκίᾳ σκελῶν.

There also Schol. says she comes out on all fours, τετραποδηδόν.

If ἴχνος means "track," it surely requires a gen., and the natural way to take it is with θηρὸς ὀρεστέρου, which makes no sense. I incline to Porson's view that we should read ἐπί χεῖρα καί ἴχνος : "setting myself on hand and foot with the movement (βάσιν adverbial acc.) of a four-footed wild beast." Thus ἴχνος would have its frequent meaning "foot." With ποίαν supply ὁδόν "what way ?."

1060. ἐξαλλάξω : "change to, turn to."

1064. τάλαιναι : "wretches." The word usually expresses rather pity.

1066. ποῖ μυχῶν : Cp. phrases like ποῦ γῆς, ποῖ λόγων ἔλθω. The acc. after πτώσσω is epic.

1067. ὀμμάτων . . . βλέφαρον : simply "eyes." βλέφαρον literally means "eyelid."

1068-9. τυφλόν . . . φέγγος : "having rid me of this blinded light," i.e. his blindness; an *oxymoron*. ἀσαφῶς εἴρηται διὰ τὴν τοῦ λέγοντος δεινοπάθειαν, Schol. ; but it is a vigorous poetic phrase.

Ἅλιε : the Sun is god of all light. Cp. 68.

1070, f. His vain efforts to catch his enemies have a *Grand Guignol* effect.

1072. ἐμπλησθῶ : an exaggeration for the sake of horror. This deliberate search for a horrible effect (ἔκπληξις) was regarded as typically Aeschylean ; but Eur. can give it an original turn.

1073. θηρῶν : "*like* a wild beast."

1074-5. " Inflicting wounds that shall pay me back for my mutilation."

1077. βάκχαις Ἅιδου : " hellish Bacchanals," because the Maenads tore animals and human beings to pieces, as they do Pentheus in *Bacchae*. For idiom, cp. Aesch., *Ag.*, 1235 : θύουσαν Ἅιδου μητέρ', and *Herakles*, 1119, Ἅιδου βάκχος, applied to H. after he has slain his family.

διαμοιρᾶσαι : Cp. 716. Inf. of *result*.

1078. σφακτά : Hermann's correction of MSS. σφακτάν. Construe w. τέκνα, above, " to be slaughtered."

1079. "A wild thing to be exposed on the mountains," i.e. for the wild beasts as well as for the tame dogs to eat.

ἐκβάλλειν, normally of exposing unwanted children, a practice common enough, though probably not as everyday a matter as New Comedy would suggest.

1080. κάμψω : simply " turn " as a runner doubling back on the second lap in a race-track.

1081. λινόκροκον: from κρέκω, " of woven linen." Polymestor here mixes his metaphors : he girds up his robe and compares himself to a ship mounting sail, in order that he may hasten to the *lair* (κοίταν) where his children lie dead.

1087. Deleted by Hermann as a repetition of 723.

1090. κάτοχον : a religious term : " possessed by."

1094. ἤ οὐδείς : scan as disyllable, by synizesis.

1100. The MSS. have αἰθέρ' ἀμπτάμενος. The deletion of αἰθέρ' is due to Hermann. The Aeolic form of the aorist ἀνέπτην, from ἀναπέτομαι, is found in Opt. ἀμπταίην and in the participle middle, as here. The latter is particularly frequent in Trag. In the Indic., it only occurs in Wilamowitz's very attractive conjecture, ψάμμος ἄμπτα, Aesch., *Ag.*, 985. ἀμ- is for Aeolic prep. ἀν, Ionic-Attic ἀνά.

1104. Orion and Sirius both rise after the summer solstice, and are thus associated with the hottest part of the year. Sirius is called " the Dog " first in Aesch., *Ag.*, 967. Later he becomes the dog of the hunter Orion, who is mentioned with him in Hesiod, *Works and Days*, 609.

For the alternative, cp. *Herakles*, 1157–8 : πτερωτὸς ἢ κατὰ χθονὸς μολών. Its earliest occurrence seems to be Soph., *Ajax*, 1192 : ὄφελε πρότερον αἰθέρα δῦναι μέγαν ἢ πολύκοινον Ἅιδαν. These are really alternative modes of *death* ; the belief that the souls of the dead go up into the αἰθήρ was common in 5th-century Athens. Cp. the Potidaean inscription, Hicks-Hill, *Manual of Greek Inscriptions*, No. 54 :

αἰθὴρ μὲμ φσυχὰς ὑπεδέχσατο, σώματα δὲ χθών,

and *Supplices*, 531, f.

1105. ἐς Ἀίδα : genitive ; ellipse of δόμον.

1107. συγγνῶσθ᾽ : for συγγνωστά ἐστι, " it is pardonable." The Chorus are suggesting suicide. Contrast *Herakles*, 1247 f., 1351, etc., where the *condemnation* of suicide is much more seriously meant. Suicide was to some extent frowned on by Greek public opinion (cp. Rohde, *Psyche*, Eng. trans., ch. v, note 33), and forbidden by the Pythagoreans and the Platonists. On the other hand, Sophocles' *Ajax* is in a sense a glorification of it ; cp. 479 :

ἀλλ᾽ ἢ καλῶς ζῆν ἢ καλῶς τεθνηκέναι
τὸν εὐγενῆ χρή,

and it became almost a point of honour among the Stoics, who derived in some measure from Socrates, but here surely perverted his teaching of καρτερία.

κρεῖσσον᾽ ἢ φέρειν : for more usual ἢ ὥστε φέρειν.

1109–1292. See note at 953. This second part of the Exodos and final scene of the tragedy takes the form of a trial and judgment, in which Agamemnon skilfully plays the part he has agreed to play (cp. 850–904) while Polymestor shows his utter baseness by his cringing and lying, and Hecuba once more exhibits her skill as a pleader. The scene ends with the discomfiture of the villain, but not until, in the fashion of a *deus ex machina*, he has malevolently prophesied the fates of his enemies. For a parallel to the trial-scene, cp. the great *Agon* in Aesch., *Eum.*, 566–577, and for the normal *deus ex machina*, cp. the conclusion of *Hippolytus* and *Bacchae*.

1109. Agamemnon comes in with his guards. This opening passage, with Agamemnon's pretended sympathy for Polymestor, is a superb piece of stage-craft.

1110. λέλακ' : Cp. 678.

1111. Ἠχώ was apparently a character in the lost *Andromeda*, as is suggested by the parody in Ar., *Thesm.*, 1008, f.

1113. πάρεσχεν : Sonnenschein, *Greek Grammar*, § 356, c, p. 195, explains this as a case " in which a Principal Clause with ἄν may be supplied in thought." He translates : " *this noise caused us no little fear* (supply *or would have done so) if we had not known.*"

1119. ἄρα : " if one but knew ! " Cp. Denniston, *Greek Particles*, p. 40. Agamemnon is laboriously ignorant.

1121. μειζόνως : " somethi g worse."

1122. τί φής : Ag. express< s elaborate surprise.

1124. τί λέξεις : Cp. 511. He cannot believe she is near him.

1126. Note the almost Aeschylean weight of this line, expressing his savage hatred.

1127. Ag. begins to show his hand.

οὗτος : " you there ! " common as a rude form of address ; more frequent w. σύ. Cp. 1280 and Soph., *O.T.*, 532, οὗτος σύ, πῶς δεῦρ' ἦλθες ; Ag. here seizes Polymestor.

τί πάσχεις : " what do you mean ? "

1128. μαργῶσαν : " raging "; only in this participial form.

1129. ἴσχ' : frequentative of ἔχω, a reduplicated present (* siskh-) like τίθημι, ἵστημι.

τὸ βάρβαρον : in contemptuous contrast with Greek discipline and moderation.

1132. λέγοιμ' ἄν: "Very well, speak 1 will."

Note the contrast between the uninstructed directness of P.'s narrative, distinguished only by its duplicity, and Hecuba's polished rhetorical manner. Hadley points out that each speaks exactly fifty lines. Such set displays are called ἐπιδείξεις, and Eur. was famous for them.

1135. ὕποπτος: active, "suspicious, apprehensive," a rare use. δή: "it would seem."

1139. "Lest he should muster Troy and make it one city again." The συνοικισμός of Athens by Theseus was the creation of the πόλις from scattered townships. Note vivid subjunctives.

1141. ἄρειαν: The opt. is less vivid, perhaps subtly implying that this is a secondary reason.

1143. γείτοσιν: "us neighbours of Troy."

1144. ἐν ᾧπερ: the κακόν is regarded as a kind of disease. νῦν, "just now."

1146. τοιῷδ': refers to what he is about to say. ὡς: common conjunction after λόγος.

1147. φράσουσα: "on the pretext that she was going to tell me."

1150. κάμψας γόνυ: perhaps to emphasise his unguarded state.

1152. ἔνθεν: "from the other side."

ὡς δή: "as if forsooth."

1153. Ἠδωνῆς: The Edoni were one of the Thracian peoples best known to Athens. In 465 they had defeated the Athenians at Drabeskos, and destroyed their first settlement at Ennea Hodoi, later Amphipolis. "The shuttle of an Edonian hand" is a poetical way of saying "the work of an Edonian loom." Thracian embroidery was famous; cp. Kazarow, C.A.H. viii, p. 543.

1154. πέπλους: generally "a woman's robe," but also used for any stately garment.

1155. κάμακα: properly "vine-pole," but already "spear-shaft" in Aesch., Ag., 66,

1156. διπτύχου στολίσματος : normally explained, after Schol., as meaning " cloak and spear." Weil points out that there is no question of P.'s cloak having been taken away, and correctly explains " my twofold equipment," i.e. the two javelins normally carried by a heroic warrior ; cp. Paris, *Iliad* iii, 18. He is thus led, however, to a needless correction of κάμακα in 1155 into a dual. There is no necessity for such literal accuracy. στόλισμα : from στόλος.

1157. ἐκπαγλούμεναι : " admiring greatly," a strong word. Like μαργῶσαν (1128) it only occurs in participial form.

1159. γένοιντο : With τέκνα, plural because subject denotes *persons*. Note absence of caesura here.

1160. πῶς δοκεῖς : A colloquialism, not found in Aesch. or Soph., but frequent in Eur., and of course in Comedy. " You can't imagine how peaceful their talk was."

1164. ἀρκέσαι : " to help." Note aorist.

1166. κόμης : " by the hair," gen. common with verbs of *holding on to*.

1168. Cp. Aesch., *Ag.*, 864, κακοῦ κάκιον ἄλλο πῆμα.

1170. πόρπας : equivalent to περόνας, Latin *fibulae*, "brooches."

1172. ἐκ δὲ πηδήσας : tmesis for ἐκπηδήσας δὲ, an epic and archaic usage permissible in a narrative ῥῆσις such as this.

1173. θὴρ ὢς : an echo of 1058.

1174. τοῖχον ὡς κυνηγέτης : queried by Verrall, whom Murray follows. The change from the wild beast turning on the dogs in the previous line to the huntsman here is abrupt, but not impossible to Eur.

Note τοῖχος, "*side* of a tent," τεῖχος, "wall."

1176. τὴν σὴν : equivalent to σοῦ w. σπεύδων intrans.

1178-82. This outburst is not of course to be taken as the poet's own serious opinion. Denunciation of women was a commonplace since Semonides of Amorgos (fr. 7, Diehl).

1179. λέγων ἔστιν : an Ionic idiom, found in Herodotus.

1181. For a magnificent elaboration of a similar theme, cp. Aesch., *Choeph.*, 585, f. : πολλὰ μὲν γᾶ τρέφει δεινὰ δειμάτων ἄχη, κ.τ.λ.

Aesch. makes women's crimes only a special case of ὑπέρτολμον ἀνδρὸς φρόνημα.

1182. αἰεί : "from time to time," as often.

1185–6. These two lines, though quoted by Stobaeus (c. 500 A.D.) along with 1183–4, are unintelligible as they stand. Not merely does πολλαί stand in the air, but there is no contrast implied between ἐπίφθονοι and τῶν κακῶν, whereas the Chorus surely mean to say that most women are good. There is either a very ancient corruption or an interpolation; but the latter, as Page remarks, cannot come from an actor (the usual source), because the lines " have no tolerable sense." For the general sentiment, as Eur. probably intended it, Weil compares fr. 658 (quoted a little before this by Stobaeus), from *Protesilaos* :

ὅστις δὲ πάσας συντιθεὶς ψέγει λόγῳ
γυναῖκας ἑξῆς, σκαιός ἐστι κοὐ σοφός,
πολλῶν γὰρ οὐσῶν τὴν μὲν εὑρήσεις κακήν
τὴν δ᾽, ὥσπερ αὕτη, λῆμ᾽ ἔχουσαν εὐγενές.

1187, f. Hecuba, in true professional style, begins by condemning her opponent's use of rhetoric. Another and closely kindred opening for a defence was to profess one's own ignorance of the art of speaking, as Socrates does in Plato's *Apology*. Here the conventional plea is strengthened by emphasis on the opponent's combination of rhetoric with a bad case. In fact, Polymestor has used very little rhetoric at all, except in a rudimentary form, more reminiscent of folk-lore than of the school, at the end of his speech. Hecuba herself, like Socrates, is a much greater master of the art than her opponent. This attack on rhetoric is not of course to be taken as a condemnation of that παιδεία which is earlier praised by Hecuba (814–820). It would be well understood by the audience to be a standard professional gambit.

1188–91. Cp. *Hipp.*, 928, f., where a very similar argument is used by Theseus against his son. Hippolytus, however, is a professional himself, and his defence (*ibid.*, 983, f.), begins with the well-known formula " unaccustomed as I am to public speaking."

1190. σαθρούς : "unsound," opp. to ὑγιής, "sound."

1192. ἠκριβωκότες : (ἀκριβόω, note quantity of i) almost 'professionals "—a clear reference to Sophists who " made the worse appear the better cause " as Socrates was accused of doing.

1194. This would be a popular argument in the Athens which saw the *Clouds* perhaps in the next year. It will be remembered that in this play the " School " of Socrates, in which he teaches the ἄδικος λόγος, is finally burnt like the Pythagorean Ιεροί οίκοι in S. Italy.

ἀπώλοντ' : gnomic aorist ; the phrase is strong, with almost the effect of a curse.

1195. φροιμίοις: " in its opening." προοίμιον was the technical term for the *exordium* of a speech ; other parts were διήγησις (narrative) πίστεις (proofs) and ἐπίλογος (conclusion). Construe τὸ σὸν ὦδ' ἔχει (τοῖς ἐμοῖς) φροιμίοις: " thus far your (Agamemnon's) share in my preamble." φροίμιον owes its initial aspirate to analogy with φρουρά, φροῦδος (from ὁρά, ὁδός).

1197. πόνον . . . διπλοῦν : " (ridding them of) a double burden," i.e. the prospect of a fresh Trojan War ; cp. 1139.

1201. τίνα . . . χάριν : take together ; " what interest did you serve by your zeal ? " an allusion to 1175. In typically Greek fashion, she shows that P. could not have been helping Ag., as he claimed, because no interest *of his own* was served by his doing so.

1202. κηδεύσων : Cp. on κηδεστής, 833. Here the verb means " make someone your kin by marriage."

1203. Note accent of τίν' : " *what* cause had you ? "

1204. ἔμελλον : understand οἱ Ἕλληνες.

1206. εἰ βούλοιο : " if you wished " (as of course you do not) you would admit that it was gold killed my boy.

1208. ἐπεί : emphatic for normal γάρ. Cp. Soph., *O.T.*, 390.

1209. εἶχ' : " protected."

1211. τί δ' : Here δέ is argumentative, not adversative ; the phrase simply resumes πῶς in 1208.

1212. χάριν θέσθαι : " acquire favour *for yourself.*"

1214. οὐκέτ' . . . ἐν φάει : " no longer living."

1215. ἐσήμην' : absolute. Edd. are reminded of Aesch., *Ag.*, 293, 497, 818. The word suggests a *beacon*, and the whole phrase can only be explained as a parenthesis. πολεμίων ὕπο then goes w. οὐκέτ᾽ ἐσμέν ἐν φάει. This explanation is due to Bernardakis.

1217. πρὸς τοῖσδε : " furthermore."

1219. τοῦδε : Polydorus.

1220. πενομένοις : " leading hard lives," of the Achaeans during the ten years' siege.

1223. τολμᾷς : " bring yourself to."

1224. καὶ μὴν : " nay, more."

1226. ἐν τοῖς κακοῖς : " in bad times."

1227. ἕκαστ᾽ : w. τὰ χρηστά, " in every case."

1228. εἰ δ᾽ ἐσπάνιζες : " if you were now in want, and Polydorus prosperous."

1230. νῦν δ᾽ : " as it is," a common use.

1232. σοὶ δ᾽ ἐγὼ λέγω : In her ἐπίλογος, or conclusion, she turns again to Ag. Cp. 1195.

1233. ἀρκέσεις : the fut. w. εἰ almost implies a threat to come.

1234–5. εὐσεβῆ corresponds to ὅσιον, πιστὸν to δίκαιον, as outer to inner and permanent qualities.

1237. She does not call him κακὸς directly, and at 1233 she has only said κακὸς φανῇ. Now she skilfully breaks off by pointing to her own helplessness.

1239. ἀφορμάς : " starting-points." Hecuba has at least partly disproved her opening contention ; " a good cause always gives scope for a good speech."

1240. Ag. would seem himself to have taken lessons in rhetoric.

1243. ἵν᾽ εἰδῇς : almost " I may as well tell you." Subjunctive of οἶδα.

1244. οὔτ᾽ οὖν Ἀχαιῶν : " no, nor for the sake of the Greeks." χάριν understood. Cp. 874.

1247. τάχ᾽ οὖν : " Perhaps, as you say."

ῥᾴδιον : " a light matter." The Thracians were notoriously fierce.

1248. ἡμῖν δέ γ' : " For us at any rate, who are Greeks " ; the order gives the emphasis. Cp. 26, and for Greek feelings about injury to strangers or guests, Aesch., *Eum.*, 269, f., Ar., *Ran.*, 145, f. It was counted along with injury to parents as a crime punishable in Hades, and the Furies pursued those guilty of it. ·

1249. μὴ ἀδικεῖν : note synizesis.

φύγω : delib. subj.

1250. οὐκ ἂν δυναίμην : emphatic ; " Impossible ! "

1251. ἐτόλμας, τλῆθι : a play on words ; cp. 562. " Since you could bear to do a wicked thing, you must also bear its unpleasant consequences." τολμᾶν, lit. " to show wicked daring."

1253. ὑφέξω δίκην : " lose my case to my inferiors." In calling H. a female slave, he is relieving his feelings by insult.

1254, f. On στιχομυθία, cp. Introduction to First Epeisodion, 216 *supra*.

οὔκουν : Cp. 251. εἴπερ, like εἴπερ γε, " if, as is the case, since " ; Latin *si quidem*.

1259. τάχ' : " maybe." νοτίς " spray."

1260. μῶν ναυστολήσῃ : The subj. follows ἡνίκ' ἂν. Hecuba's interruption is of course sarcastic ; she means " are you threatening me with the prospect of a voyage to Greece ? " which of course has no terrors for her.

· 1261. μὲν οὖν : " no, but," as often. Latin *immo, immo vero*.

καρχησίων : καρχήσιον occurs first in Sappho, 51, 3, where it means a kind of " narrow-waisted " drinking-cup. The meaning " masthead," which it has here, occurs first in Pindar, *Nem.* 5, 51, and appears to be a nautical slang-derivation from its original sense, due to some peculiarity of shape. Latin *carchesium*, whence Ital. *calcese*, Fr. *calcet* (Boisacq.).

1262. An elaborate way of saying " who will push me ? "

1263. ἀμβήσῃ : second person, fut. of ἀναβαίνω. On Aeolicism, cp. 1100.

πρὸς ἱστόν : "up the mast."

`1264. Again heavily sarcastic.

1265. πύρσ' : πυρσός, Attic πυρρός, lit. "fiery," as here. As a proper name, Πύρρος, "red-head," it is paroxytone. The metamorphosis of Hecuba into a dog with fiery eyes is described, as we might expect, in Ovid, *Met*. xiii, 565, f., where she is said to have undergone it after having been stoned to death by Thracians in revenge for Polymestor. According to another version (Schol. Lycophron, 1181) she was stoned by the Greeks; Dion of Prusa (ed. von Arnim, xxxiii, 59) says she was changed by the Erinyes, and Nicander (3rd cent, B.C., quoted by Schol. on 3 *supra*) that she sprang into the sea after the fall of Troy. We have no means of judging the relative ages of these stories nor of deciding how far Eur. may have added to older legend. In any case, this story, and its connection with the spot called κυνὸς σῆμα (probably marked by a great heap of stones, whence the detail about the manner of her death), point to some original kinship between Hecuba and the Asiatic goddess Hecate, who was thought to be accompanied by howling demon-dogs or to take a dog's form herself, and who was propitiated by throwing a stone on a cairn at cross-roads. Hecuba may well have begun as a local form of this dreaded goddess of earth and the underworld.

1267. Herod. vii, 111, tells of an oracle of Dionysus among the Satrae, a Thracian tribe. The Greeks also regarded him as a god of prophecy ; cp. *Bacchae*, 298, f. It is not unlikely that the prophetic *deus ex machina* was originally Dionysus himself, and that Aeschylus, in his *Lykourgeia*, was the first poet to make him a Thracian. In *Bacchae*, where he prophesies, he comes from Lydia.

1268. Once more sarcastic.

1270. This line is very puzzling as it stands. Murray marks it suspect, and indeed it requires drastic interpretation to give it sense. Weil's conjecture φάτιν for βίον seems the simplest remedy : Hecuba asks for the conclusion of the oracle she has interrupted.

1272. ἐπῳδόν : The meaning "called after," required by the context, is unique for this word, which normally means either "charmer" or "song" or "verse." There seems to be a curious confusion between συνῳδόν and ἐπώνυμον.

1275. καὶ σήν γ': "yes, and what is more, your daughter, C., must die." The reference is of course to the story told in *Odyssey*, xi, 420, f., and in Aesch., *Ag.*

1276. ἀπέπτυσ': "instantaneous" aorist. The meaning is of course "*absit omen.*" ταῦτα means the death referred to; her gesture (or rather formula) is intended to turn it back on P. himself.

1277. ἄλοχος: Clytemnestra.

πικρά: "guardian of his house who will bring him bitter death"; an *oxymoron.*

1278. μήπω: a pious understatement of her wish, instead of μήποτε; *litotes.*

1280. Cp. 1127.

1281. κτεῖν': "go on, kill," the *durative* sense of the present.

λουτρά: Agamemnon was killed in his bath. ἀμμένει: Aeolicism; cp. 1100.

1282. οὐχ ἕξετ': for the idiom, cp. 579.

1283. ἐφέξετε: "check."

1284. ἐγκλήετ': note present; "go on, close my mouth."

1285. νήσων: partitive gen. w. που.

1287. Cp. word order at 372.

1291. This prayer is "ironical" coming, as it does, after Polymestor's prophecy.

1293-5. The final anapaests are usually quite brief; in *Alcestis, Andromache, Helen,* the same verses are repeated.

VOCABULARY

The principal tenses of Compound Verbs will be found under the Simple Verb.

ᾰ, ᾱᾱ, *interj.*, ah, ha! alas!

ᾱ, *Dor. for* ἡ, *from* ὁ, ἡ, τό.

ᾱ, *Dor. for* ἥ, *from* ὅς, ἥ, ὅ.

ἀγαθοί = οἱ ἀγαθοί.

ἀγαθός, -ή, -όν, good, excellent, brave.

ἄγαλμα, -ατος, *n.*, glory, honour, 461; statue, 560.

Ἀγαμέμνων, -ονος, *m.* Agamemnon, son of Atreus, king of Mycenae, commander of Greeks at Troy.

ἀγαστός, -ή, -όν, *verbal adj. of* ἄγαμαι, desirable.

ἀγγελθείς. *See* ἀγγέλλω.

ἀγγελία, -ας, *f.*, message, news.

ἀγγέλλω, -ελῶ, ἤγγειλα, ἤγγελκα, announce, report.

ἀγείρω, -ερῶ, gather, collect.

ἀγέραστος, -ον, unrewarded.

ἀγησαι (*Dor.*) = ἡγῆσαι, 1 *aor. mid. imperat.*

ἄγκυρα, -ας, *f.*, anchor.

ἀ-γνωσία, -ας, *f.*, ignorance.

ἄγρα, *f.*, booty, spoils.

ἄγριος, -α, -ον, wild.

ἄγω, ἄξω, ἤγαγον, lead, bring; spend, pass (364); carry off, 937.

ἀγωγός, -όν, *adj.*, bringing up, *used as subst.* (536).

ἀγών, -ῶνος, *m.*, contest, struggle.

ἀγωνία, -ας, *f.*, struggle, 314.

ἀδ' (*Dor.*) = ἥδε.

ἀ-δάκρυτος, -ον, tearless.

ἀδελφή, *f.* sister.

ἀδελφός, *m.*, brother; ἀδελφώ, brother and sister, 896.

ἀ-δικέω, -ήσω, act wrongly *or* unjustly.

ἄ-δικος, -ον, unjust, wrong.

ἀ-δοξέω, be of no reputation.

ἀ-δώρητος, -ον, unrequited.

ἀεί, *adv.*, always, ever; from time to time.

ἀείρω, ἀρῶ, raise, support.

ἀηδών, -όνος (-οῦς), *f.*, nightingale.

Ἀθάνᾱ (*Dor.*) = Ἀθήνη, *f.*, Athene, patron goddess of Athens.

Ἀθῆναι, -ῶν, *f.*, Athens.

Ἀθηναῖος, -αία, Athenian, 467.

ἄθλιος, -α, -ον, wretched.

ἄ-θραυστος, -ον, unbroken, unhurt.

ἀθρέω, gaze upon, inspect.

ἀθροίζω, -σω, ἤθροισα, gather, muster.

ἄθροισις, -εως, *f.*, mustering, gathering.

αἶα, *f.*, land.

αἰαῖ, alas! ah, me!

Αἴγυπτος, Aegyptus, king of Egypt. *See* 886, *note.*

Αἴδα (*Dor.*) = Αἴδου.

αἰδέομαι, -έσομαι, ᾐδέσθην, revere, respect.

Ἅιδης (Ἀίδης *and* ᾄδης), -ου, *m.*, Hades, God of underworld.

135

αἰδώς, -οῦς, f., reverence, shame.

αἴθαλος, m., smoky flame.

αἰθήρ, -έρος, m., upper air, air.

αἷμα, -ατος, n., blood.

αἱμάσσω, -ξω, ᾕμαξα, make bloody.

αἱματόεις, -εσσα, -εν, adj., bloody.

αἵμων, -ον, -ονος, adj., bloody.

αἰνέω, -έσω, ᾔνεσα, praise.

αἰνό-παρις, -ῐδος, wicked Paris, 946, note.

αἱρέω, -ήσω, εἷλον, ᾕρηκα, -μαι, ᾑρέθην, take ; catch, get into one's power ; slay (886).

αἴρω, ἀρῶ, ᾖρα, lift, raise ; αἴ. πόδα, walk, 965 ; αἴ. στόλον, get together expedition, 1141 ; excite, 69.

αἰσθάνομαι, αἰσθήσομαι, ᾐσθόμην, ᾔσθημαι, see, perceive, understand.

ἀίσσω (and ᾄσσω), ἀίξω (ᾄξω), rush, 1105 ; float, 31, note.

αἰσχρός, -ά, -όν, base, disgraceful, shameful ; superl. αἴσχιστος. Superl. adv., αἴσχιστα, most shamefully.

αἰσχύνη, f., shame, disgrace.

αἰσχύνω, αἰσχυνῶ, ᾐσχύνθην, trans. shame ; mid., be ashamed.

αἰτέω, -ήσω, ᾔτησα, ask, ask for, beg, demand ; mid., ask for oneself, 390.

αἰτία, f., reason, ground.

αἴτιος, -α, -ον, he (or that) which causes ; neut. αἴτιον, the cause, 974.

αἰχμ-αλωτίς, -ίδος, f., female captive ; used as adj. at 1016, etc.

αἰχμ-άλωτος, -ον, captive.

αἰχμή, f., spear-point.

αἰχμητής, -οῦ, adj., armed with spear.

ἀίω, hear.

αἰών, -ῶνος, m., life, lifetime.

αἰωρέω. lift up ; pass., hover.

ἄκᾰτος, f., light vessel, ship.

ἀκέομαι, -έσομαι, heal.

ἄ-κλαυστος, -ον, unwept, unlamented.

ἀκμή, f., point (of time), crisis.

ἀκοίτᾱν (Dor.) = ἀκοίτην.

ἀκοίτης, -ου, m., husband.

ἀ-κόλαστος, -ον, undisciplined.

ἀκούω, -σομαι, ἤκουσα, ἀκήκοα, ἠκούσμαι, -σθην, hear, listen, trans. and intrans.

ἀκραιφνής, -ές, unmixed, pure.

ἀκρῑβόω, make accurate, 1192, (perf. part. ἠκριβωκώς).

ἄκρος, -α, -ον, at furthest point, topmost, outermost ; ἄ. χῶμα, top of mound, 524 ; ἄ. καρδία, surface of my heart, 242. See 94, 558.

ἀκτή, f., beach, strand.

ἀκτίς, -ῖνος, f., ray.

ἀλάστωρ, -ορος, m., avenging demon.

ἀλγέω, suffer, be in pain or grief.

ἄλγος, -ους, n., pain, grief.

'Αλέξανδρος, name of Paris (lit. defender of men).

ἀ-ληθής, -ές, adj., true ; τὰ ἀληθῆ, truth, 1206.

ἀ-λίαστος, -ον, unceasing. See note, 85.

ἁλι-ήρης, -ες, sweeping over sea.

ἀ-λίμενος, -ον, harbourless.

ἅλιος, -α, -ον, of sea.

ἅλιος, Dor. for ἥλιος.

ἅλις, adv., enough, with gen., 278.

ἁλίσκομαι, ἁλώσομαι, ἑάλων (part. ἁλούς), ἑάλωκα, pass., am taken.

ἀλκή, f., strength.

ἀλλά, adv., but.

ἄλλα, from ἄλλος.

ἀλλάσσω, -ξω. change.

ἄλλος, -η, -ο, adj., other; ἄλλος τις, some one else; οὐδὲν ἄλλο, nothing else; ἄλλος πρὸς ἄλλῳ, one in addition to another ; *with article*, the rest ; *adv. acc.* τὰ ἄλλα, in all other respects.

ἄλλοτε, *adv.*, at another time.

ἀλλότριος, -α, -ον, of *or* belonging to another.

ἄλλως, *adv.*, otherwise, idly, in vain.

ἄλμα, -ἄτος, *n.*, leap.

ἄ-λοχος, *f.*, spouse, wife.

ἀλούς. *See* ἀλίσκομαι.

ἅλς, ἁλός, *f.*, sea, 26 ; sea-water, 610.

ἅλωσις, -εως, *f.*, capture, taking.

ἅμα, *adv.*, at same time.

ἀ-μαθία, *f.*, ignorance, folly.

ἁμαρτάνω, -τήσομαι, ἥμαρτον, -τηκα, err, fail to get, miss, *with gen.*, 594.

ἀμ-βήσει, *syncopated form of* ἀνα-βήσει, *fut. of* ἀνα-βαίνω.

ἀ-μέγαρτος, -ον, unenviable, *hence* direful.

ἀμείβω, exchange, hand on ; *mid.*, answer, 1196.

ἀμείνων, -ον, *comp. of* ἀγαθός.

ἀμέρα, *Dor. for* ἡμέρα.

ἀμέρδω, -σω, deprive, rob.

ἀ-μέτρητος, -ον, measureless, numberless.

ἀ-μήχανος, -ον, inconceivable.

ἄμιλλα, *f.*, contest, conflict.

ἀμιλλάομαι, contend, strive.

ἀμμένει ἀναμένει.

ἄμ-μορος, -ον, without share in.

ἄ-μορφος, -ον, unsightly.

ἀμ-πτάμενος, *syncopated form of* ἀνα-πτάμενος, *aor. of* ἀνα-πέτομαι.

ἄμπυξ, -ῦκος, *c.*, headband, snood.

ἀμύνω, -νῶ, ἤμυνα, ward off, *hence* (*with dat.*), defend, help.

ἀμφί, *prep. with acc.*, round, near, beside ; concerning ; *with gen.*, about, concerning.

ἀμφι-κρύπτω, hide on every side, surround.

ἀμφι-πίπτω (*tenses like* πίπτω), fall around.

ἀμφί-πῦρος, -ον, blazing all round.

ἀμφι-τίθημι (*tenses like* τίθημι), put around, wrap round.

ἀμφί-χρῦσος, -ον, gilded all over.

ἄν Particle ; *w. vbs.*, conditional ; *w. pronouns, etc.*, indef.

ἄν, Dor. for ἦν = ἐάν.

ἀν' = ἀνά.

ἄν (*Dor.*) = ἦν.

ἀνά, *prep. with acc.*, through, throughout.

ἀνα-βαίνω (*tenses like* βαίνω), climb up.

ἀνάγκᾱ (*Dor.*) = ἀνάγκη.

ἀναγκάζω, compel, constrain.

ἀναγκαῖος, -ον, necessary ; τὸ ἀ., necessity.

ἀνάγκη, *f.*, necessity ; ties of relationship ; ἀν. (ἐστι), it is necessary.

ἀνά-δετος, -ον, binding up (*the hair*).

ἀν-αθρέω, *aor.* ἀνήθρησα, gaze upon, behold.

ἀνα-μένω, await.

ἄν-ανδρος, -ον, husbandless.

ἄναξ, -κτος, *m.*, king, lord.

ἀνα-πέτομαι, -πτήσομαι, -επτάμην (-επτόμην), fly up.

ἀναρπαστάν, *Dor. for* -τήν.

ἀν-αρπαστός, -ή, -όν, dragged (*torn*) away.

ἀνα-ρ-ρήγνυμι, -ρήξω, break through.

ἀν-αρχία, *f.*, lawlessness.

ἄνασσα, *f.*, queen, lady.

ἀνα-στένω, groan aloud, bewail.

ἀνδρο-φόνος, -ον, man-slaying, murderous.

ἀν-εκτός, -όν, endurable ; οὐκ ἀ., unendurable.

ἀν-έρχομαι (tenses as ἔρχομαι), go or come up.

ἀν-έσχον, aor. of ἀνέχω.

ἀν-έχω (tenses as ἔχω), hold up, maintain, uplift, 459 ; ἀνέχων λέκτρα, ever holding in honour, 123.

ἀν-ήμερος, -ον, wild, cruel.

ἀνήρ, ἀνδρός, m., man (esp. as opp. to woman), hero, warrior.

ἀνθ' = ἀντί.

ἀνθ-αιρέομαι (tenses like αἱρέομαι), dispute, lay claim to.

ἀνθ-άπτομαι, grasp in turn, with gen.

ἀνθέω, ἤνθουν, flourish, prosper.

ἀνθό-κροκος, -ον, flower-bespangled.

ἄνθρωπος, m., man (esp. as opp. to animals) ; pl., men=mankind.

ἀνθρωπο-σφαγέω, slay human being.

ἀν-ίστημι (tenses like ἵστημι), set up ; intrans., be destroyed, 494, note ; mid., ἀνίστασο, rise.

ἄ-νοια, f., folly.

ἀν-οίκτως, adv., without pity.

ἀν-όνητα, adv., to no purpose.

ἀν-όσιος, -ον, unholy.

ἀντ-ακούω, hear in turn.

ἀντ-απο-κτείνω, kill in return, in revenge.

ἀντί, prep. with gen., instead of, in place of ; ἀνθ' ὅτου, wherefore, for what reason.

ἀντι-δίδωμι, give in return.

ἀντί-ποινα, -ων, pl. (ποινή), retribution.

ἀντι-σηκόω, lit. weigh over against, hence compensate for, 57, note.

ἄντλος, m., bilge-water, sea, 1025, note.

ἀν-υμέναιος, -ον, without bridal song, i.e., unwedded.

ἄ-νυμφος, -ον, unwedded.

ἀνύτω and ἀνύω, -σω, effect, accomplish.

ἄνω, adv., up, upwards, on high ; τοὺς ἄ., (gods) above, 791.

ἀν-ωνόμαστος, -ον, nameless, indescribable.

ἀξία, f., worth, desert.

ἄξιος, -α, -ον, worthy, worth ; οὐ γὰρ ἄξιον (408), it is not meet.

ἀξιόω, deem worthy, honour ; perf. pass. ἠξίωμαι.

ἀξίωμα, -ατος, n. that of which one is thought worthy, reputation.

ἀξίως, worthily.

ἄξω, from ἄισσω.

ἀπ-αγγέλλω, bring back word, report, announce.

ἀπ-άγω, carry away, bear back.

ἄ-παις, -δος, adj., childless.

ἀπ-αιτέω, ask back, ask in return.

ἀπ-αλλάσσω, put or take away.

ἀ-πάρθενος, -ον, adj., not a maiden.

ἀπᾶς, ἄπασα, ἄπαν, all, whole.

ἀπ-ειμι (see εἶμι), go away, depart.

ἀπ-ειμι (see εἰμί), be away, be distant.

ἀπ-εῖπον, aor. forbid, renounce ; give in, 942.

ἀπ-ελαύνω (tenses like ἐλαύνω), drive away.

Ἀπιδανός, river in Thessaly, 454.

ἀ-πιστέω, mistrust.

ἄ-πιστος, -ον, incredible.

ἀπό prep. with gen., from ; after case μητρὸς ἁρπασθεῖσ' ἄπο, 513.

ἀπο-βαίνω (tenses as βαίνω), go away from, depart from.

ἀπό-βλεπτος, -ον, gazed upon, admired. *See note*, 355.

ἀπο-κείρω, -κερῶ, -κέκαρμαι, shear off.

ἀπο-κουφίζω, lighten.

ἀπο-κτείνω (*tenses as* κτείνω), slay, kill.

ἀ-πόλεμος, -ον, unwarlike.

ἄ-πολις, -ι, *adj.*, without city or state, cityless.

ἀπ-όλλυμι (*tenses as* ὄλλυμι), ruin, destroy, kill; *mid.*, be undone, perish.

ἀπο-ξενόω, drive into exile.

ἀπο-πέμπω, send away; avert; *mid.*, send away from myself, hence abhor, shrink from.

ἀπο-πτύω, spit away, hence loathe, spurn.

ἀ-πόρθητος, -ον, unsacked.

ἀπο-σκοπέω, gaze at.

ἀπο-σπάω, -σπάσω, -έσπασα, -εσπάσθην, tear (drag) away.

ἀπο-σταθείς. *See* ἀφ-ίστημι.

ἀπο-στέλλω, send off.

ἀπο-στη-. *See* ἀφ-ίστημι.

ἀπ-ουσία, *f.*, absence.

ἅπτω, ἅψω, ἧψα, *mid.* ἅψομαι, ἡψάμην, take hold of, touch; grasp with the mind (*with gen.*), 675.

ἀπύσω, Dor. for ἠπύσω.

ἀπ-ωθέω, thrust away, reject; *mid.*, abandon, 1242.

ἀπ-ωλ-. *See* ἀπ-όλλυμι.

ἀπ-ωσ-. *See* ἀπ-ωθέω.

ἄρα, *particle*, so then, perhaps, after all.

ἆρα. *Interrog. particle.*

ἀράμενος, *from* αἴρω.

ἀράσσω, smite.

Ἀργεῖος, -α, -ον, man of Argos, hence Argive, Greek.

Ἄργος, -ους, *n.* town in Peloponnesus.

ἄργυρος, *m.*, silver.

ἄρδην, *adv.* (αἴρω), wholly, altogether.

ἄρειαν. *See* αἴρω.

Ἄρης, -εος, *m.*, Ares.

ἄρθρον, *n.*, joint, limb.

ἀριθμός, *m.*, number.

ἀριστερός, -όν, on left hand.

ἄριστος, -η, -ον, best, bravest; *used as superl. of* ἀγαθός.

ἀρκέω, -έσω, ἤρκεσα, ward off defend.

ἀρκούντως, sufficiently.

ἅρμα, -ατος, *n.*, chariot.

ἀρνέομαι, deny.

ἄρνυμαι (*only in pres. in imperf.*), win for myself.

ἁρπάζω, -σω (*and* -ξω), ἡρπάσθην, snatch, seize.

ἄρρητος, -ον, unspeakable, unutterable, horrible.

ἄρσην, -ενος, *adj.*, male.

Ἄρτεμις, -ιδος, *f.*, huntress goddess, daughter of Zeus and Leto, born and worshipped at Delos with Apollo.

ἀρτι-μαθής, -ές, having just learnt.

ἀρτίως, *adv.*, recently, just now.

ἀρχαῖος, -α, -ον, ancient, venerable.

ἄρχω, ἄρξω, ἦρξα, rule (*with gen.*); *mid.*, begin.

ἀ-σθενής, -ές, *adj.*, weak.

Ἀσία, Asia; generally restricted to Asia Minor.

ἄσπασμα, -ατος, *n.*, embrace.

ἀ-στένακτος, -ον, without a groan.

ἄστυ, -εος, *n.*, town.

ἀ-σφαλής, -ές, safe, secure; ἐν ἀσφαλεῖ, in safety, 981.

ἀ-σφαλῶς, safely.

ἀ-σχημονέω, be put to shame (ἀσχήμων, unseemly).

ἀτάρ, but, yet.

ἄ-ταφος, -ον, unburied.

ἄ-τεκνος, -ον, childless.

ἄτερ, prep. with gen., without.

ἀ-τέρμων, -ονος, adj., boundless.

ἄτη, f., ruin, destruction.

'Ατρείδης, -ον, m., son of Atreus.

αὖ, again, on the other hand.

αὐγάζω (αὐγή), shine upon.

αὐγή, f., beam.

αὐδάν, Dor. for αὐδήν.

αὐδάω, speak, utter.

αὐδή, f., voice.

αὐθ'=αὐτά, 1227.

αὖθις, again, back again.

αὐλή, f., courtyard, palace.

αὔξομαι, αὐξήσομαι, ηὐξήθην, grow.

αὔρα, f., breeze.

ἀϋτέω, utter, shout.

αὐτίκα, forthwith, immediately.

αὐτός, -ή, -ό, self, him-, her-,
itself, themselves ; in oblique
cases him, her, it, etc. ; ὁ αὐτός,
the same.

αὐτός=ὁ αὐτός (crasis).

αὐτοῦ, adv., there, here.

αὐτοῦ=ἑαυτοῦ.

αὐχήν, -ένος, m., neck, throat.

ἀφ-αιρέω (tenses as αἱρέω), take
away from (with double acc.),
285.

ἀφ-ειλόμην, from ἀφ-αιρέω.

ἀφ-εῖμαι, from ἀφ-ίημι.

ἀφ-έλκω (tenses as ἕλκω), drag
away.

ἀφ-ίημι (tenses as ἵημι), send
forth ; cast or fling forth ;
πνεῦμα, give up ghost, die, 571 ;
leave, 117 ; give up, resign,
367 ; release, 1292.

ἀφ-ικνέομαι (tenses as ἱκνέομαι),
come, arrive at.

ἀφ-ίστημι (tenses as ἵστημι), put

away, remove ; in intrans.
tenses and mid., keep away
from, 980 ; stand away from,
807 ; get out of way of (with
dat.), 1054.

ἀφ-ορμή, f., starting-point,
occasion.

'Αχαιϊκός, -ή, -όν, Achaean.

'Αχαιοί, Achaeans, i.e., Greeks.

ἀχάριστος, -ον, thankless.

ἀχθεινός, -ή, -όν, burdensome,
troublesome.

'Αχιλεύς ('Αχιλλεύς), -έως, m.,
Achilles, son of Peleus and
Thetis, chief warrior of Greeks
at Troy.

'Αχίλλειος, -ον, of Achilles.

ἄχος, -ους, n., grief, woe.

ἄ-ωρος, -ον, untimely, 425.

ἀχώ, f., Dor.=ἠχώ.

βαίνω, βήσομαι, ἔβην, βέβηκα, walk,
advance.

βάκτρον, n., staff.

βακχεῖος, -α, -ον, Bacchic,
frenzied.

βάκχη, f., frenzied devotee of
Bacchus ; prophetess (used
of Cassandra), 123.

βαλιός, -ά, -όν, dappled.

βάλλω, βαλῶ, ἔβαλον, βέβλημαι,
ἐβλήθην, throw, cast, hurl,
shoot ; 574, bestrew.

βάπτω, dip.

βάρβαρος, -ον, adj., not Greek,
foreign, hence wild, savage ;
τὸ βάρβαρον, 1129, note ; subst.,
foreigner, barbarian, 328.

βάρος, -ους, n., weight, load.

βαρύς, -εῖα, -ύ, adj., heavy,
grievous, cruel.

βασιλεύς, -έως, m., king.

βασιλίς, -ίδος, f., queen, princess.

βάσις, -εως, f., stepping, step.

βέλος, -ους, n., shaft, blow, 1041, note.

βία, f., violence, force; πρὸς βίαν, βίᾳ, by force.

βίαιος, -α, -ον, forced, compulsory.

βίος, m., life, livelihood, sustenance.

βιοτή, f., life.

βλάπτω, harm, injure.

βλάστημα, -ατος, n., sprout, crop.

βλέπω, see, behold, 585 ; with or without φῶς, see light of day, be alive.

βλέφᾰρον, n., eyelid.

βλώ-σκω, μολοῦμαι, ἔμολον, μέμβλωκα, come, go.

βοάω, -ήσω, cry out.

βοή, f., loud cry.

βου-θυτέω, sacrifice oxen.

βούλευμα, -ατος, n., purpose, plan.

βουλεύω, plot, plan.

βούλομαι, -ήσομαι, βεβούλημαι, ἐβουλήθην, wish, desire, be willing.

βούτης, -ου, m., herdsman.

βραδύ-πους, -ποδος, adj., slow-footed.

βραδύς, -εῖα, -ύ, adj., slow.

βραχίων, -ονος, m., arm.

βροτός, -οῦ, m., mortal.

βωμός, -οῦ, m., altar.

γαῖα, f., land, ground, earth.

γαληνός, -όν, adj., gentle, calm.

γάμος, m., marriage (often in pl.).

γάρ, for.

γε, particle, enclitic, at least, surely ; sometimes equivalent to yes. See notes on 246, etc.

γέγηθα. See γηθέω.

γεγώς, γεγῶσα, γεγώς, perf. part. of γίγνομαι.

γείτων, -ονος, c., neighbour.

γενεά, f., race.

γενειάς, -άδος, f., beard.

γένειον, n., chin.

γέννα, -ης, f., child, offspring.

γενναῖος, -α, -ον, noble.

γένος, -ους, n., race, kind, stock.

γένυς, -υος, f., cheek.

γεραιός, -ά, -όν, aged ; subst., γεραιά, an old woman, 389.

γέρας, -ως, n., gift, gift of honour.

γέρων, -οντος, adj., aged, old ; subst., old man.

γεύομαι, taste, experience (with gen.).

γῆ, f., earth, land, country.

γηθέω, -ήσω, ἐγήθησα, γέγηθα, rejoice.

γηραιός, -ά, -όν, aged ; γηραιά, old woman.

γῆρας, -ως, n., old age.

γι-γνώ-σκω, γνώσομαι, ἔγνων, ἔγνωκα, -σμαι, learn, ascertain ; hence know, recognise.

γί-γν-ομαι, γενήσομαι, ἐγενόμην, γέγονα, γεγένημαι, ἐγενήθην, become, turn out, happen.

γλῶσσα, f., tongue.

γνώμη, f., will, purpose, judg-ment; κατὰ γνώμην, 867.

γοερός, -ά, -όν, wailing, mournful.

γόνος, m., child.

γόνυ, -ατος, n., knee.

γόος, m., wailing, lamentation.

γουνάτων = γονάτων.

γραῖα, f., old woman.

γραῖος, -α, -ον, old, aged.

γραῦς, γρᾱός, f., old woman.

γραφεύς, -έως, m., painter.

γραφή, f., writing; νόμων γραφαί, written laws, 866.

γύης, -ου, m., piece of land.

γυμνός, -ή, -όν, naked ; γυμνὸν τιθέναι, strip (of arms).

γυμνόω, strip naked.

γυνή, -αικός, *f.*, woman; lady (*used as title of respect*).

'γω=ἐγώ (*prodelision*).

δαιδάλεος, -ον, cunningly wrought.

Δαίδαλος, *m.*, mythical artist of Crete, 838, *note*.

δαίμων, -ονος, *m.* and *f.*, deity, god, goddess.

δαί-νῡμι, δαίσω, ἔδαισα, feast; *mid.*, feast upon.

δαίς, δαιτός, *f.*, feast.

δάκρυ, *n.*, tear.

δάκρυον, *n.*, tear.

δακρύω, weep.

δάμαρ, -αρτος, *f.*, spouse, wife.

Δαναΐδαι, *m.*, descendants of Danaus, Greeks.

Δαναοί, -ῶν, *m.*, name used for Greeks.

δᾱρόν (*Dor.*)=δηρόν, *adv.*, long, for long time.

δάφνη, *f.*, laurel- *or* bay-tree.

δάω, obsolete present. *See* ἐδάην.

δέ, *particle*, but. *Often answers* μέν, *but also merely connects sentences*.

δεῖ, δεήσει, it is necessary; needful; ὧν σε δεῖ, which you need, 1021.

δείδω, δείσω, ἔδεισα, δέδοικα (δέδια), fear, dread.

δείκ-νῡμι, δείξω, show, point out.

δείλαιος, -α, -ον, miserable, wretched.

δεῖμα, -ατος, *n.*, terror, horror.

δειμαίνω, fear, dread.

δεινός, -ή, -όν, dreadful; *also* wonderful, strange.

δεῖπνον, *n.*, meal, banquet.

δειρή, *f.*, neck.

δέμας (*only in nom. and acc. sing.*), *n.*, body, form.

δεξιός, -ά, -όν, right, on right; δεξιά, *subst.*, right hand.

δέπας, -αος, *n.*, cup, goblet.

δέργμα, -ατος, *n.*, look, glance.

δέρη (=δειρή), *f.*, neck, throat.

δέρκομαι, -ξομαι, ἔδρακον, δέδορκα, behold.

δέσποινα, *f.*, lady, mistress.

δεσπόσυνος, -ον, of our masters.

δεσπότης, -ου, *m.*, master, lord.

δεῦρο, *adv.*, hither.

δεύτερον, *adv.*, in next place.

δέχομαι, δέξομαι, δέδεγμαι, ἐδέχθην, receive, accept, listen to.

δή, *particle*, in truth, indeed; ποῖ δή, whither then? τί δή, pray what?

δηκ-τήριος, -ον, biting (*with gen.*) (δάκνω, bite).

Δηλιάς, -άδος, *f.*, *adj.*, Delian, of Delos (sacred isle in Aegean).

δημ-ηγόρος, -ον, *adj.*, addressing the people; δημηγόρους τιμάς (254), a speaker's honours.

δημο-χαρίστης, -ον, *m.*, one who seeks to please the people.

δήποτε, lately.

δῆτα, *adv.*, surely, indeed; οὐ δῆτα, no indeed! forsooth, *in irony*, 623; *in question*, 247.

Δία, *from* Ζεύς.

διά, *prep.* (*with gen.*, through; *with acc.*, on account of); *of time*, διὰ μακροῦ, long-lasting, 320; by means of, 442, 1004; διὰ χερός, 673; διὰ τέλους, continually, throughout; δι' οἴκτου ἔχειν, 851.

δια-βάλλω (*tenses as* βάλλω), slander, speak evil of.

δια-δοχή, *f.*, succession.

διά-δοχος, -ον, *adj.*, bringing succession. *See note*. 588.

δί-αιμος, -ον, *adj.*, bloody (αἷμα), 656, *note*.

δια-κωλύω, hinder.

δια-μοιράω, -άσω, tear limb from limb.

δια-ρ-ροή, f., pipe, channel, 567; πνεύματος δ. = windpipe.

δια-σπάω, -σπάσω, tear in pieces.

δια-τέμνω, cut in pieces; aor. διέτεμον.

δί-αυλος, ό, double course, note, 29.

δια-φέρω (tenses as φέρω), make difference, 599.

δια-φθείρω (tenses as φθείρω), destroy, corrupt, 598.

δίδαξις, -εως, f., teaching.

δι-δά-σκω, -ξω, εδίδαξα, teach, inform; δίδαξον τοῦτο, tell me this; διδάσκου, be advised.

δί-δω-μι, δώσω, ἔδωκα, δέδωκα, ἐδόθην, give, grant, bring forth, give up, etc.; δίκην δ., pay penalty.

δι-εργάζομαι, destroy, kill.

δι-ερείδομαι, mid., lean upon.

δίκαιος, -α, -ον, just, fair, right; τὸ δίκαιον, justice.

δικαίως, justly.

δίκη, f., justice, law, right, just penalty; δ. διδόναι (ὑπέχειν), pay penalty, 803, etc.; πολεμίων δίκην, like enemies, 1162.

δι-όλλυμι, destroy utterly.

Διόνυσος, m., Dionysus, Bacchus.

δι-ορίζω, mark off, define, determine.

Διός, from Ζεύς.

δῖος, -α, -ον, divine.

Διόσ-κοροι, Castor and Polydeuces, sons of Zeus and Leda, and brothers of Helen.

διπλοῦς, -ῆ, -οῦν, adj., twofold, double.

δί-πτυχος, -ον, twofold; pl., two, 1287.

δίς, twice.

δισσός, -ή, -όν, twofold.

δίχα, asunder.

διώκω, pursue.

δι-ώλεσα. See δι-όλλυμι.

δμωίς, -ίδος, f., female slave.

δμώς, -ωός, m., slave.

δοκέω (tenses formed from δοκ-), think, deem, suppose; with inf., seem, appear; πῶς δοκεῖς 1160, note; impersonal δοκεῖ, it seems, seems good; ἔδοξε, it was determined; οἱ δοκοῦντες, men of repute, 295.

δόλος, m., craft, treachery.

δόμος, m., house, dwelling, home.

δόξα, f., opinion.

δοξάζω, suppose.

δορι-θήρᾱτος, -ον, captured by spear.

δορί-κτητος, -ον, won by spear.

δόρυ, -ατος, n., spear.

δουλεία, f., slavery.

δούλειος, -α, -ον, of slaves, of slavery.

δουλεύω, be a slave.

δούλη, f., female slave.

δοῦλος, m., slave; adj. = δούλειος; τὸ δοῦλον, slavery, 332.

δουλόσυνος, -ον, enslaved.

δράω, δράσω, ἔδρασα (ἔδρᾱν), δέδρᾱκα, do, accomplish; καλῶς δ., benefit.

δρύπτω, tear; mid., tear (oneself), 655.

δρῦς, δρυός, f., oak.

δύναμαι, -ήσομαι, ἐδυνήθην, am able, can.

δύναμις, -εως, f., power, strength.

δύο, two.

δύρομαι = ὀδύρομαι, lament.

δυσ-μαχος, -ον, hard to fight against, irresistible.

δυσ-μενής, -ές, hostile; τὸ δυσμενές, hostility, 745.

δύσ-νοια, f., ill-will, dislike.

δύσ-τᾰνος, Dor. for δύστηνος.

δύσ-τηνος, -ον, wretched, unhappy.

δυσ-τυχέω, to be unfortunate.

δυσ-τυχής, -ές, unfortunate.

δυσ-φημέω, use words of evil omen (with acc. of person addressed), 182.

δύσ-φημος, -ον, ill-omened.

δύσ-φορος, -ον, hard to bear.

δυσ-χλαινία, f., mean clothing (χλαῖνα=cloak).

δῶμα, -ατος, n., house, hall, home; often in pl.

δωρέομαι, give, present.

Δωρίς, -ίδος, f. adj., Dorian.

ἔα, interj., ha!

ἐᾷ, from ἐάω.

ἐάν, conj.=εἰ ἄν, if, with subj.; ἐὰν μή, except.

ἑαυτόν, -ήν, pron. refl., him-, herself.

ἐάω, -άσω, allow, let be.

ἐγγύς, adv., near.

ἐγ-κλήω, shut up.

ἐγ-κλίνω, turn.

ἐγ-κονέω, hasten.

ἔγχος, -ους, n., sword.

ἐγώ, pron., I.

ἐδάην, I understand. See δάω.

ἔζη, from ζάω.

ἐθέλω, -ήσω, be willing, wish.

ἐθρέφθην, ἔθρεψα, from τρέφω.

εἰ, conj., if, with ind. and opt.; oh that! (with opt.), 836, whether, 988, 992; καὶ εἰ, 318, even if.

εἰδείην, εἰδέναι, from οἶδα.

εἶδον, used as aor. of ὁράω.

εἶδος, -ους, n., form.

εἴδωλον, n., phantom.

εἶεν, adv., well then!

εἴθε, oh that!

εἰκότως, adv. of εἰκώς, perf. part. of ἔοικα, in seemly way.

εἰλάτινος, -η, -ον, adj., of pine or fir.

εἶλον. See αἱρέω.

εἷμα, -ατος, n., cloak.

εἶμι, imperf. ᾖα, I will go; in other moods than the ind. has pres. force, come, go, etc.

εἰμί, ἔσομαι, ἦν, I am; impers. ἐστι(ν), it is allowed, 234; I live, 284, etc.

εἶπα, aor. See εἶπον.

εἴπερ, if indeed.

εἶπον, used as aor. of ἀγορεύω or φημί, say, speak.

εἴργω, εἴρξω, εἶρξα, prevent, restrain.

εἴρηκα, εἴρημαι, εἰρήσομαι, perf. and fut. tenses of εἴρω, speak, say, tell, etc.

εἰς (ἐς), prep. with acc., into, against, to, towards.

εἷς, μία, ἕν, one.

εἰσ'=εἰσί, from εἰμί.

εἰσ-άγω, lead into.

εἰσ-ακούω, hear.

εἰσ-εῖδον, used as aor. of following: εἰσ-οράω, look upon, behold.

εἶτ'=εἶτα.

εἶτα, then.

εἴ-τε, generally doubled, εἴτε . . . εἴτε, whether . . . or.

εἶχον. See ἔχω.

εἴωθα, perf. from unused ἔθω), am accustomed; part., familiar.

ἐκ (ἐξ), prep. with gen., out of, from; (agent) by, at hands of. ἐξ ἀριστερᾶς, on left hand; ἐκ δείπνων, after supper.

Ἑκάβη, f., Hecuba.

ἕκαστος, -η, -ον, each.

ἑκᾱτι, adv., for the sake of (with gen.).

ἐκ-βάλλω, cast forth; shed tear, 298 ; burst or break out, 1044.

ἐκ-βλητος, -ον, cast up.

ἐκ-βολή, f., that which is cast forth.

ἐκ-γονος, m., child.

ἐκεῖ, there.

ἐκειθ' = ἐκειτο.

ἐκεῖθεν, from thence.

ἐκεῖνος, -η, -ο, that, he, she, it.

ἐκεῖσε, thither.

ἐκ-κρῐτος, -ον, picked out, chosen.

ἐκ-λογίζομαι, reckon, consider.

ἐκ-παγλέομαι, wonder at, admire, 1157.

ἐκ-πέμπω, send out, send out from.

ἐκ-πηδάω, bound forth.

ἐκ-πίμ-πλη-μι, -πλήσω, etc., fill ; βίον, live out life.

ἐκ-πίπτω, fall out from, lose (with gen.).

ἐκ-ποδών, adv., out of the way.

ἐκ-πράττω, kill, 515.

ἐκ-πρεπής, -ές, pre-eminent.

ἐκ-πτήσσω (aor. ἐξ-ἐπτηξα), scare out of.

ἐκ-τείνω, aor. ἐξ-ἐτεινα, stretch out.

ἐκ-τήκω, trans., melt ; perf. intr. ἐκτέτηκα, pine away.

Ἕκτωρ, -ορος, m., son of Priam ; chief warrior of Troy.

ἐκ-φέρω, cast up, bring out.

ἐκ-φθείρω, utterly destroy.

ἑκών, -οῦσα, -όν, adj., willing, willingly.

ἐλάσσων, used as comp. of μικρός, less.

ἔλαφος, f., hind.

Ἑλένη, Helen, daughter of Zeus and Leda, wife of Menelaus, king of Sparta. Being carried off by Paris she caused the Trojan War.

Ἕλενος, Helenus, son of Priam, a seer.

ἐλεύθερος, -α, -ον, free.

ἑλκόω, wound.

ἕλκω, ἕλξω, εἵλκυσα, drag, drag away.

Ἑλλάς, -άδος, adj., Hellenic, Greek ; subst., Hellas, Greece.

Ἕλλην, -ηνος, adj., Hellenic, Greek ; subst., a Hellene, Greek. Ἑλληνίς, -ίδος, f., adj.

Ἑλληνικός, -ή, -όν, Hellenic, Greek.

ἐλπίζω (aor. opt. -σαιμι), hope.

ἐλπίς, -ίδος, f., hope, expectation.

ἐμᾶς, Dor. for ἐμῆς.

ἐμ-αυτόν, -ήν, refl. pron., myself.

ἐμ-βαίνω, go into, enter.

ἐμ-βατεύω, enter, set foot in.

ἐμ-βεβώς, perf. part. of ἐμβαίνω.

ἔμολον. See βλώσκω.

ἐμός, -ή, -όν, adj., my, mine.

ἔμ-παλιν, adv., backwards, away, 343 ; τὸ ἔμπαλιν, the contrary, 789.

ἐμ-πίμπλημι, -πλήσω, fill, glut ; aor. pass. ἐνεπλήσθην.

ἐμ-πίπτω (tenses as πίπτω), fall upon (with dat.).

ἐμ-πλησθῶ. See ἐμ-πίμπλημι.

ἐμ-ποδών, in the way (with dat.).

ἐν, prep with dat., in, among. ἐν Ἅιδου, 418.

ἐν, from εἰς.

ἐν-άλιος, -α, -ον, sea-dipped.

ἐναντίον, adv., opposite, in face.

ἐνδεής, -ές, lacking in (with gen.).

ἐν-δίδωμι, afford, supply.

ἐνδίκως, rightly, justly.

ἔνδον, adv., within.

ἐνεγκ-. *See* φέρω.

ἕνεκα, *adv.*, for the sake of (*with gen.*).

ἔνθα, *adv.*, there, where.

ἐνθάδε, *adv.*, thither, there.

ἔνθεν, *adv.*, thence, on the other side.

ἐνθένδε, *adv.*, hence ; τὸ ἐνθένδε, from henceforth.

ἐν-θνῄσκω (*aor.* ἐν-θανεῖν), die away, grow numb in.

ἕν-νυχος, -ον, by night, nightly.

ἔν-οπλος, -ον, in arms, armed.

ἔν-οπτρον, mirror.

ἐνταῦθα, *adv.*, there, thereupon.

ἐν-τίθημι, put in.

ἐντός, within.

ἐν-τυγχάνω (*aor. part.* ἐντυχών), light upon.

ἔν-υπνος, -ον, *adj.*, in sleep.

ἐξ-αίρω (*aor. part.* ἐξ-άρας), raise aloft.

ἐξ-αιτέομαι (*aor.* ἐξῃτησάμην), demand.

ἐξ-αλείφω, smear out, wipe out.

ἐξ-αλλάσσω, take in exchange, take in turn.

ἐξ-αλύσκω, -ύξω, ἐξ-ήλυξα, flee, escape.

ἐξ-αν-ίστημι, raise, lift up, 1165.

ἐξ-απ-αλλάσσω, set free from, rid of.

ἐξ-άρασα. *See* ἐξ-αίρω.

ἐξ-αυδάω, speak out.

ἐξ-εῖλκον. *See* ἐξ-έλκω.

ἐξ-ειργασάμην. *See* ἐξ-εργάζομαι.

ἐξ-έλκω, *imperf.* -εῖλκον, draw forth.

ἐξ-έπτᾱξας. *See* ἐκ-πτήσσω.

ἐξ-εργάζομαι, wreak, accomplish.

ἐξ-έρχομαι, come out.

ἔξ-εστι(ν), *impers.*, it is lawful.

ἐξ-ευρίσκω, find out.

ἐξ-έφθαρμαι. *See* ἐκ-φθείρω.

ἐξ-ήλυξα. *See* ἐξ-αλύσκω.

ἐξ-ηνεγκ-. *See* ἐκ-φέρω.

ἐξ-ῃτησάμην. *See* ἐξ-αιτέω.

ἐξ-ιστορέω, question, investigate.

ἐξ-οικίζω, ἐξ-ῴκισα, exile ; depopulate

ἔξω. *See* ἔχω.

ἔξω, *adv.*, outside, without (*with gen.*).

ἐξ-ῴκισα. *See* ἐξ-οικίζω.

ἔοικα, *part.* εἰκώς, *perf. with pres. meaning*, seem, seem likely ; *impers.* ἔοικε, it seems.

ἔοιχ' = ἔοικε.

ἐπ-άγω, bring to ; induce (260).

ἐπ-αίρω, raise.

ἐπ-άσσω, ἐπῇξα, rush.

ἐπ-άρκεσις, -εως, *f.*, aid, succour.

ἐπ-αρκέω, -έσω, help, aid (*with dat.*).

ἐπ-αρωγός, *m.*, helper, aider.

ἐπ-έζεσα. *See* ἐπιζέω.

ἐπεί, *of time*, when, since ; *causal*, since, seeing that ; *as connective*, for, 1208.

ἐπειδ-άν, *conj.*, whenever (*with subj.*).

ἐπει-δή, *conj.*, when, seeing that.

ἐπ-εῖδον, *used as aor. of* ἐφοράω.

ἔπ-ειμι, be over, superintend.

ἐπεί-περ, *conj.*, seeing that.

ἐπ-εισ-πίπτω (*aor. subj.* -πέσω), rush in.

ἔπειτα, *adv.*, thereupon, then.

ἐπ-ερείδω, press. *See* 112, *note*.

ἐπ-ερρόθουν. *See* ἐπιρροθέω.

ἐπ-έστην. *See* ἐφ-ίστημι.

ἐπ-εύχομαι (*aor.* -ηυξάμην), join in prayer, 542.

ἐπ-έχω (*tenses like* ἔχω), stay, stop, delay.

ἐπ-ήγαγον. *See* ἐπ-άγω.

ἐπί, *prep. with* 3 *cases ; with acc.*,
against, over, to, with regard
to, for ; *with dat.*, on, at, by ;
for, 648 ; *with gen.*, upon.

ἐπι-βαίνω, mount upon (*with gen.*).

ἐπ-ιδεῖν. *See* ἐφ-οράω.

ἐπι-δέμνιος, -ον, on a bed, 927.

ἐπι-ζέω, -ζέσω, -έζεσα, boil *or*
surge up.

ἐπι-κουρία, *f.*, aid.

ἐπι-λανθάνομαι *or* ἐπι-λήθομαι,
-λήσομαι, forget (*with gen.*).

ἐπι-ρ-ροθέω, applaud loudly.

ἐπί-σημος, -ον, remarkable, well
marked.

ἐπι-σκήπτω, urge.

ἐπι-σκοπέω, -σκέψομαι, supervise,
watch.

ἐπίσταμαι, -στήσομαι, know.

ἐπι-στάτης, -ου, *m.*, overseer.

ἐπι-σφάζω, -άξω, slay at.

ἐπι-σχ-. *See* ἐπ-έχω.

ἐπι-τίμια, -ων, *n. pl.*, recom-
pense, requital.

ἐπί-φθονος, -ον, open to hatred.

ἐπ-οικτείρω, ἐπῴκτειρα, pity.

ἕπομαι, ἕψομαι, ἑσπόμην, follow,
pursue (*with dat.*).

ἔπος, -ους, *n.*, word.

ἐπ-ῳδός, -όν, called after, 1272,
note.

ἐπ-ωμίς, -ίδος, *f.*, shoulder strap
of tunic, 558, *note.*

ἔραμαι, ἐρασθήσομαι, ἠράσθην, love,
long for.

ἐράω, *only in pres. and imperf.*,
love, long for ; covet (*with
gen.*), 996.

ἐργάζομαι, do, perform, accomplish ; *perf. pass. or depon.*
εἴργασμαι.

ἔργον, *n.*, deed.

ἐρευνάω, search.

ἐρημία, *f.*, solitude, solitary place,

981 ; (*with gen.*), absence,
1017. ·

ἔρημος, -ον, lonely, desolate.

ἐρημόω, abandon, quit.

ἐρήσομαι. *See* ἔρομαι.

ἔρις, -ιδος, *f.*, strife, contest.

ἔρομαι, -ήσομαι, ask.

ἕρπω, *lit.*, creep, *hence* come, go.

ἔρρεον, *imperf. of* ῥέω. (529,
note.)

ἔρχομαι, ἐλεύσομαι, ἦλθον, ἐλήλυθα,
come go.

ἐρῶ, *used as fut. of* φημί.

ἐρωτάω, ask.

ἐς, *short form of* εἰς.

ἐσεῖδον (*subj.* ἐσίδω), *aor. of* εἰσοράω.

ἐσήμηνα, 1*st. aor. of* σημαίνω.

ἐσθλός, -ή, -όν, noble, brave,
good, etc.

ἑσπόμην, *aor. of* ἕπομαι.

ἑστία, *f.*, hearth.

ἔσω, within.

ἐτάμετο, 2*nd aor. mid. of* τέμνω.

ἕτερος, -α, -ον, other (of two).

ἔτι, *adv.*, still ; *with neg.*, any
longer.

ἔτλης, 2*nd aor. of* τλάω.

ἕτοιμος, -η, -ον, ready.

εὖ, *adv.*, well.

εὐ-γένεια, *f.*, noble birth.

εὐ-δαίμων, -ονος, *adj.*, prosperous.

εὐ-δοξία, good repute.

εὕδω, -ήσω, sleep.

εὐθύνω, direct, rule.

εὐθύς, *adv.*, immediately.

εὔ-ιππος, -ον, well-horsed, war-
like.

εὐ-κάρδιος, -ον, stout of heart.

εὐ-καρδίως, *adv.*, with good heart.

εὐ-λογέω, speak well of, praise.

εὐ-μενής, -ές, well-disposed,
friendly.

εὐνή, f., couch, bed.
εὔ-παις, -παιδος, adj., blest with children.
εὐ-πραξία, f., prosperity.
εὐ-πρεπής, -ές, adj., beauteous.
εὕρημα, -ατος, n., invention.
εὑρίσκω, εὑρήσω, ηὗρον, ηὕρηκα, -μαι, ηὑρέθην, find, find out, discover.
εὔ-ροος, -ον, fair flowing, 650.
Εὐρώπη, f., Europe.
Εὐρώτᾱς, -ου, m., river of Sparta.
εὐ-σεβής, -ές, pious.
εὐ-σχήμως, adv., becomingly.
εὔ-τεκνος, -ον, blest with children.
εὐ-τρεπής, -ές, ready.
εὐ-τυχέω, prosper.
εὐ-τυχής, -ές, fortunate.
εὐ-φημέω, speak words of good omen.
εὐφρόνη, f., night.
ἐφ' = ἐπί.
ἐφ-εστάναι, perf. inf. of ἐφ-ίστημι.
ἐφ-ίημι (aor. inf. ἐφ-εῖναι), lay upon, 1128.
ἐφ-ίστημι, trans. tenses, put over ; intrans. tenses, stand over.
ἐφ-οράω, aor. ἐπ-εῖδον, look upon, behold.
ἔχηθ' = ἔχητε.
ἔχθιστος, superl. of ἐχθρός.
ἐχθρός, -ά, -όν, hated, hateful ; subst., enemy (private).
ἐχρῆν, imperf. of χρή.
ἐχρησε(ν), aor. of χράω.
ἔχω, ἕξω, σχήσω, ἔσχον, ἔσχηκα, trans., have, hold, stop ; with inf., have power to, be able ; intrans., σχές (963), hold ! forbear ! ὧδε ἔχει (1195), so the matter stands ; mid. ἔχομαι (with gen.), cling to.
ἕως, adv., so long as.

ζάω, ζῆς, etc., part. ζῶν, inf. ζῆν, live.
ζεύγ-νῦμι, ζεύξω, yoke.
Ζεύς, Διός, m., Zeus.
ζέω, ζέσω, boil.
ζῇ, ζῆν. See ζάω.
ζῆλος, m., rivalry.
ζηλόω, strive for.
ζητέω, seek.
ζόη, f., life (poetic form of ζωή).
ζυγόν (ζυγός), n., yoke.
ζωή, f., life.
ζώνη, f., girdle.

ἤ, interrogative particle.
ἤ, or, ἤ . . . ἤ, either . . . or.
ἡ, from ὁ, ἡ, τό.
ἥ, from ὅς, ἥ, ὅ.
ἡγεμών, -όνος, c., guide.
ἡγέομαι, -ήσομαι, ἥγημαι, think, consider ; with dat., lead.
ἠδέ, and.
ἥδε, from ὅδε, ἥδε, τόδε.
ἡδέως, adv., gladly.
ἤδη, adv., now, immediately, already.
ἡδύ-λογος, -ον, sweet-speaking, sweet-voiced.
ἡδύς, -εῖα, -ύ, sweet.
Ἠδωνός, -όν, Edonian. See 1153, note.
ἥκιστα, adv., least ; hence in an answer, by no means.
ἠκριβωκώς. See ἀκριβόω.
ἥκω, imperf. ἧκον, am come.
ἦλθον. See ἔρχομαι.
ἥλιος, m., sun.
ἥλυσις, f., going, gait.
ἦμαρ, -ατος, n., day.
ἡμέρα, f., day ; καθ' ἡμέραν, daily.
ἦμος, when, 915.
ἦν, imperf. of εἰμί.

ἥν = ἐάν.

ἥνεγκον, aor. of φέρω.

ἡνίκα, when, 239.

ἡπύω, say, utter.

ἡράσθην. See ἔραμαι.

ἦσμεν. See οἶδα.

ἡσσάομαι, be worsted.

ἧσσον, adv., less.

ἥσυχος, -ον, adj., calm, idle, silent.

ἥσω, fut. of ἵημι.

ἠχώ, -ους, f., sound, 156; Echo (personified).

θ' = τε.

θᾶκος, m., seat.

θάλαμος, m., bridal chamber.

θαλάσσιος, -α, -ον, of the sea.

θαλασσό-πλαγκτος, -ον, sea-tossed.

θάμβος, -ους, n., amazement.

θανάσιμος, -ον, deadly.

θάνατος, m., death.

θάπτω, bury.

θαρσέω, be of good courage.

θάρσος, -ους, n., confidence.

θάσσω (only pres.), sit.

θαῦμα, n., marvel.

θαυμάζω, intrans., wonder; trans., admire, honour.

θεά, f., goddess.

θεάομαι, -άσομαι, gaze at.

θεῖος, -α, -ον, inspired by god.

θέλω = ἐθέλω.

θεό-δμητος, -ον, god-built.

θεό-θεν, adv., from the gods.

θεός, m., a god; πρὸς θεῶν, by the gods.

θεράπαινα, f., handmaid.

θεράπνη (Dor. θεράπνα), f., dwelling. See note, 482.

θεσπι-ῳδός, -όν, chanting in prophetic strain, inspired.

Θέτις, -ιδος, f., daughter of sea-god Nēreus, wife of Pēleus, mother of Achilles.

θήκη, f., chest.

θῆλυς, -υ, (and -υς, -εια, -υ), female.

θήρ, θηρός, m., wild beast.

θησαυρός, m., treasure.

Θησείδης, -ου, m. Son of Athenian hero Theseus, 123, note.

θιγ-γάνω, θίξομαι, ἔθιγον, touch (with gen.).

θνῄσκω, θανοῦμαι, ἔθανον, τέ-θνηκα, die, be slain.

θνητός, -ή, -όν, mortal; subst., a mortal.

θοίνη, f., feast.

θοός, -ά, -όν, swift.

θόρυβος, m., noise, clamour.

θρασύνομαι, be over-bold or insolent.

θρασυ-στομέω, be bold (insolent) of tongue.

θρεφθῆναι, aor. inf. pass. of τρέφω.

Θρήκη, f., Thrace, mod. Bulgaria.

Θρήκιος, -α, -ον, Thracian.

Θρῇξ, Θρηκός, adj. and subst., Thracian.

θρηνέω, wail for, lament.

θρῆνος, m., lamentation, dirge.

θυγάτηρ, -τρός, f., daughter.

θῦμα, -ατος, n., sacrifice.

θῡμός, m., wrath.

θυμόομαι, am angry; τὸ θυμούμενον, wrath.

θυσία, f., sacrifice.

θυσιᾶν, Dor. gen. pl. of θυσία.

θωύσσω, cry out, shout.

Ἴδη, Dor. Ἴδᾱ, f. Ida, mountain near Troy.

Ἰδαῖος, -α, -ον, of Ida; βούτης Ἰ. = Paris, 646.

ἰδίᾳ, adv. dat., in private, individually.

ἴδιος, -α, -ον, private, individual, personal.

ἰδοῦ, imperat. of εἰδόμην.

ἰδού, adv., lo ! behold !

ἱερεύς, -έως, m., priest.

ἱερός, -ά, -όν, sacred.

ἵζω (only in pres. tenses), sit.

ἵημι, ἥσω, ἧκα, εἷκα, εἷμαι, εἵθην, send ; utter (338) ; intrans., betake oneself, rush.

ἴθι, imperat. of εἶμι.

ἱκέσιος, -α, -ον, of suppliants.

ἱκετεύω, trans. and intrans., supplicate, entreat.

ἱκέτις, -ιδος, f. (female) suppliant.

ἱκνέομαι, ἵξομαι, ἱκόμην, ἷγμαι, come to.

Ἰλιάς, -άδος, f. adj., of Ilion ; subst., (a) Trojan woman, (b) Troy.

Ἴλιον, n., Ilion, Troy.

Ἴλιος, -α, -ον, Ilian, Trojan.

ἵνα, conj., in order that, with subj. and opt. ; adv., where, wherein. See note 818 for special use with indic.

ἱππότης, -ου, m., horseman.

ἱρά, neut., for ἱερά, sacred things (rites).

ἴσος, -η, -ον, equal, hence fair, just.

ἵ-στη-μι, στήσω, ἔστησα, (ἔστην), ἕστηκα, ἐστάθην, trans. tenses, make to stand, set, place ; intrans., stand.

ἱστός, m., mast.

ἰσχύω, be strong ; πλέον ἰ., be stronger than, prevail over (with gen.).

ἴσχω (only in pres. tenses, reduplicated form of ἔχω), hold, stop.

ἴσως, adv., equally, perhaps.

ἴχνος, -ους, n., track, hence foot.

ἰώ, interj., oh ! ah ! alas !

κἀγώ, κἀγωγε = καὶ ἐγώ (crasis).

καθ' = κατά.

καθ-αιμάσσω, aor. καθήμαξα, make bloody [αἷμα].

καθ-αιρέω, overpower.

καθ-εῖλον, aor. of καθ-αιρέω.

καθ-είς, aor. part. of καθ-ίημι.

καθ-έξω, fut, of κατ-έχω.

καθ-ίημι, let down, lower.

καθ-οράω, κατόψομαι, κατεῖδον, behold.

καί, conj., and, also, even.

καὶ δή. See note, 758.

καὶ μήν. See note, 216.

καινός, -ή, -όν, new, fresh, strange.

καί-περ, adv., although (with part.).

καιρός, m., point of time, season, crisis ; ἐς καιρόν, at suitable time.

κακόγλωσσος, -ον, adj., ill-tongued.

κακός,.-ή, -όν, bad, evil ; subst., κακά, evils, reproaches, abuse.

κακύνομαι, behave badly.

κακῶς, badly, ill, miserably.

καλέω, καλῶ, ἐκάλεσα, κέκληκα, -μαι, ἐκλήθην, κεκλήσομαι, call.

καλλί-διφρος, -ον, of the fair chariot.

κάλλιστα, superl. of καλῶς, most gloriously.

κάλλος, -ους, n., beauty.

καλός, -ή, -όν, fair, beautiful, good, noble.

καλῶς, adv., nobly, honourably. See δράω.

κἄμ' = καὶ ἐμέ (crasis).

κάμαξ, -ακος, f., spear-shaft, lance.

κάμνω, καμοῦμαι, ἔκᾰμον, κέκμηκα, grow weary, suffer.

κάμπτω, κάμψω, bend; intrans., turn.

κᾶν = καὶ ἄν. κἀν = καὶ ἐν (crasis).

κἀνάθρησον = καὶ ἀνάθρησον (crasis).

κανών, -όνος, m., rule, standard.

κἀπεί = καὶ ἐπεί (crasis).

κἄπειτα = καὶ ἔπειτα (crasis).

καπνός, m., smoke.

κάρα (only in nom. and acc.), head; Κασάνδρας κάρα, 676, note.

καρδία, f., heart.

καρπός, m., fruit.

κἄρσένων = καὶ ἀρσένων (crasis).

καρτερέω, persist, continue.

κᾱρύξᾱσ(α), Doric for κηρύξασα.

καρχήσιον, n., lit. a drinking cup, hence (from its shape), mast-head of a ship, 1261, note.

κᾆς = καὶ ἐς (crasis).

Κασάνδρα, Cassandra, daughter of Priam, gifted with prophecy by Apollo, went to Greece with Agamemnon, and was there slain by Clytaemnestra.

κἀσθενεῖς = καὶ ἀσθενεῖς (crasis).

κάσις, -ιος, c., brother, 428; sister, 361, 944.

κᾆτ(α) = καὶ εἶτα (crasis).

κατά, prep.; with gen., down from; with acc., throughout (κατ᾽ ἄστυ), in (κατὰ Θρήκην). κατ᾽ ἴχνος, on track; καθ᾽ ἡμέραν, day by day; so κατ᾽ ἦμαρ.

κατα-θνήσκω, die, be slain.

κατα-κέχρωσμαι, perf. of κατα-χρώννῡμι.

κατα-κτείνω, slay, kill.

κατα-παύω, make to cease.

κατάρα, f., curse.

κατ-άρᾱτος, -ον, accursed.

κατ-άρχομαι, begin, commence (dirge), 685, note.

κατα-σκάπτω, dig down, overthrow; aor. pass. κατε-σκάφην.

κατά-σκοπος, m., spy.

κατα-στάζω, -ξω, shed, let flow, wet.

κατα-τείνω, strive; part. = vehement, contentious.

κατα-χρώ-ννῡμι, -κέχρωσμαι, -εχρώσθην, stain.

κατ-εῖπον (aor. with no pres.), denounce, betray.

κατ-εῖχον. See κατ-ἔχω.

κατ-έκταν, poetic aor. of κατα-κτείνω.

κατ-ερείπω, -ερείψω, -ηρείφθην, overthrow.

κατ-εσκάφην, aor. pass. of κατα-σκάπτω.

κατ-έσχον. See κατ-ἔχω.

κατ-έχω, καθέξω (κατα-σχήσω), κατέσχον, hold back, detain, restrain, seize, occupy, dwell in.

κατα-θανεῖν, aor. inf. of κατα-θνῃσκω.

κᾆτι = καὶ ἔτι (crasis).

κάτ-οχος, -ον, subject to.

κατ-όψομαι. See καθ-οράω.

κάτω, adv., below, esp. referring to the under-world.

κατ-ῶρυξ, -υχος, f., cavern, pit (ὀρύσσω, dig).

καὐτός = καὶ αὐτός (crasis).

κεῖμαι, κείσομαι, lie, lie low.

κεῖνος = ἐκεῖνος.

κέκαρμαι. See ἀπο-κείρω.

κέκτημαι, perf. of κτάομαι.

κέλαδος, m., din, shout.

κέλευσμα, -ατος, n., command.

κελεύω, bid, command.

κέλλω, κέλσω, ἔκελσα, run to land, 1057, note.

κενός, -ή, -όν, empty, devoid of

(*with gen.*), 230; . useless, vain, 824.

κεντέω, pierce, stab.°

κερδαίνω, -δανῶ, ἐκέρδᾱνα, gain.

κέρδος, -ους, *n.*, gain.

κερκίς, -ίδος, *f.*, rod by which threads of woof driven home ; garment spun by loom, 1153 ; *in pl.*, loom, 363.

κευθμών, -ῶνος, *m.*, hiding-place., κεύθω, κεύσω, ἔκευσα, κέκευθα, hide.

κέχρωσμαι, *perf. pass.* of χρώννυμι.

κηδεστής, -οῦ, *m.*, kinsman ; 834, *note.*

κηδεύω, make a marriage-alliance, marry.

κηλητήριος, -α, -ον, propitiatory.

κηλίς, -ίδος, *f.*, stain.

κήρυγμα, -ατος, *n.*, announcement.

κῆρυξ, -ῦκος, *m.*, herald, messenger.

κηρύσσω, announce, proclaim, invoke (148).

κίδναμαι (*only in pres. tenses*), be spread ; 916, *note.*

κίνδυνος, *m.*, danger.

κῑνέω, move, disturb.

Κισσεύς, -έως, *m.* Cisseus, Thracian king, father of Hecuba.

κισσός, *m.*, ivy.

κλαίω, κλαύσομαι, -σοῦμαι, ἔκλαυσα, κέκλαυμαι, weep ; *trans.*, lament for.

κλέμμα, *n.*, a thing stolen, 618, *note* (κλέπτω, steal).

κλέος, *n.*, (*only in nom. and acc. sing. and pl.*), fair fame, reputation.

κληρόω, apportion by lot.

κλίνη, *f.*, couch.

κλύδων, -ωνος, *m.*, wave, billow.

κλυδώνιον, *n.*, wavelet (*diminutive*).

κλύω, ἔκλυον, *aor. imperat.* κλῦθι, hear, listen, listen to.

κοιμίζω, lull to sleep, *i.e.*, kill, 474 ; *mid.*, sleep, 826.

κοινός, -ή, -όν, common, joint.

κοίτη, *f.*, bed, *hence* lair (of wild beasts).

κολεός, *m.*, sheath (of sword).

κόμη, *f.*, hair (of head), *usually pl.*

κομίζω, bring, conduct, escort, carry, carry off.

κομιστήρ, -ῆρος, *m.*, conductor.

κόμπος, *m.*, boast.

κόνις, -εως ΄(-εος), *f.*, dust.

κόπις, -εως, *m.*, prater, cunning speaker, 134, *note.*

κόρη, *f.*, girl, daughter ; pupil of the eye, 972.

κορμός, *m.*, log.

κορυφή, *f.*. top.

κόσμος, *m.*, decoration.

κού, κούκ = καὶ οὐ(κ) (*crasis*).

κούρη = κόρη.

κραίνω, κρανῶ, ἔκρανα, ἐκράνθην, accomplish, carry (a vote).

κρᾶτα, *n.*, (*nom.* κράς *not found*), head.

κρατέω, have power, might ; *with gen.*, prevail over, rule, overpower.

κράτος, -ους, *n.*, might ; *with gen.*, mastery over, 883.

κραυγή, *f.*, outcry, shouting.

κρείσσων, -ον, used as *comp.* of ἀγαθός, stronger, better ; κρείσσονα ἢ φέρειν, too great to be borne (*lit.* to bear), 1107.

κρίνω, κρινῶ, ἔκρῑνα, κέκρικα, -μαι, ἐκρίθην, judge, decide, (89) interpret.

κρόκεος, -ον, saffron-coloured.

Κρονίδης, -ου, *m.*, son of Cronos.

κρουνός, *m.*, spout.

κρυπτός, -ή, -όν, stealthy.

κρύπτω, -ψω, ἔκρυψα, κέκρυμμαι,
ἐκρύφθην, hide, conceal, *with
double acc.*, 570 ; hide in the
ground, bury.

κρύφιος, -α, -ον, by stealth.

κταν-. *See* κτείνω.

κτάομαι, κτήσομαι, κέκτημαι, ἐκτήθην,
get, win ; *in perf.*, have, own ;
κτηθείς, *pass. sense*, bought,
449, *note*.

κτείνω, κτενῶ, ἔκτεινα, ἔκτᾰνον, kill,
slay.

κτύπος, *m.*, outcry, din.

κύκλος, *m.*, circle, orb.

κυκλόομαι, encircle.

κῦμα, -ατος, *n.*, wave, billow.

κυν-ηγέτης, -ου, *m.*, hunter ; *lit.*
dog-leader.

Κύπρις, -ιδος, *f.*, Cypris, name of
Aphrodite, derived from
Cyprus, where she was especially worshipped ; *hence* love,
825.

κῦρέω, meet with, obtain ;
intrans., happen, follow, 690,
note.

κύων, κυνός, *c.*, dog, hound.

κῶλον, *n.*, limb.

κώπη, *f.*, handle, *hence* oar, 456 ;
hilt (of sword), 543.

λαγών, -όνος, *f.*, side, flank.

Λαερτιάδης, -ου, *m.*, son of
Laërtes, king of Ithaca, *i.e.*,
Odysseus.

Λαέρτιος, *m.* Laërtius = Laërtes.

λαθών, *aor. part. of* λανθάνω.

λάθρᾳ, secretly.

λαιμός, *m.*, throat.

λαιμό-τομος, -ον, with the throat
cut.

λαῖφος, -ους, *n.*, a sail.

λαιψηρός, -ά, -όν, swift.

Λάκαινα, Laconian (Spartan)
woman, 441, 651.

λαμβάνω, λήψομαι, ἔλαβον, εἴληφα,
-μμαι, ἐλήφθην, take, get, receive,
seize, take hold of.

λαμπρός, -ά, -όν, bright.

λανθάνω, λήσω, ἔλᾰθον, λέληθα,
-σμαι, escape the notice of
(*with acc.*).

λᾱός, *m.*, a people ; *pl.*, host,
553.

λάσκω, λακήσομαι, ἐλάκησα (ἔλᾰκον),
λέλᾱκα, speak of, mention,
678 ; cry aloud, 1110.

λάτρις, -ιος, *f.*, handmaiden, 609,
note.

Λᾱτώ, Dor. *for* Λητώ.

λέγω, λέξω, ἔλεξα (εἶπον), εἴρηκα,
ἐλέχθην, say, speak, declare ;
speak to, address, speak of ;
pass., be reported.

λε-ηλατέω, drive off booty (λεία,
booty ; ἐλα-, drive).

λείπω, -ψω, ἔλιπον, λέλοιπα,
λέλειμμαι, ἐλείφθην, leave.

λεκτός, -ή, -όν, chosen, picked.

λέκτρον, *n.*, couch, *esp.* marriage-
couch.

λέλᾱκα. *See* λάσκω.

λευρός, -ά, -όν, smooth.

λεύσσω, gaze, gaze at.

λέχος, -ους, *n.*, couch, marriage-
couch.

λέχριος, -α, -ον, *lit.* slanting,
sideways. *See* 1026, *note*.

λεώς, -ώ, *m.*, host.

Λῆμνος, *f.*, Lemnos, island in
Aegean.

Λητώ, -οῦς, *f.*, Leto, mother of
Apollo and Artemis.

λιάζομαι, ἐλιάσθην, bend *or* turn
aside. *See notes*, 85, 98.

λίαν, *adv.*, very, excessively ;
τὸ λ., excess.

λιμήν, -ένος, *m.*, harbour.

λίμνη, *f.*, pool, lake, sea.

λινό-κροκος, -ον, flax-woven.

λιπαίνω, make fat, enrich.

λίσσομαι, pray, entreat.

λιτή, f., prayer, entreaty.

λογάς, -άδος, selected, chosen.

λόγος, m., word, argument, story, speech, conversation.

λόγχη, f., spear, lance.

λογχο-φόρος, -ον, lance-bearing.

λοιδορέω, rail at.

λοιπός, -ή, -όν, left, remaining.

λοίσθιος, -α, -ον, left, remaining; τὸ λοίσθιον, at last.

λουτρόν, n., (usually in pl.), water (for washing), bath, washing.

λούω, wash.

λύκος, m., wolf.

λύμη, f., shame, outrage.

λῡπέω, trans., pain, grieve.

λύπη, f., pain, grief.

λυπρός, -ά, -όν, grievous.

λύω, loosen, unfurl; pass., be relaxed, fail.

λώβη, f., outrage, ruin.

μ' = με, from ἐγώ.

μάθημα, -ατος, n., learning, science; see, note, 814.

μαίνομαι, μανοῦμαι, μέμηνα, ἐμάνην, am mad.

μάκαρ, -αρ or -αιρα, -αρ, blessed (of the gods).

μακρός, -ά, -όν, long; διὰ μακροῦ, at long interval.

μάλα, adv., much.

μάλιστα, adv., most, especially, certainly (superl. of μάλα).

μᾶλλον, adv., more, rather, (compar. of μάλα).

μανείην, aor. opt. of μαίνομαι.

μανθάνω, μαθήσομαι, ἔμαθον, μεμάθηκα, learn, learn of.

μαντι-πόλος, -ον, adj., inspired.

μάντις, -εως, m., seer.

μάνυσον, Dor. for μήνυσον.

μαργάω, rage, 1128, note.

μάρπτω, -ψω, seize.

μαστεύω, seek.

μαστός, m., breast.

ματεύω, seek.

μάτην, adv., in vain, to no purpose.

μάτηρ, Dor. for μήτηρ.

μάχομαι, μαχοῦμαι, ἐμαχεσάμην, μεμάχημαι, fight.

μέγα, adv., greatly, very.

μέγας, -άλη, -α, great.

μεθ' = μετά.

μεθ-ῆχ' = μεθ-ῆκε, aor. of μεθίημι.

μεθ-ίημι, -ήσω, let go, release; throw, fling; suffer, allow; mid., leave hold of (with gen.), 400; μέθες (λόγον), cease, 888.

μειζόνως, compar. adv., more, worse.

μείζων, -ονος, greater.

μελάγ-χρως, -ωτος, dark-skinned, swarthy.

μέλαθρον, dwelling; μ. οὐράνιον, the hall of heaven.

μελαν-αυγής, -ές, dark-gleaming.

μελανό-πτερος, -ον, black-winged.

μελανο-πτέρυξ, -υγος, black-winged.

μέλας, -αινα, -αν, black, dark.

μέλει, it is a care or concern; οὐδὲν μέλει μοι = I care nothing.

μέλεος, -ον or -α, -ον, wretched, hapless.

μέλλω, -ήσω, be about to; hesitate, delay, 726; τὸ μέλλον, what is to be.

μέλος, -ους, n., limb, also strain, song.

μέμνημαι, remember, perf. of μιμνήσκομαι.

μέμφομαι, find fault with, blame

(acc. of person, gen. of cause) ;
think poorly of, 885.

μέν, particle ; word or clause
in which it stands answers
to following word or clause,
introduced by δέ : μέν . . δέ =
on the one hand . . . on the
other, but μέν may often be
left untranslated. Combined,
μὲν οὖν, nay rather, so then,
798; μέντοι. nevertheless, after
all, 600.

μένω, μενῶ, ἔμεινα, μεμένηκα, remain,
wait.

μέριμνᾰ, f., care, source of care.

μέρος, -ους, n., part, share ; ἐν
μέρει, in turr !130 ; τὸ ἐκείνου
μ., with re . l to him, 989.

μεσο-νύκτιος, -ον, at midnight.

μέσος, -η, -ον, middle, middle of ;
ἐν μέσοις, in their midst, 531 ;
ἐν μέσῳ, in middle, 1150.

μέσως, adv., moderately ; οὐ μέσως
(1113)=considerably.

μετά, prep. ; with acc., after, in
quest of ; with gen., with,
among ; with dat., among,
amidst, 355, note (poetical).

μετα-κλαίω, lament.

μεταξύ, adv.=prep., between.

μετα-πέμπω, send after.

μετ-άρσιος, -ον, upright.

μετά-στασις, -εως, f., change.

μετα-στείχω, come after, seek.

μετ-έρχομαι, -ἦλθον, come after,
come to fetch.

μέτ-εστι (from μέτ-ειμι), there is a
share. .

μή, not, especially used with
imperatives, in conditions and
wishes. μὴ σύ γε (ποίησῃς),
do not so ; εἰ μή, if not, unless,
except.

μη-δέ, and not, nor yet, not
even.

μηδ-είς, μηδεμία, μηδέν, no one,

nothing ; adv, neut., μηδέν, in
no way, not at all.

μήθ' = μήτε.

μήν, particle used to strengthen
asseverations ; ἦ μήν, in very
truth ; καὶ μήν, and look you,
216, note.

μηνύω, reveal, declare.

μή-ποτε, adv., lest ever, never.

μή-πω, adv., not yet.

μή-τε, and not, neither, nor ;
μήτε . . . μήτε, neither . . . nor.

μήτηρ, -τρός, f., mother.

μιαι-φόνος, -ον, blood-defiled.

μῖκρός, -ά, -όν, little, small ;
comp. ἐλάσσων.

μι-μνη-σκω, μνήσω, ἔμνησα, μέμνημαι,
ἐμνήσθην, remind ; mid., remember.

μισθός, m., hire, pay, reward.

μίτρα, f., snood, headband.

μολ-. See βλώσκω.

μολπή, f., song, strain.

μόνον, adv., only.

μονό-πεπλος, -ον, wearing only one
garment, 933, note.

μόνος, -η, -ον, alone.

μόρος, m., doom, fate.

μορφή, f., shape, form.

μόσχος, f., young heifer, 205 ;
hence, maiden, 526.

μοχθέω, toil.

μόχθος, m., toil, labour.

μῦθος, m., word, speech, counsel.

μυρίος, -α, -ον, countless, vast.

μυχός, m., innermost part, recess.

μῶν = μὴ οὖν (crasis), interrog. adv.
expecting answer No ; surely
not ?

ναίω (only in pres. and impf.
tenses), dwell.

νᾱός, m., temple ; also gen. of
ναῦς, 1263.

νασμός, m., stream.

νᾶσος, Dor. for νῆσος.

ναύ-λοχος, -ον, harbouring ships.

ναῦς, νεώς (ναός), f., ship.

ναυ-στολέω, go by ship, sail.

ναύτης, -ου, m., sailor; used as adjective, 921.

ναυτικός, -ή, -όν, of sailors.

ναυτίλος, m., sailor, seafarer.

νεᾱνίας, -ου, m., young man.

νεᾱνις, -ίδος, f., maiden.

νεκρός, m., dead body, corpse.

νέμω, -ῶ, ἔνειμα, νενέμηκα, attribute, assign.

νέος, -α, -ον, young, new, strange.

νεο-σφαγής, -ές, fresh slain.

νέρθε(ν), adv., below; τούς γῆς ν., gods of underworld.

νεύω, nod, beckon.

νέφος, -ους, n., cloud; hence, multitude.

νεῶν, from ναῦς.

νεωστί, adv., lately; τούς ν. δεσπότας, our new masters.

νή-νεμος, -ον, still, silent (νή, not; ἄνεμος, wind).

νῆσος, f., island.

νικάω, conquer, surpass.

νιν=him, her, 265, note.

νομίζω, be accustomed, 326, note.

νόμος, m., custom, usage, law; song, 686, note.

νόστιμος, -ον, returning.

νόστος, m., return home.

νοτίς, -ίδος, f., water.

νοῦς (νόος), νοῦ, m., mind.

νύκτερος, -ον, nightly, by night.

νύμφη, f., bride.

νυμφίος, m., bridegroom.

νῦν, adv., now.

νυν, enclitic, so, therefore, then. See 996, note.

νύξ, νυκτός, f., night.

νῶτον, n., usually pl., back.

ξεῖνος, Ionic = ξένος.

ξενία, f., relation of guest-friend, hospitality.

ξενο-κτονέω, slay guest.

ξένος, m., subst, guest-friend, guest, host; adj., -ον or -η, -ον, foreign.

ξίφος, -ους, n., sword.

ξυγγ-, ξυμ-, ξυν-. See συ-.

ξυν-εχώρουν. See συγ-χωρέω.

ξυστόν, spear, 920, note.

ὁ, ἡ, τό, article, the; with inf., τὸ κατθανεῖν, death, 356; cp. 260, 378, 600; with adj., τὸ δοῦλον, slavery, 332; τὸ θυμούμενον, wrath, 299; with participles, translated by relative and verb, τούς κάτω σθένοντας, those who rule in underworld; οἱ μέν . . . οἱ δέ, some . . . others; (rel.) τήν=ἥν, 636.

ὅ, from ὅς, ἥ, ὅ.

ὀγκόομαι, be puffed up, be vain.

ὅδε, ἥδε, τόδε, this, often used to point at person, 339, 860; especially referring to oneself, 202; τῇδε, thus, 1007.

ὁδός, f., way.

ὀδυρμα, -ατος, n., ὀδυρμός, m., lamentation, complaint.

ὀδύρομαι, lament.

Ὀδυσσεύς, (Ὀδυσεύς) -έως, m., Odysseus, king of Ithaca.

ὄζος, m., offshoot, scion.

οἱ, ah! alas!

οἵ'=οἷα.

οἱ, from ὁ, ἡ, τό.

οἵ, from ὅς, ἥ, ὅ.

οἷάπερ=οἷά περ, such things as.

οἶδα, pluperf. ᾔδη, know.

οἶδμα, -ατος, n., surge, swell.
οἰζύς, -ύος f., woe.
οἴκαδε, homewards.
οἰκίζω (aor. ᾤκισα, perf. mid. ᾤκισμαι), cause to dwell, mid., dwell.
οἶκος, m., house, family; pl., tents.
οἰκ-ουρός, f., house-keeper, mistress.
οἰκτείρω, pity (aor. ᾤκτειρα).
οἰκτίζω, pity (aor. mid. ᾠκτισάμην).
οἶκτος, m., pity, compassion; δι' οἴκτου ἔχειν, regard with pity.
οἰκτρός, -ά, -όν, piteous, pitiable.
οἰκτρότατος, superl. of οἰκτρός.
οἰκτρῶς, adv., piteously, pitiably.
οἴ-μοι, ah me! woe is me!
οἰμωγή, f., wailing, lamentation.
οἶος, -α, -ον, relative pron., correl. of τοῖος, of such a kind as, such as; of what kind, what; οἷός τε, able.
οἶσθα, from οἶδα.
οἴσω, from φέρω.
οἴχομαι, imperf. ᾠχόμην, οἰχήσομαι, be gone, lost; perish, be undone.
ὄλβιος, -ον, or -α, -ον, happy, blessed.
ὄλβος, m., happiness.
ὀλέθριος, -ον, deadly.
ὄλλῡμι, ὀλῶ, ὤλεσα, ὀλώλεκα, ὠλόμην (ὄλωλα=I am undone); destroy; mid., perish.
ὁμ-αρτῇ, adv., together.
ὅμ-ῑλος, m., crowd.
ὄμ-μα, -ατος, n., eye; sight, 1045.
ὁμό-δουλος, f., fellow-slave.
ὅμοιος, -α, -ον, like, similar.
ὀμφαλός, m., navel.
ὁμῶς, adv., nevertheless.

ὁμῶς, adv., equally.
ὄν, from ὤν.
ὄν, from ὅς, ἥ, ὅ.
ὀναίμην, aor. opt. mid. of ὀνίνημι.
ὀνειδίζω (aor. ὠνείδισα), blame, upbraid.
ὄνειρον (ὄνειρος, 89), n., dream.
ὀνειρό-φρων, -ονος, adj., wise in dreams, 709, note.
ὄνη-σις, -εως, f., benefit, profit.
ὀνίνημι, ὀνήσω, ὤνησα, ὠνήμην, ὠνήθην, benefit; mid., enjoy, with gen., 997.
ὄνομα, n., name.
ὄνυξ, -υχος, m., nail.
ὀπ-, acc. ὄπα, defective noun voice, word.
ὀπάων, -ονος, m., attendant.
ὅπλα, n., pl., arms, weapons.
ὁποῖος, -α, -ον, of what kind; adv. acc., ὁποῖα, like, 398.
ὅπου, adv., where, when.
ὅπως, conj., in order that; adv., as.
ὁράω, ὄψομαι, εἶδον, ἑώρᾱκα, -αμαι (ὦμμαι), ὤφθην, see, look at; look for, await.
ὄρειος, -ον or -α, -ον, of the mountain.
ὀρέστερος, -α, -ον, of the mountain.
ὀρθός, -ή, -όν, upright, undestroyed; steep, lofty, 221. See note, 972.
ὀρθόω, support, raise.
ὁρίζω, ὁριῶ, ὤρισα, perf. pass. ὥρισμαι, determine, define, 801; part, sever, 941; pass (vote), 259.
ὅρισμα, n., boundary.
ὁρμάω, set in motion; hurry away, 145; mid., be hurled, 1041.
ὅρμος, m., anchorage.
ὄρνις, -ῑθος, c., bird.

ὄρ-νῡμι, ὄρσω, ὦρσα, ὄρωρα, arouse.

ὄρος, m., boundary ; district.

ὀρρωδέω, dread, fear.

ὀρφᾰνός, -όν or -ή, -όν, bereft of.

ὅς, ἥ, ὅ, rel. pron., who, which ;
ὅ=δι' ὅ, wherefore, 13 ; ἔστιν
ᾗ, there is a point in which,
857, note.

ὅσιος, -α, -ον, holy, righteous.

ὅσος, -η, -ον, as great (much)
as, how great (much) ; pl.,
how many, as many as ; adv.
acc., ὅσον, as much as ; ὅσον
οὔ, almost, 141, note ; ὅσον
τάχος, with all speed, 1284.

ὅσ-περ, ἥπερ, ὅπερ, who, which.

ὄσσε, -ων (dat. -οις), eyes.

ὅσ-τε, ἥτε, ὅτε, who, which.

ὅσ-τις, ἥτις, ὅ τι (who, which),
whoever, whichever.

ὀστοῦν, ὀστέον, n., a bone.

ὅτ' = ὅτε.

ὅτ-αν, whenever, when, with
subj.

ὅτε, when.

ὅτου, gen. ; ὅτῳ, dat. of ὅστις.

οὐ, οὐκ, adv., not, used especially
in statements and with ind. ;
οὐ μή, see note, 1039.

οὗ, adv., where.

οὖδος, -εος, n., the ground.

οὐ-δέ, and not, nor yet, not
even.

οὐδ-είς, οὐδεμία, οὐδέν, no one.

οὐδέ-ποτε, never.

οὐδέ-πω, not yet.

οὐκ-έτι, no longer.

οὐκ-οῦν, therefore.

οὔκ-ουν, not therefore ; used in
asking question, 251, note.

οὑμοί = οἱ ἐμοί (crasis).

οὑμός = ὁ ἐμός (crasis).

οὖν, so, then, therefore.

οὕνεκα, for the sake of, following
gen.

οὔ-περ, where.

οὔ-ποτε, never.

οὔ-πω, not yet.

Οὐρᾰν-ίδης, -ου, m., son of Ouranos,
(heaven) ; pl., the gods.

οὐράνιος, -α, -ον, of heaven.

οὔρειος, -α, -ον, on the mountains

οὐρί-θρεπτος, -η, -ον, mountain
bred.

οὔριος, -α, -ον, fair, favourable.

οὔ-τε, and not, neither, nor ;
οὔτε . . . οὔτε, neither . . . nor.

οὔτι, not at all, 1039.

οὔ-τις, οὔτι, no one, nothing.

οὔτοι, by no means.

αὕτοι, from οὗτος.

οὗτος, αὕτη, τοῦτο, this ; with 2nd
pers. pron., expressed or understood = " you there ! " " ho
there ! " 1127, note.

οὕτω, οὕτως, thus, so.

οὐχί = οὐ.

ὀφείλω, -ήσω, ὠφείλησα, (ὤφελον),
ὠφείληκα, -θην, owe ; with inf.,
be obliged (to do), ought ;
imperf. and aor., would that.
See 395, note.

ὀφλισκάνω, ὀφλήσω, ὦφλον, ὤφληκα,
-μαι, incur the charge of, 327,
note.

ὄχλος, m., crowd, mob ; heap,
1014.

ὄψις, -εως, f., vision.

ὄψομαι. See ὁράω.

πᾶ, Dor. for πῆ.

πάγ-χρυσος, -ον, all of gold.

παθ-. See πάσχω.

πάθος, n., suffering, woe, disaster.

παῖς, παιδός, c., child, son or
daughter ; servant (like our

"boy "). *In* 59 παῖδες = female attendants of Hecuba.

παίω, strike, smite.

παλαιός, -ά, -όν, ancient, of old time.

πάλιν, *adv.*, again ; back again ; π. καὶ πρόσω, backwards and forwards.

Παλλάς, -άδος, *f.*, Pallas, epithet and synonym of Athene.

πάλ-λευκος, -ον, quite white.

πάλλω, sway, brandish ; toss, dandle.

παν-άθλιος, -α, -ον, all-forlorn.

πάν-δυρτος, -ον, all-plaintive.

παν-οῦργος, -ον, villain, wretch.

παν-τάλας (*like* τάλας), all-wretched, all-forlorn.

πανταχοῦ, *adv.*, everywhere.

παν-τλάμων, *Dor. for* παν-τλήμων.

παν-τλήμων, -ον = παντάλας.

παντοῖος, -α, -ον, of all kinds.

πάνυ, *adv.*, altogether, quite.

παν-ύστατος, -η, -ον, very last ; *adv.*, -τον, for the last time.

παρά (πάρα *when after its case*), *prep.* ; *with gen.*, from side of ; *with acc.*, to side of ; *with dat.*, at side of—*thus with acc.*, to, 559 ; beyond, contrary to, 680 ; *with dat.*, with, in house of, 19 ; in presence of, among ; *with gen.*, from, 615.

πάρα = πάρεστι, is here.

παρα-βαίνω, pass by, escape.

παρ-αιρέω (*aor.* -εῖλον), take away.

παρα-καλέω, -έσω, call to one's side, call aside.

παρα-στάς. *See* παρ-ίστημι.

παρά-σχες. *See* παρ-έχω.

παρά-φορος, -ον, erring, unsteady (*lit.* borne on one side).

παρα-ψῡχή, *f.*, refreshment, comfort.

πάρ-εδρος, -ον, seated near.

παρειά, *f.*, cheek.

παρ-εῖλον. *See* παρ-αιρέω.

πάρ-ειμι, be near, be present.

πάρεστι, it is possible. *Part.* παρών, -οῦσα, -όν (τὸ παρόν, my present estate, 997).

παρ-έχω (*same tenses as* ἔχω), afford ; cause ; offer.

παρ-ηγορέω, advise, counsel.

παρηΐς -ίδος, *f.*, cheek.

παρθένος, *f.*, maiden, virgin.

Πάρις, -ιδος, *m.* Paris, son of Priam and Hecuba, whose rape of Helen caused the Trojan War.

παρ-ίστημι (*tenses like* ἵστημι), set near ; *intransitive tenses*, stand by ; be at hand.

πάροιθε (-θεν), *adv.*, before ; *with article = adj.*, former.

πάρος, *adv.*, formerly ; *as prep.*, in front of, δωμάτων π.

παρ-ουσία, *f.*, presence.

πᾶς, πᾶσα, πᾶν, all, every ; πάντα (*n. pl.*), in every way.

πάσσαλος, *m.*, peg.

πάσχω, πείσομαι, πέπονθα, ἔπαθον, suffer, experience ; *with adv.*, εὖ, οἰκτρά πάσχειν, experience good or pitiable treatment. *Phrases*, τί πάθω; 614, what am I to do ? τί πάσχεις ; what ails you ? 1127.

πατήρ, πατρός (*acc.* πατέρα) *m.*, father.

πάτρα, *f.*, fatherland.

πάτριος, -α, -ον, handed down from forefathers, ancestral.

πατρίς, -ίδος, *f. adj.*, native.

πατρ-ῷος, -ον *or* -α, -ον, paternal ancestral.

πεδίον, *n.*, ground, plain.

πείθ-ω, persuade ; *mid.*, be persuaded ; obey (*with dat.*).

πειθώ, -οῦς, f., persuasion.

πειρ-άομαι, make trial of (with gen.).

πεῖσμα, -ἄτος, n., cable, esp. stern-cable.

πελάγιος, -α, -ον, of the sea.

πέλαγος, n., sea, esp. open sea

πελάζω, come near.

πέλας, adv., near; with gen., 486.

πέλεκυς, m., axe.

πέμπω, send; convey (πεμπομέναν κώπᾳ, sped by the oar); in mid., send for.

πένομαι, be poor, be in need.

πεντήκοντα, fifty.

πέπλος, m., robe; 466, note.

πέπρωται, it is fated; part. πεπρωμένος fated; ἡ πεπρωμένη, fate, destiny.

περ, particle adding emphasis and exactness to word; common with relatives.

πέρα, beyond, exceeding; with gen., 714.

πέραω, -άσω, pass, cross.

πέρθω, sack, waste; aor. part. πέρσας.

περί, with acc. and dat., about, around; gen., about, concerning.

πέριξ, adv., all around.

περι-πίπτω (tenses like πίπτω), fall into, fall in with (with dat.).

περι-πτύσσω, enfold, envelop.

περι-πτυχή, f., lit. something enfolding; fence.

περισσός, -ή, -όν, excessive, odd; adv., περισσά (n. pl.), very, exceedingly.

Περσεφόνη, f., Persephone, daughter of Demeter, queen of lower world.

πέσημα, -ἄτος, n., lit. falling; victim, 699, note.

πέτρα, f., rock.

πεύκινος, -η, -ον, of pine.

πῆ, where or whither ?

Πηλείδης (patronymic), son of Peleus = Achilles.

Πήλειος, -α, -ον, of Peleus. See 190, note.

Πηλεύς, -έως, m. Peleus of Thessaly, father of Achilles.

πῆμα, -ἄτος, n., woe, suffering, trouble.

πημονή, f., suffering, trouble.

πήνη, f., thread; in pl., web, 471.

πικρός, -ά, -όν, bitter, harsh, cruel.

πίνω, πίομαι, ἔπιον, πέπωκα, drink.

πίπτω, πεσοῦμαι, πέπτωκα, ἔπεσον, fall, throw oneself; π. εἰς χεῖρας, fall into hands of.

πιστός, -ή, -όν, faithful; trustworthy.

πίτνω, fall.

πλάθω (collat. form of πελάζω), draw near; aor. pass. πλαθείς, 890.

πλάξ, πλακός, f., level place, plain.

πλάτη, f., oar.

πλεῖστος, -η, -ον, superl. of πολύς.

πλέον, πλέων, comp. of πολύς.

πλευρά (πλευρόν), f. (n.), rib, side.

πλέω, πλεύσομαι and πλευσοῦμαι, ἔπλευσα, sail.

πλῆθος, -ους, n., multitude, crowd.

πλήν, adv., save, except.

πλήρης, -ες, full.

πληρ-όω, fill, fulfil; complete, heap up.

πλησίον, near. See 996, note.

πλόκαμος, m., lock of hair, tress.

πλοῦς (contr. from πλόος), m., sailing, voyage (πλέω, sail).

πλούσιος, -α, -ον, rich.

πνεῦμα, -ἄτος, n., breath.

πνοή, f., breeze; wind.

πόθεν, adv., whence ?

ποθέν, adv. enclitic, from some quarter.

ποθέω, desire, long for.

ποῖ, adv., whither ? with gen., esp. in phrase ποῖ γῆς ; sometimes nearly = ποῦ, e.g. 419.

ποι, adv. enclitic, some whither ; like ποῖ, with gen., 1285.

ποιέω, make, do, perform. In mid., consider, regard, account

ποικίλλω, embroider (lit. work in various patterns : ποικίλος).

ποικιλό-φρων, -ον, adj., versatile ; generally in bad sense, shifty, crafty.

ποῖος, -α, -ον, adj., of what sort, what ? (almost = τίς, 160).

πολέμιος, -α, -ον, adj., hostile ; as subst., enemy. Superl. πολεμιώτατος, 848 (strictly public enemy, opp. to ἐχθρός).

πολιός, -όν or -ά, -όν, grey, hoary.

πόλις, -εως (-εος), f., city, town, state.

πολίτης, -ου, m., citizen.

πολλ-άκις, adv., many times, often.

πολυ-δάκρυτος, -ον, tearful.

Πολύδωρος, Polydorus, youngest son of Priam and Hecuba : murdered by Polymestor.

Πολυμήστωρ, -ορος, m., Thracian king, guardian and murderer of Polydorus.

πολύ-μοχθος, -ον, full of labour, full of sorrow.

Πολυξένη (or -ξείνη), Polyxena, daughter of Priam and Hecuba, sacrificed to spirit of Achilles.

πολύ-πονος, -ον, full of suffering, full of toil. Superl. -πονώτατος.

πολύς, πολλή, πολύ, adj., many, much ; οἱ πολλοί, the mob ; αἱ π. πόλεις, most cities. Adv.

forms, πολύ, πολλά. Comp. πλείων (πλέων), more (adv. πλέον) ; superl. πλεῖστος, most.

πολύ-χρυσος, -ον, adj., with much gold, rich.

πόμπιμος, -ον, favourable (πέμπω, send).

πομπός, m., messenger.

πονέω, work (with cognate acc. πόνον, 779).

πονηρός, -ά, -όν, troublesome ; bad, worthless, evil.

πόνος, m., labour, suffering, evil.

ποντιάς, -άδος, f., adj., of the sea.

πόντιος, -ον or -α, -ον, of the sea ; ἀφῆκε πόντιον, flung into the sea, 797, note.

ποντο-πόρος, -ον, seafaring.

πόντος, m., sea.

πορ-εύω, make go or pass ; in pass.; go, move.

πορθμός, m., ferry ; strait.

πόρπη, f., brooch, 1170.

πόσις, m., husband.

πότε, interrog., at what time ? when ?

ποτε, enclitic part., at some time, ever ; formerly, once ; often in questions "pray."

πότερα, interrog, adv., whether.

πότερος, -α, -ον, whether of two.

πότμος, m., fate, destiny.

πότνια, f., adj., revered ; 70, note.

ποῦ, where ? in what way ?

που, enclitic, anywhere ; perhaps ; ἦ που, I suppose, 775.

πούς, ποδός, dat. pl. ποσί, m., foot ; (of a ship) sheet, 1020, note.

πρᾶγμα, -ατος, n., matter, business, act, deed.

πράσσω, πράξω, do, commit ; fare (with qualifying adv., as κακῶς, 56 ; καλῶς, 820).

πρέπω, *esp. as impers.* πρέπει, it is seemly, right.

πρέσβυς, -εως, *m.*, old man.

πρεσβῦτις, -ιδος, *f.*, old woman.

πρεσβύτης, -ου, *m.*, old man, 323, *note.*

πρευμενής, -ές, *adj.*, gentle, kind ; favourable.

Πριαμίδης, -ου, *m.*, son or descendant of Priam (*patronymic*).

Πρίαμος, *m.*, Priam, king of Troy, husband of Hecuba.

πρίν, *conj.*, before that ; *usually with inf.* ; *with ind. when action in past. As adv. with article = adj.*, former. *See* 622, φρονήματος τοῦ πρίν.

πρό, *prep.* (*with gen.*), before, *of time or place.*

προ-βάλλω (*tenses like* βάλλω), put forward (as plea), 825.

προ-θυμέομαι, desire, be anxious

πρό-θυμος, -ον, *adj.*, eager, desirous.

προ-κόπτω, advance (*lit.* cut down before, as a pioneer), 961, *note.*

προ-λείπω, leave ; swoon, 438.

προ-μηθία, *f.*, forethought ; consideration, 795, *note.*

πρό-νοια, *f.*, forethought.

προ-πετής, -ές, *adj.*, fallen in front of.

πρός, *prep.* : *with acc.*, to, towards, π. οἶκον, π. οὖδας π. τὸ δεινόν ; *adv.*, π. βίαν, by force ; *with gen.*, from, at hands of ; (of oaths) π. θεῶν, by the gods ; *with dat.*, at, near ; in addition to.

προσ-αρκέω, -έσω, help.

προσ-βάλλω (*tenses like* βάλλω), lay by side of.

προσ-βλέπω, look at.

πρόσ-ειμι, -έσομαι, be added to, be on, be near.

προσ-εῖπον, *strong aor.*, speak to, address.

πρόσθε (-θεν), *adv.*, before, formerly, once ; ἐς πρόσθεν κακῶν, 961, *note.*

προσ-θιγγάνω, -θίξομαι, -έθιγον, touch.

προσ-ίζω, sit near (as suppliant).

προσ-λάζυμαι, grasp, take hold of (*with gen.*), 64, *note.*

προσ-οιστέος, -α, -ον, *verbal adj. from* φέρω, to be added.

προσ-οράω, -όψομαι, -εῖδον, look at.

προσ-πίπτω (*tenses like* πίπτω), fall at.

προσ-πίτνω = *foreg.*, fall before (as suppliant).

προσ-τάσσω (*tenses like* τάσσω), assign.

προσ-τίθημι (*tenses like* τίθημι), *lit.* add to ; *thus* impose on, 362 ; consign, 368 ; *mid.*, bring on oneself (in addition), 742.

πρόσ-φαγμα, -ατος, *n.*, victim (σφάζω).

πρόσ-φθεγμα, -ατος, *n.*, word.

προσ-φιλής, -ές, *adj.*, dear, beloved.

πρόσ-φορος, -ον, *adj.*, helpful, serviceable.

πρόσω, *adv.*, forward ; *with gen.*, πρόσω πατρός, far from their father.

πρόσωπον, *n.*, visage, face.

προ-τίθημι (*tenses like* τίθημι), put forward, 67 ; *in mid.*, lay out (of corpse), 613, *note.*

πρότονοι, *m.*, halyards (τείνω).

πρό-φασις, -εως, *f.*, pretext (φημί).

πρύμνα, *f.*, stern (of ship).

πρωτό-γονος, -ον, first-created.

πρῶτος, -η, -ον, first, pre-eminent ;
adv. πρῶτον, τὸ πρῶτον.

πτόλις, -ιος, f., city (=πόλις).

πτόρθος, m., young branch, shoot,
sapling.

πτώσσω, crouch ; with acc. of
person, cower before.

πύλη, f., gate.

πῦρ, πυρός, n., fire.

πυρά, -ᾶς, f., pyre.

πύργος, m., tower, wall.

πυρ-σός, -ή, -όν, fiery-red.

πω, enclitic, as yet.

πῶλος, m. and f., colt, foal ;
young girl, 144.

πῶμα, -ἄτος, n., draught.

πῶς, adv., how ? πῶς δοκεῖς ;
see note, 1160.

πως, enclitic adv., somehow.

ῥᾴδιος, -α, -ον, easy.

ῥέω, ῥεύσομαι, ἐρρύηκα, flow.

ῥήγνυμι, ῥήξω, tear, rend.

ῥήτωρ, -ορος, m., orator, speaker.

ῥίπτω, throw, toss.

ῥυθμίζω, set in order ; in mid.
924, arrange (of hair).

σαθρός, -ά, -όν, rotten ; unsound,
1190, note.

σαίρω, sweep.

σάλος, m., swell (of sea).

σάρξ, σαρκός, f., flesh.

σᾶς, Dor. for σῆς. See σός.

σαυτοῦ, -τῷ. See σεαυτοῦ.

σαφής, -ές, adj., clear, manifest.

σεαυτοῦ, -τῆς, reflexive pron., of
thyself.

σέβω, worship, reverence.

σέθεν, gen. of σύ.

Σείριος (i.e. ἀστήρ), m., Sirius,
the dog-star, 1104, note.

σεμνός, -ή, -όν, adj., reverend.

σεύω, hurry ; in pass., hasten.

σῆμα, -ἄτος, n., tomb, monument ;
κυνὸς σῆμα, see note, 1265.

σημαίνω, show by sign, indicate,
announce, declare.

σημεῖον, n., sign.

σθένω, am strong, have force ;
οὐ ταὐτὸν σ., has not same force,
295 ; τοὺς κάτω σθένοντας, powers
below, 49.

σῖγα, adv., silently, in silence.

σιγάω, be silent.

σιγή, f., silence.

σιδήρεος, -α, -ον, of iron.

σίδηρος, m., iron ; sword, 567.

Σιμουντίς, -ίδος, adj., of Simois,
rivulet in Troad, hence Trojan.

σιτο-ποιός, -όν, adj., bread-
making ; σ. ἀνάγκη, task of
making bread.

σιωπάω, be quiet, silent.

σκηνή, f., tent.

σκήνωμα, -ἄτος, n., tent, encamp-
ment.

σκίδναμαι, be shed ; pres. pass.
of σκίδνημι =σκεδάννυμι.

σκίπων, -ωνος, m., stick, staff.

σκίρτημα, -ἄτος, n., bounding,
struggling.

σκολιός, -ά, -όν, adj., crooked,
bent.

σκοπιά, f., hill-top, 931, note.

σκότιος, -α, -ον, dark.

σκότος, m., darkness.

σκῦλον, n., spoils (in pl.), 1014.

σκύμνος, m., and f., cub, whelp.

σμικρός, -ή, -όν (μικρός), adj.,
small ; in 318 σμικρά, a little.

σός, σή, σόν, possessive pron.,
thine.

σόφισμα, -ἄτος, n., device, trick.

σοφός, -ή, -όν, adj., wise, clever.

σοφῶς, adv., wisely, cleverly.

σπανίζω, lack, need (*with gen.*).

σπάνις, -εως, *f.*, deficiency, lack.

σπαραγμός, *m.*, rending.

σπάω, -άσω, ἔσπακα (*aor. pass.* ἐσπάσθην), tear away, wrench away.

σπείρω, sow, cultivate.

σπέρμα, -ἄτος, *n.*, seed ; children, race.

σπεύδω, hasten ; set forward ; strive for ; make haste.

σπορά, *f.*, race ; θῆλυς σπορά, race of women.

σπουδάζω, be zealous, eager, hasten.

σπουδή, *f.*, hot haste ; σπ. ἔχειν =σπουδάζεσθαι, 673 ; contention.

σταλαγμός, *m.*, drop.

στάς, 2*nd aor. part. of* ἵστημι.

στάχυς, -υος, *m.*, ear of corn.

στέγη, *f.* (*lit.* covered place), in *pl.*, tent, cavern.

στείχω, go, advance, walk.

στέλλω, *v.a.*, make ready ; gather up (robe) ; in *mid.*, set sail, start (on expedition), depart.

στεναγμός, *m.*, groaning, lament.

στένω, groan, lament.

στέργω, love ; am content, 789.

στερίσκω (*pass.* στέρομαι, στερίσκομαι), deprive. (*Tenses as if from* στερέω, *but pass. aor.* στερηθῆναι, 338, στερέντες, 623.)

στέρνον, *n.*, breast.

στεροπή (-ά *Dor.*), *f.*, lightning, lightning flash.

στερρός, -όν or -ά, -όν, *adj.*, fixed, hard, stern.

στεφάνη (-α *Dor.*), *f.*, crown, diadem (of towers).

στέφανος, *m.*, crown, chief prize.

στεφανόω, crown, honour.

στόλισμα, -ἄτος, *n.*, garment ;

armament, equipment (*see note*, 1156).

στόλος, *m.*, expedition.

στόμα, -ἄτος, *n.*, mouth.

στράτευμα, -ἄτος, *n.*, army, host.

στρατιά, *f.*, army.

στρατός, *m.*, army, host.

στρέφω, turn ; revolve in mind.

σύ, *pron.*, 2*nd pers.*, thou.

συγ-γενής, -ές, *adj.*, kindred, akin ; *as subst.*, kinsman.

συγ-γνωστός, -όν, *adj.*, pardonable.

σύγ-γονος, -ον, *adj.*, akin ; *subst.*, *f.*, sister, 441.

συγ-κλείω, συγκλήσω, *perf. pass.* συγκέκλημαι, enclose, wrap up.

συγ-χωρέω, agree, consent.

συθείς, *aor. part. pass. of* σεύω.

συμ-βούλομαι, -βουλήσομαι, agree in wishing.

σύμ-μαχος, *m.*, ally.

συμ-παίω, *fut.* -παίσω, clash.

σύμ-πας (*like* πᾶς), all together, all, whole.

συμ-πίπτω *or* συμπίπτω, come together, meet ; coincide, happen, 846 ; 1029, *note.*

συμ-πονέω, work with, co-operate.

συμ-φονεύω, to kill at same time with.

συμ-φορά, *f.*, event, chance, misfortune, disaster.

σύν (ξύν), *prep.* : *with dat.*, with, in co-operation with ; σ. ὅπλοις, in arms ; σ. δόλῳ, by treachery.

συν-αρπάζω (*aor.* συνήρπᾰσα), seize together.

συν-δουλεύω, be slave with.

συν-δράω, -άσω, do with, co-operate.

σύν-ειμι (*tenses like* εἰμί), be with.

συν-εξ-έρχομαι (*tenses like* ἔρχομαι), come out with.

συν-ἐσται, 3*rd sing. fut. of* σύνειμι.

συν-θνήσκω (tenses like θνήσκω), die with.

σύν-ισθι, imperat. of σύνοιδα.

σύν-οδος, f., assembly, 109.

σύν-οιδα (tenses like οἶδα), be conscious of, aid, abet.

συν-οικίζω, help in colonising (aor. συνῴκισα).

συν-τείνω, tend.

συν-τέμνω, curtail, cut short ; συντεμών, in brief.

συν-τίθημι (tenses like τίθημι), place together, include in one.

συν-τυγχάνω (tenses like τυγχάνω), meet with, fall in with.

συν-τυχία, f., chance, fate.

σφαγή, f., slaughter, murder ; deadly wound.

σφάγιον, n., victim.

σφάζω, σφάξω, ἔσφαξα (aor. pass. ἐσφάγην), slay, slaughter.

σφακτός, -ή, -όν, slaughtered.

σφε = σφᾶς. See 260, note.

σφεῖς, ibid.

σχεδία, f., raft, ship.

σχές, 2nd aor. imperat. of ἔχω.

σχέτλιος, -α, -ον, adj., wretched, unhappy.

σχῆμα, -ατος, n., form, fashion. See 619, note.

σχολάζω, act leisurely, delay.

σῴζω, save, keep safe.

σῶμα, -ατος, n., body, person.

σῶς, σῶν, adj., safe.

τᾷ, Dor. for τῇ.

ταλαίπωρος, -ον, adj., wretched, ill-starred.

τάλας, -αινα, -αν, adj., wretched, unhappy.

Ταλθύβιος, Talthybius, Greek herald.

τάν = τὰ ἐν (crasis).

ταπεινός, -ή, -όν, adj., humble, lowly.

ταραγμός, m., disturbance, perplexity ; confusion.

ταρβέω, -ήσω, etc., be frightened, quail.

τάσσω (τάττω), order, appoint.

τάφος, m., tomb, burial.

τάχα, adv. soon, quickly ; perhaps, possibly.

τάχος, -ους, n., speed ; ὅσον τάχος, with all speed.

ταχύς, -εῖα, -ύ, adj., swift ; comp. θάσσων, superl. τάχιστος ; superl. adv., τάχιστα, with ὡς, as soon as possible.

τε, conj. (enclitic), and ; τε . . . τε, both . . . and.

τέγγω, τέγξω, wet ; bedew.

τείνω, stretch ; stretch out, prolong ; design, intend.

τεῖχος, -ους, n., wall.

τέκμαρ, n. (only in nom. and acc.), mark, beacon.

τέκνον, n., child.

τέκος, -ους, n., child.

τεκών, -οῦσα, -όν, 2nd aor. part. of τίκτω ; as subst., parent.

τελευτάω, end, finish.

τέλος, -ους, n., end ; διὰ τέλους, for ever ; ἐς τέλος, to utmost.

τέμνω, cut down, destroy ; waste ; mid., cut down for oneself (aor. ἐταμόμην).

τετρά-πους, -ποδος, adj., four-footed.

τεύξομαι, fut. of τυγχάνω.

τεῦχος, -ους, n., vessel, urn.

τέχνη (in pl.), f., art, device skill.

τῇδε, adv., in this way, thus. See ὅδε.

τήμῇ = τῇ ἐμῇ (crasis).

τητάομαι, be deprived of, be without.

τίθημι, θήσω, ἔθηκα, τέθεικα, τέθειμαι, set, place ; make ; mid., place, dispose of ; regard, account ; lay up for oneself, 1212, note.

τιθήνη, f., nurse.

τίκτω, τέξομαι, τέτοκα, ἔτεκον, beget ; bear, bring forth.

τιμάω, honour, esteem.

τιμή, f., honour.

τίμιος, -α, -ον, adj., honourable.

τιμωρέω (with dat.), avenge ; mid., avenge oneself on, punish (with acc.).

τιμωρός, -όν, helping ; as subst. m., avenger.

τις, τι, τινος, enclitic, some ; some one, any one ; τι (as adverb), in some measure, somewhat.

τίς, τί (τίνος τοῦ, τίνι τῷ), interrog., who, what ? τί, why ?

Τιτάν, -ᾶνος, m., Titan (giants who rebelled against Zeus).

τλάμων, Dor. for τλήμων.

τλᾱτός, Dor. for τλητός.

τλάω, τλήσομαι, τέτληκα, ἔτλην, dare, venture, suffer.

τλήμων, -ονος, adj. ; original sense, enduring, patient ; hence wretched, miserable, in 562, brave (see note).

τλητός, -ή, -όν, verbal adj., endurable.

τοι, enclitic particle, assuredly.

τοῖος, -α, -ον, adj., such ; of such a sort.

τοιόσδε, -άδε, -όνδε, adj., such ; of such kind, esp. referring to what follows.

τοιοῦτος, -αύτη, -οῦτο, adj., such, esp. referring to what goes before ; τοιαῦτα, just so ! 776.

τοῖχος, m., wall ; side of tent, 1174.

τοκάς, -άδος, f., mother.

τοκεύς, -έως, m., parent.

τόλμᾰ, -ης, f., boldness, rashness ; rash deed.

τολμάω, venture, be bold ; endure, put up with.

τοξεύω, shoot ; aim at.

τόξον, n., bow ; pl., arrows.

τόσος, -η, -ον, adj., so great, so many, so much.

τοσόσδε, -ήδε, -όνδε, adj., so great ; adv., τοσόνδε, so greatly.

τοσοῦτος, -αύτη, -οῦτο, adj., so much, so great.

τότε, adv., then ; τὴν τότε χάριν, 276, note.

τοὐμόν = τὸ ἐμόν (crasis).

τοὔμπαλιν = τὸ ἔμπαλιν (crasis).

τοὐνθένδε = τὸ ἐνθένδε (crasis).

τράπεζα, f., table, board.

τρέπω, τρέψω, τέτροφα, ἔτραπον, turn ; mid., betake oneself.

τρέφω, θρέψω, ἔθρεψα, τέτροφα, τέθραμμαι, ἐθρέφθην, nurture, nourish, bring up.

τρέχω, δραμοῦμαι, ἔδραμον, run.

τρίβω, rub ; lay waste, 1142.

τρισσός, -ή, -όν, adj., threefold ; three.

τριταῖος, -α, -ον, on third day ; 32, note.

Τροία, f., Troy.

τρόπος, m., way, method ; humour, character, 867, note.

τροφή, f., nurture, training.

Τρῳάς, -άδος, adj., of Troy ; fem. subst., Trojan woman.

Τρῶες, -ων, m., Trojans.

Τρωιάς, -άδος, f., Trojan woman.

Τρωικός, -ή, -όν, of Troy, Trojan.

τυγχάνω, τεύξομαι, ἔτυχον, light upon, meet with, obtain, usually with gen., but also with acc. ; succeed ; (with part.) τυγχάνω ὤν, happen to be ; τυγχάνει περῶσα (665) ; τυγχάνω ἀπών (963).

τύμβος, m., tomb.

Τυνδαρίς, -ίδος, f., (patronymic), daughter of Tyndareus, king of Sparta (=Helen, 269, Clytemnestra, 1278).

τυραννικός, -ή, -όν, kingly, royal.

τύραννος, m. and f., king, monarch; queen, princess.

τυφλός, -ή, -όν, adj., blind.

τυφλόω, make blind, blind.

τύφω, smoulder, smoke.

τύχη, f., fortune ; see 786, note.

τῷ = τίνι.

ὑβρίζω, insult, be insolent.

ὕδωρ, -ατος, n., water.

ὕλη, f., wood, timber.

ὑμεῖς, -ᾶς, -ῶν, -ῖν, pl. of σύ.

ὑπάρχω, lit. begin to be ; hence be.

ὑπ-έγγυος, -ον, adj., under pledge (ἐγγύη = pledge), responsible ; τὸ ὑπέγγυον, responsibility, liability.

ὑπ-εκ-πέμπω, send away secretly (aor. ὑπεξέπεμψα), 6, note.

ὑπ-εξ-άγω, withdraw stealthily.

ὑπέρ, prep. : with acc., above, beyond ; with gen., above : on behalf of, for sake of.

ὑπερ-θρῴσκω, -θοροῦμαι, -έθορον, leap over.

ὑπερ-τέλλω, rise above.

ὑπερ-φέρω (tenses like φέρω), excel.

ὑπ-έχω (tenses like ἔχω), undergo ; ὑπ. δίκην, undergo punishment.

ὑπ-ηρετέω, serve, help, with dat.

ὑπ-ηρέτης, -ου, m., servant,

minister (lit. under-rower : ἐρέτης).

ὕπνος, m., sleep.

ὑπό, prep. : with acc., under, usually with verb implying "motion to ") ; τοὺς ὑπὸ γαῖαν, gods of nether world ; with gen., from under, ὑ. σκηνῆς, from within tent, 53 ; with pass. verbs, of agent, by, at hands of ; under hands of, 1215 ; with dat., under.

ὑπο-πέμπω, send beneath.

ὑπό-πτερος, -ον, adj., winged.

ὑπ-οπτος, -ον, adj., suspicious, fearful of, with gen. ; 1135, note.

ὕστατος, -η, -ον, last.

ὑφέξω, fut. of ὑπέχω.

ὑψι-πέτης, -ες, adj., lofty.

φαίνω, perf. pass. πέφασμαι, aor. ἐφάνην, show ; mid. and pass., be seen, show oneself, appear.

φάμα, Dor. for φήμη.

φάντασμα, -ατος, n., shade, ghost.

φάος (only in nom. and acc. sing.), n., light, esp. light of life.

φάρμακον, n., drug, poison.

φᾶρος, -ους, n., cloak : robe.

φάσγανον, n., sword.

φάσμα, -ατος, n., phantom, vision (φαίνω).

φέγγος, -ους, n., light. (See note. 368.)

φείδομαι, spare, desist.

φερτός, -ή, -όν, verbal adj., bearable.

φέρω, οἴσω, ἐνήνοχα, ἤνεγκα, ἤνεγκον, bear, carry ; bring, fetch : produce ; carry off, plunder : mid., win ; pass., be carried on, rush. 1075.

φεῦ, interj., ah ! alas ! woe !

φεύγω, φεύξομαι, ἔφυγον, πέφευγα, fly from, escape.

φήμη, f., rumour, report.

φημί, φήσω, ἔφην, say.

φθέγγομαι, speak aloud, utter.

φθείρω, destroy, spoil.

Φθιάς, -άδος, f. adj., of Phthia (in Thessaly).

φθίμενος. See φθίω.

φθίω, φθίσω, ἔφθικα, ἔφθιμαι, consume, destroy; 2nd aor. part., οἱ φθίμενοι, the dead.

φθογγή, f., voice, note.

φθόγγος, m., voice, cry.

φθονέω, grudge; with gen. and dat.

φθόνος, m., ill-will; envy. See 288, note.

φιλέω, love; be wont.

φίλιος, -α, -ον, adj., friendly, dear.

φίλ-ιππος, -ον, adj., horse-loving.

φίλος, -η, -ον, adj., loving, dear; as subst., friend; n., pl., φίλα, welcome news (comp. φίλτερος, superl. φίλτατος).

φιλο-ψῦχέω, be a coward (be fond of life).

φιλό-ψῦχος, -ον, adj., cowardly (lit. life-loving).

φίλτρον, -ον, n., charm, love-charm.

φλόγεος, -α, -ον, burning, flaring.

φλογμός, m., blaze.

φλόξ φλογός, f., flame.

φοβερός, -ά, -όν, adj., terrible.

φόβος, m., fear, alarm.

Φοιβάς, -άδος, f., priestess of Phoebus, prophetess.

φοῖνιξ, -ῖκος, m., palm-tree.

φοίνιος, -α, -ον, adj., blood-stained.

φοινίσσω, redden, make red.

φονεύς, -έως, m., murderer.

φόνιος, -ον or -α, -ον, adj., murderous, bloody.

φόνος, m., murder, death; blood.

φορέω, carry to and fro.

φράζω, say, declare; in mid., observe, notice (546, note).

φρήν, φρενός, f., mind, heart.

φρίσσω, shiver, shudder.

φροίμιον, n., prelude, opening (for προ-οίμιον).

φρονέω, think; be minded (with adv. or n. adj.).

φρόνημα, -ατος, n., thought; temper, spirit.

φροντίζω, think, consider, take care, take heed.

φροντίς, δος, f., thought, care.

φροῦδος, -η, -ον, adj., gone, departed, out of the way (πρό, ὁδοῦ). See 160, note.

φρουρέω, guard.

Φρύξ, -ῠγός, m., Phrygian; Trojan. Φρυγῶν πόλις = Troy.

φυγάς, -άδος, c., fugitive.

φυγή, f., flight.

φυλακή, f., watch, guard.

φύλαξ, -ακος, m., guard, keeper.

φύλλον, n., leaf.

φύρω (aor. ἔφυρσα and ἔφυρα), mix together, confuse; 958, note; defile, 496.

φύσις, -εως, f., nature, disposition, temper.

φύω (intrans. tenses, πέφυκα, ἔφυν), produce, beget; intrans., be born, be.

φωνή, f., voice.

φῶς, φωτός, n., light.

φώς, φωτός, m., man.

χαίρω, χαιρήσω, ἐχάρην, rejoice, be glad; imper. and inf., farewell.

χᾱλᾷ, Dor. for χηλῇ.

χαλάω, -άσω, loosen, slacken ; *intrans.*, be indulgent to (403), *with dat.*

χαλινωτήρια, -ων, *n. pl.*, cables (for mooring).

χαρακτήρ, -ῆρος, *m.*, impress, stamp. *See note*, 379.

χάρις, -ιτος, *f.*, thanks, grace, kindness, benefit ; χάριν, *with gen.*, for sake of ; χάριν ἐμήν, 874, for my sake ; πρὸς χάριν (τινί) to win favour.

χἀτέρων = καὶ ἐτέρων (*crasis*).

χείρ, χερός *and* χειρός, *f.*, hand, arm.

Χερσονήσιος, -α, -ον, *adj.*, of Chersonesê.

Χερσό-νησος, *f.*, Chersonese in Thrace (Gallipoli peninsula), opposite Troy (χερσό-νησος = land-island).

χηλή, *f.*, hoof ; claw.

χθόνιος, -α, -ον, *adj.*, of lower world.

χθών, χθονός, *f.*, land, country.

χιονώδης, -ες *adj.*, snowy.

χλωρός, -ά, -όν, fresh, new.

χοή, *f.*, libation (χέω = pour).

χόλος, *m.*, anger, wrath.

χορο-ποιός, -όν, choral.

χραίνω, defile.

χράω, χρήσω, *act.*, declare ; *mid.*, use, treat (*with dat.*) : κέχρημαι, *with gen.*, be in need of.

χρεία, *f.*, need.

χρέος, -ους, *n.*, need ; business ; *see* 892, *note*.

χρεών (*sc.* ἐστί), it is meet, it must be.

χρή, *impers.*, ἐχρῆν *or* χρῆν (η *in* contraction preserved *throughout*), it must be, it is right ; τὸ χρῆν, necessity, *see* 260, *note*.

χρῄζω, wish, desire.

χρῆμα, -ατος, *n.*, matter ; τί χ., what in world ? 754, *note* ; *in pl.*, money, wealth.

χρηστός, -ή, -όν, *adj.*, good, kind ; (of land) rich, fertile ; τὰ χρηστά, prosperity.

χρόνος, *m.*, time.

χρύσεος, -έα *or* -ῆ, -ον, *adj.*, golden.

χρῦσός, *m.*, gold.

χρυσο-φαής, -ές, *adj.*, with golden light.

χρυσο-φόρος, -ον, *adj.*, wearing gold.

χρώς, χρωτός (χροός, χροί, etc.), *m.* flesh.

χὠ = καὶ ὁ (*crasis*).

χῶμα, -ατος, *n.*, mound.

χώρα, *f.*, place ; region.

χωρέω, *intrans.*, go ; go *or* come forth ; spread abroad ; depart.

χωρίζω, separate.

χωρίς, *adv.*, apart ; *with gen.*, far from.

ψάμαθος, *f.*, sand.

ψαύω, touch.

ψευδής, -ές, *adj.*, false.

ψεύδω, deceive, cheat.

ψῆφος, *f.*, vote, sentence (*lit.* pebble for voting).

ψόγος, *m.*, blame.

ψυχή, *f.*, soul : life.

ὤ, *vocative particle.*

ὧδε, *adv.*, thus.

ὠδίς, -ῖνος, *f.*, travail.

ὠθέω, ὤσω, ἔωσα, thrust away.

ὤμοι, woe is me !

ὠμός, -ή, -όν, *adj.*, fierce, cruel, (*lit.* raw).

ὤν, οὖσα, ὄν, part. of εἰμί.

ὠνέομαι, buy.

ὠνητός, -ή, -όν, verbal adj., bought.

'Ωρίων, -ωνος, m., Orion (ι short in Attic), mighty hunter who became constellation. See 1104, note.

ὦρσα, aor. of ὄρνυμι.

ὡς, adv., as ; with superl., ὡς τάχιστα, as soon as possible ;

how ; conj., (a) final, so that, that ; ὡς ἄν, 330, note ; (b) causal, since ; (c) after verb of saying, that ; with part. (esp. fut.) implies intention or purpose.

ὡς = (with persons), to.

ὡς, thus.

ὥστε adv., just as, like ; conj., so that, with inf. and ind. (consecutive).